PENGUIN BOOKS

WRITERS AT WORK

FIRST SERIES

The Paris Review, founded in 1953 by a group of young Americans including Peter Matthiessen, Harold L. Humes, George Plimpton, Thomas Guinzburg, and Donald Hall, has survived for twenty-seven years—a rarity in the literary-magazine field, where publications traditionally last for a few issues and then cease. While the emphasis of *The Paris Review*'s editors was on publishing creative work rather than nonfiction (among writers who published their first short stories there were Philip Roth, Terry Southern, Evan S. Connell, Samuel Beckett), part of the magazine's success can be attributed to the public interest in its continuing series of interviews on the craft of writing. Reasoning that it would be preferable to replace the traditional scholarly essay on a given author's work with an interview conducted with the author himself, the editors found a form which attracted considerable comment—from the very first interview, with E. M. Forster, which appeared in the initial issue, in which the distinguished author, then considered the greatest novelist in the English language, divulged why he had not been able to complete a novel since 1926. Since that early interview the magazine has continued to complement its fiction and poetry selection with interviews from a wide range of literary personages, which in sum constitute an authentic and invaluable contribution to the literary history of the past few decades.

WRITERS AT WORK

The *Paris Review* Interviews

Writers

at

Work

The *Paris Review* Interviews

FIRST SERIES

Edited, and with an Introduction, by

MALCOLM COWLEY

PENGUIN BOOKS

Penguin Books Ltd, Harmondsworth,
Middlesex, England
Penguin Books, 40 West 23rd Street,
New York, New York 10010, U.S.A.
Penguin Books Australia Ltd, Ringwood,
Victoria, Australia
Penguin Books Canada Limited, 2801 John Street,
Markham, Ontario, Canada L3R 1B4
Penguin Books (N.Z.) Ltd, 182–190 Wairau Road,
Auckland 10, New Zealand

First published in the United States of America by
The Viking Press 1958
First published in Great Britain by
Martin Secker & Warburg Ltd 1958
Viking Compass Edition published 1959
Reprinted 1960, 1961, 1963, 1964, 1965, 1967, 1968, 1969, 1971, 1973, 1975
Published in Penguin Books 1977

Reprinted 1979, 1981, 1983

LIBRARY OF CONGRESS CATALOGING IN PUBLICATION DATA
Main entry under title:
Writers at work.
First published in 1958.
1. Authors—Interviews.   I. Cowley, Malcolm,
1898–   . II. The Paris review.
[PN453.P3 1977b]   808   77-8443
ISBN 0 14 00.4540 6

Printed in the United States of America by
The Murray Printing Company, Westford, Massachusetts
Set in Linotype Electra

Contents

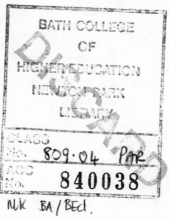

Writers at Work

INTRODUCTION

How Writers Write

THIS IS THE best series of interviews with writers of our time that I have read in English. The statement, though sweeping, isn't quite so eulogistic as it sounds. As compared with Continental Europeans, the English since Boswell, who was Scottish, and the Americans from the beginning have seldom been good at literary interviews. Everything in their background has been against the development of the form. Editors haven't been willing to give it much space because of a probably justified feeling that their public was not interested in literary problems. Authors have been embarrassed or reticent, often at the wrong places, and interviewers by and large have been incompetent. I can think of recent exceptions, but most of the interviewers either have had no serious interest in literature or else have been too serious about themselves. Either they have been reporters with little knowledge of the author's work and a desire to entrap him into making scandalous remarks about sex, politics, and God, or else they have been ambitious writers trying to display their own sophistication, usually at the expense of the author, and listening chiefly to their own voices.

In this book the literary conversations are of a different order, perhaps because of the changing times. The interviewers belong to a new generation that has been called "silent," though a better word for it would be "waiting" or "listening" or "inquiring." They have done their assigned reading, they have asked the right questions, or most of them, and have listened carefully to the answers. The authors, more conscious of their craft than authors used to be, have talked about it with an engaging lack of stuffiness. The editors of *The Paris Review* have been generous with their time and space, and the result is a series that seems to me livelier and more revealing than others of its kind. Unlike most of the others it is concerned primarily with the craft of fiction. It tells us what fiction writers are as persons, where they get their material, how they work from day to day, and what they dream of writing.

The series started with the first issue of *The Paris Review* in the spring of 1953. The new quarterly had been founded by young men lately out of college who were in Europe working on their first novels or books of poems. Their dream of having a magazine of their very own must have been more luminous than their picture of what it should be, yet they did have a picture of sorts. They didn't want their magazine to be "little" or opinionated (*engagé*, in the slang of the year) or academic. Instead of printing what were then the obligatory essays on *Moby Dick* and Henry James's major phase, they would print stories and poems by new authors—and pay for them too, as long as the magazine kept going. They wanted to keep it going for a long time, even if its capital was only a thousand dollars, with no subventions in sight. They dreamed that energy and ingenuity might take the place of missing resources.

At this point *The Paris Review* took a different direction from that of other magazines published by Americans in Europe. Like them it wanted to present material that was new, uncommercial, "making no compromise with the public taste," in the phrase sanctified by *The Little Review*, but unlike the others it was willing to use commercial devices in getting the material printed and talked about. "Enterprise in the service of art" might have been its motto. The editors compiled a list, running to thousands of names, of Americans living in Paris and sent volunteer salesmen to ring their doorbells. Posters were printed by hundreds and flying squadrons of three went out by night to paste them in likely and unlikely places all over the city. In June 1957 the frayed remnants of one poster were still legible on the ceiling of the lavatory in the Café du Dôme.

The series of interviews was at first regarded as another device—more dignified and perhaps more effective too—for building circulation. The magazine needed famous names on the cover, but couldn't afford to pay for the contributions of famous authors. "So let's talk to them," somebody ventured—it must have been Peter Matthiessen or Harold Humes, since they laid the earliest plans for the *Review*—"and print what they say." The idea was discussed with George Plimpton, late of the *Harvard Lampoon*, who had agreed to be editor. Plimpton was then at King's College, Cambridge, and he suggested E. M. Forster, an honorary fellow of King's, as the first author to be interviewed. It was Forster himself who gave a new direction to the series, making it a more thoughtful discussion of the craft of fiction than had at first been planned. Forster began by saying that he would answer questions if they were given to him in advance so that he could brood over them. The questions were submitted, and a few days later when the interviewers appeared, Forster gave his answers so methodically and slowly that his guests had no trouble keeping up with him. It was a simple interview to transcribe, and it furnished the best of patterns for the series that followed.

Interviewers usually worked in pairs, like FBI agents. Since no recording equipment was available for the early interviews, they both jotted down the answers to their questions at top speed and matched the two versions afterward. With two men writing, the pace could be kept almost at the level of natural conversation. Some of the later interviews—with Frank O'Connor, for example —were done with a tape recorder. After two or three sessions the interviewers typed up their material; then it was cut to length, arranged in logical order, and sent to the author for his approval. Sometimes he took a special interest in the text and expanded it with new questions of his own. There were important additions to some interviews, including those with Mauriac, Faulkner, and Moravia, while this volume was being edited.

It seems strange that famous authors should have devoted so much of their time to a project from which they had nothing to gain. Some of them disliked the idea of being interviewed but consented anyway, either out of friendship for someone on the *Review* or because they wanted to help a struggling magazine of the arts, perhaps in memory of their own early struggles to get published. Others—notably Simenon, Cary, Warren, and O'Connor—were interested in the creative process and glad to talk about it. Not one of the interviewers had any professional experience in the field, but perhaps their inexperience and youth were positive advantages. Authors are sometimes like tomcats:they distrust all the other toms, but they are kind to kittens.

"Kind" in this case means honest and painstaking in one's own fashion. Rereading the interviews, this time as a group, I was impressed by the extreme diversity of the characters and talents they present. The sixteen authors have come from the ruling class, the middle class, or the working class of five different countries. They are Catholic, Protestant, Jewish, or agnostic; old or young; married, single, or divorced; and they have had all sorts of education, from those who never finished secondary school (Simenon, Faulkner) to those who are university professors or fellows. One started life as a gunman, another as a bindle stiff, another as a soldier and government official; several went straight into professional writing. All have strongly marked personalities which are revealed —asserted, one might say—in their simplest remarks, and no personality resembles any other. Yet in spite of their diversity, what emerges from the interviews is a composite picture of the fiction writer. He has no face, no nationality, no particular background, and I say "he" by grammatical convention, since two of the authors are women; but they all have something in common, some attitude toward life and art, some fund of common experience.

Let us see how they go about their daily task of inventing stories and putting them on paper.

There would seem to be four stages in the composition of a story. First comes the germ of the story, then a period of more or less conscious meditation, then the first draft, and finally the revision, which may be simply "pencil work," as John O'Hara calls it—that is, minor changes in wording—or may lead to writing several drafts and what amounts to a new work.

The germ of a story is something seen or heard, or heard about, or suddenly remembered; it may be a remark casually dropped at the dinner table (as in the case of Henry James's story, *The Spoils of Poynton*), or again it may be the look on a stranger's face. Almost always it is a new and simple element introduced into an existing situation or mood; something that expresses the mood in one sharp detail; something that serves as a focal point for a hitherto disorganized mass of remembered material in the author's mind. James describes it as "the precious particle . . . the stray suggestion, the wandering word, the vague echo, at a touch of which the novelist's imagination winces as at the prick of some sharp point," and he adds that "its virtue is all in its needle-like quality, the power to penetrate as finely as possible."

In the case of one story by the late Joyce Cary, the "precious particle" was the wrinkles on a young woman's forehead. He had seen her on the little boat that goes around Manhattan Island, "a girl of about thirty," he says, "wearing a shabby skirt. She was enjoying herself. A nice expression, with a wrinkled forehead, a good many wrinkles. I said to my friend, 'I could write about that girl . . .'" but then he forgot her. Three weeks later, in San Francisco, Cary woke up at four in the morning with a story in his head—a purely English story with an English heroine. When he came to revise the story he kept wondering, "Why all these wrinkles? That's the third time they come in. And I suddenly realized," he says, "that my English heroine was the girl on the

Manhattan boat. Somehow she had gone down into my subconscious, and came up again with a full-sized story."

The woman with the wrinkled forehead could hardly have served as the germ of anything by Frank O'Connor, for his imagination is auditive, not visual. "If you're the sort of person," he says, "that meets a girl in the street and instantly notices the color of her eyes and of her hair and the sort of dress she's wearing, then you're not in the least like me. . . . I have terribly sensitive hearing and I'm terribly aware of voices." Often his stories develop from a remark he has overheard. That may also be the case with Dorothy Parker, who says, "I haven't got a visual mind. I hear things." Faulkner does have a visual mind, and he says that *The Sound and the Fury* "began with a mental picture. I didn't realize at the time it was symbolical. The picture was of the muddy seat of a little girl's drawers in a pear tree, where she could see through a window where her grandmother's funeral was taking place and report what was happening to her brothers on the ground below. By the time I explained who they were and what they were doing and how her pants got muddy, I realized it would be impossible to get all of it into a short story and it would have to be a book." At other times the precious particle is something the author has read—preferably a book of memoirs or history or travel, one that lies outside his own field of writing. Robert Penn Warren says, "I always remember the date, the place, the room, the road, when I first was struck. For instance, *World Enough and Time*. Katherine Anne Porter and I were both in the Library of Congress as fellows. We were in the same pew, had offices next to each other. She came in one day with an old pamphlet, the trial of Beauchamp for killing Colonel Sharp. She said, 'Well, Red, you better read this.' There it was. I read it in five minutes. But I was six years making the book. Any book I write starts with a flash, but takes a long time to shape up."

The book or story shapes up—assumes its own specific form, that is—during a process of meditation that is the second stage in composition. Angus Wilson calls it "the gestatory period" and says that it is "very important to me. That's when I'm persuading myself of the truth of what I want to say, and I don't think I could persuade my readers unless I'd persuaded myself first." The period may last for years, as with Warren's novels (and most of Henry James's), or it may last exactly two days, as in the extraordinary case of Georges Simenon. "As soon as I have the beginning," Simenon explains, "I can't bear it very long. . . . And two days later I begin writing." The meditation may be, or seem to be, wholly conscious. The writer asks himself questions—"What should the characters do at this point? How can I build to a climax?"—and answers them in various fashions before choosing the final answers. Or most of the process, including all the early steps, may be carried on without the writer's volition. He wakes before daybreak with the whole story in his head, as Joyce Cary did in San Francisco, and hastily writes it down. Or again—and I think most frequently—the meditation is a mixture of conscious and unconscious elements, as if a cry from the depths of sleep were being heard and revised by the waking mind.

Often the meditation continues while the writer is engaged in other occupations: gardening, driving his wife to town (as Walter Mitty did), or going out to dinner. "I never quite know when I'm not writing," says James Thurber. "Sometimes my wife comes up to me at a dinner party and says, 'Dammit, Thurber, stop writing.' She usually catches me in the middle of a paragraph. Or my daughter will look up from the dinner table and ask, 'Is he sick?' 'No,' my wife says, 'he's writing.' I have to do it that way on account of my eyes." When Thurber had better vision he used to do his meditating at the typewriter, as many other writers do. Nelson Algren, for example, finds his plots simply by writing page after page, night after night. "I always figured," he says, "the only way I could finish a book and get a plot was just to keep making it longer and longer until something happens."

The first draft of a story is often written at top speed; probably that is the best way to write it. Dorothy Canfield Fisher, who is not among the authors interviewed, once compared the writing of a first draft with skiing down a steep slope that she wasn't sure she was clever enough to manage. "Sitting at my desk one morning," she says, "I 'pushed off' and with a tingle of not altogether pleasurable excitement and alarm, felt myself 'going.' I 'went' almost as precipitately as skis go down a long white slope, scribbling as rapidly as my pencil could go, indicating whole words with a dash and a jiggle, filling page after page with scrawls." Frank O'Connor explains the need for haste in his own case. "Get black on white," he says, "used to be Maupassant's advice—that's what I always do. I don't give a hoot what the writing's like, I write any sort of rubbish which will cover the main outlines of the story, then I can begin to see it." There are other writers, however, who work ahead laboriously, revising as they go. William Styron says, "I seem to have some neurotic need to perfect each paragraph—each sentence, even—as I go along." Dorothy Parker reports that it takes her six months to do a story: "I think it out and then write it sentence by sentence—no first draft. I can't write five words but that I change seven."

O'Connor doesn't start changing words until the first draft is finished, but then he rewrites, so he says, "endlessly, endlessly, endlessly." There is no stage of composition at which these authors differ more from one another than in this final stage of preparing a manuscript for the printer. Even that isn't a final stage for O'Connor. "I keep on rewriting," he says, "and after it's published, and then after it's published in book form, I usually rewrite it again. I've rewritten versions of most of my early stories, and one of these days, God help, I'll publish these as well." Françoise Sagan, on the other hand, spends "very little" time in revision. Simenon spends exactly three days in revising each of his short novels. Most of that time is devoted to tracking down and crossing out the literary touches—"adjectives, adverbs, and every word which is there just to make an effect. Every sentence which is there just for the sentence. You know, you have a beautiful sentence—cut it." Joyce Cary was another deletionist. Many of the passages he crossed out of his first drafts were those dealing explicitly with ideas. "I work over the whole book," he says, "and cut out anything that does not belong to the emotional development, the texture of feeling." Thurber revises his stories by rewriting them from the beginning, time and again. "A story I've been working on," he says, ". . . was rewritten fifteen complete times. There must have been close to two hundred and forty thousand words in all the manuscripts put together, and I must have spent two thousand hours working at it. Yet the finished story can't be more than twenty thousand words." That would make it about the longest piece of fiction he has written. Men like Thurber and O'Connor, who rewrite "endlessly, endlessly," find it hard to face the interminable prospect of writing a full-length novel.

For short-story writers the four stages of composition are usually distinct, and there may even be a fifth, or rather a first, stage. Before seizing upon the germ of a story, the writer may find himself in a state of "generally intensified emotional sensitivity . . . when events that usually pass unnoticed suddenly move you deeply, when a sunset lifts you to exaltation, when a squeaking door throws you into a fit of exasperation, when a clear look of trust in a child's eyes moves you to tears." I am quoting again from Dorothy Canfield Fisher, who "cannot conceive," she says, "of any creative fiction written from any other beginning." There is not much doubt, in any case, that the germ is precious largely because it serves to crystallize a prior state of feeling. Then comes the brooding or meditation, then the rapidly written first draft, then the slow revision; for the story writer everything is likely to happen in more or less its proper order. For the novelist, however, the stages are often confused. The meditation may have to be repeated for each new episode. The revision of one chapter may precede or follow the first draft of the next.

That is not the only difference between writing a short story and writing a novel. Reading the interviews together, I was confirmed in an old belief that the two forms are separate and that mere length is not their distinguishing feature. A long short story —say of forty thousand words—is not the same as a novel of forty thousand words, nor is it likely to be written by the same person. Among the authors interviewed, the division that goes deepest is not between older and younger writers, or men and women writers, or French and English writers; it is the division between those who think in terms of the short story and those who are essentially novelists.

Truman Capote might stand for those who think in terms of the short story, since he tells us that his "more unswerving ambitions still revolve around this form." A moment later he says, "I invariably have the illusion that the whole play of a story, its start and middle and finish, occur in my mind simultaneously—that I'm seeing it in one flash." He likes to know the end of a story before writing the first word of it. Indeed, he doesn't start writing until he has brooded over the story long enough to exhaust his emotional response to the material. "I seem to remember reading," he says, "that Dickens, as he wrote, choked with laughter over his own humor and dripped tears all over the page when one of his characters died. My own theory is that the writer should have considered his wit and dried his tears long, long before setting out to evoke similar reactions in a reader." The reactions of the reader, not of the writer, are Capote's principal concern.

For contrast take the interview with Simenon, who is a true novelist even if his separate works, written and revised in about two weeks, are not much longer than some short stories. Each of them starts in the same fashion. "It is almost a geometrical problem," he says. "I have such a man, such a woman, in such surroundings. What can happen to them to oblige them to go to their limit? That's the question. It will be sometimes a very simple incident, anything which will change their lives. Then I write my novel chapter by chapter." Before setting to work Simenon has scrawled a few notes on a big manila envelope. The interviewer asks whether these are an outline of the action. "No, no," Simenon answers. ". . . On the envelope I put only the names of the characters, their ages, their families. I know nothing whatever about the events which will occur later. Otherwise"—and I can't help putting the statement in italics—"*it would not be interesting to me.*"

Unlike Capote, who says that he is physically incapable of writing anything he doesn't think will be paid for (though I take it that payment is, for him, merely a necessary token of public admiration), Simenon would "certainly," he says, continue writing novels if they were never published. But he wouldn't bother to write them if he knew what the end of each novel would be, for then *it would not be interesting.* He discovers his fable not in one flash, but chapter by chapter, as if he were telling a continued story to himself. "On the eve of the first day," he says, "I know what will happen in the first chapter. Then day after day, chapter after chapter, I find what comes later. After I have started a novel I write a chapter each day, without ever missing a day. Because it is a strain, I have to keep pace with the novel. If, for example, I am ill for forty-eight hours I have to throw away the previous chapters. And I never return to that novel." Like Dickens he lets himself be moved, even shattered, by what he is writing. "All the day," he says, "I am one of my characters"—always the one who is driven to his limit. "I feel what he feels. . . . And it's almost unbearable after five or six days. That is one of the reasons why my novels are so short; after eleven days I can't—it's impossible. I have to— It's physical. I am too tired."

Nobody else writes in quite the same fashion as Simenon. He carries a certain attitude toward fiction to the furthest point that it can be carried by anyone who writes books to be published and read. But the attitude in itself is not unusual, and in fact it is shared to some extent by all the true novelists who explain their methods in this book. Not one of them starts by making a scene-by-scene outline, as Henry James did before writing each of his later novels. James had discovered what he called the "divine principle of the Scenario" after writing several unsuccessful plays, and in essence the principle, or method, seems to be dramatistic rather than novelistic. The dramatist, like the short-story writer, has to know where he is going and how he will get there, scene by scene, whereas all the novelists interviewed by *The Paris Review* are accustomed to making voyages of exploration with only the roughest of maps. Mauriac says, "There is a point of departure, and there are some characters. It often happens that the first characters don't go any further and, on the other hand, vaguer, more inconsistent characters show new possibilities as the story goes on and assume a place we hadn't foreseen." Françoise Sagan says that she has to start writing to have ideas. In the beginning she has "a character, or a few characters, and perhaps an idea for a few of the scenes up to the middle of the book, but it all changes in the writing. For me writing is a question of finding a certain rhythm." (One thinks of Simenon and his feeling that he has to keep pace with the novel.) "My work," says Moravia, ". . . is not prepared beforehand in any way. I might add, too, that when I'm not working I don't think of my work at all." Forster does lay plans for his work, but they are subject to change. "The novelist," he says, "should, I think, always settle when he starts what is going to happen, what his major event is to be. He may alter this event as he approaches it, indeed he probably will, indeed he probably had better, or the novel becomes tied up and tight. But the sense of a solid mass ahead, a mountain round or over which or through which the story must go, is most valuable and, for the novels I've tried to write, essential. . . . When I began A *Passage to India* I knew that something important happened in the Malabar Caves, and that it would have a central place in the novel—but I didn't know what it would be."

Most novelists, one might generalize on this evidence, are like the chiefs of exploring expeditions. They know who their companions are (and keep learning more about them); they know what sort of territory they will have to traverse on the following day or week; they know the general object of the expedition, the mountain they are trying to reach, the river of which they are trying to discover the source. But they don't know exactly what their route will be, or what adventures they will meet along the way, or how their companions will act when pushed to the limit. They don't even know whether the continent they are trying to map exists in space or only within themselves. "I think that if a man has the urge to be an artist," Simenon muses, "it is because he needs to find himself. Every writer tries to find himself through his characters, through all his writing." He is speaking for the novelist in particular. Short-story writers come back from their briefer explorations to brood over the meaning of their discoveries; then they perfect the stories for an audience. The short story is an *exposition*; the novel is often and perhaps at its best an *inquisition* into the unknown depths of the novelist's mind.

Apparently the hardest problem for almost any writer, whatever his medium, is getting to work in the morning (or in the afternoon, if he is a late riser like Styron, or even at night). Thornton Wilder says, "Many writers have told me that they have built up mnemonic devices to start them off on each day's writing task. Hemingway once told me he sharpened twenty pencils; Willa Cather that she read a passage from the Bible—not from piety, she was quick to add, but to get in touch with fine prose; she also regretted that she had formed this habit, for the prose rhythms of 1611 were not those she was in search of. My springboard has always been long walks." Those long walks alone are a fairly common device; Thomas Wolfe would sometimes roam through the streets of Brooklyn all night. Reading the Bible before writing is a much less common practice, and, in spite of Miss Cather's disclaimer, I suspect that it did involve a touch of piety. Dependent for success on forces partly beyond his control, an

author may try to propitiate the unknown powers. I knew one
novelist, an agnostic, who said he often got down on his knees and
started the working day with prayer.

The usual working day is three or four hours. Whether these
authors write with pencils, with a pen, or at a typewriter—and
some do all three in the course of completing a manuscript—an
important point seems to be that they all work with their hands;
the only exception is Thurber in his sixties. I have often heard it
said by psychiatrists that writers belong to the "oral type." The
truth seems to be that most of them are manual types. Words are
not merely sounds for them, but magical designs that their hands
make on paper. "I always think of writing as a physical thing,"
Nelson Algren says. "I am an artisan," Simenon explains. "I need
to work with my hands. I would like to carve my novel in a piece
of wood." Hemingway used to have the feeling that his fingers
did much of his thinking for him. After an automobile accident
in Montana, when the doctors said he might lose the use of his
right arm, he was afraid he would have to stop writing. Thurber
used to have the sense of thinking with his fingers on the keyboard
of a typewriter. When they were working together on their play
The Male Animal, Elliott Nugent used to say to him, "Well,
Thurber, we've got our problem, we've got all these people in the
living room. What are we going to do with them?" Thurber would
answer that he didn't know and couldn't tell him until he'd sat
down at the typewriter and found out. After his vision became too
weak for the typewriter, he wrote very little for a number of years
(using black crayon on yellow paper, about twenty scrawled words
to the page); then painfully he taught himself to compose stories
in his head and dictate them to a stenographer.

Dictation, for most authors, is a craft which, if acquired at all,
is learned rather late in life—and I think with a sense of jumping
over one step in the process of composition. Instead of giving dictation, many writers seem to themselves to be taking it. "I listen
to the voices," Faulkner once said to me, "and when I've put
down what the voices say, it's right. I don't always like what they

say, but I don't try to change it." Mauriac says, "During a creative period I write every day; a novel should not be interrupted. When I cease to be carried along, when I no longer feel as though I were taking down dictation, I stop." Listening as they do to an inner voice that speaks or falls silent as if by caprice, many writers from the beginning have personified the voice as a benign or evil spirit. For Hawthorne it was evil or at least frightening. "The Devil himself always seems to get into my inkstand," he said in a letter to his publisher, "and I can only exorcise him by pensful at a time." For Kipling the Daemon that lived in his pen was tyrannical but well-meaning. "When your Daemon is in charge," he said, "do not try to think consciously. Drift, wait, and obey."

Objects on the writing table, which is the altar of the Daemon, are sometimes chosen with the same religious care as if they were chalices and patens. Kipling said, "For my ink I demanded the blackest, and had I been in my Father's house, as once I was, would have kept an ink-boy to grind me Indian-ink. All 'blue-blacks' were an abomination to my Daemon. . . . My writing-blocks were built for me to an unchanged pattern of large, off-white, blue sheets, of which I was most wasteful." Often we hear of taboos that must be observed—even by Angus Wilson, although he is as coolly rational as any fiction writer who ever set pen to paper (the pen in his case is medium and the paper is, by preference, a grammar-school exercise book). "Fiction writing is a kind of magic," Wilson says, "and I don't care to talk about a novel I'm doing because if I communicate the magic spell, even in an abbreviated form, it loses its force for me." One of the interviewed authors—only one, but I suspect there are others like him—makes a boast of his being superstitious. "I will not tolerate the presence of yellow roses," Capote says—"which is sad because they're my favorite flower. I can't allow three cigarette butts in the same ashtray. Won't travel on a plane with two nuns. Won't begin or end anything on a Friday. It's endless, the things I can't and won't. But I derive some curious comfort from these primitive concepts." Perhaps they are not only comforting but of practical

service in helping him to weave his incantations. I can't help
thinking of the drunk who always carried a ventilated satchel.
"What's in it?" said his neighbor on a bus. "Just a mongoose. To
kill snakes." The neighbor peered into the satchel and said,
"There's nothing in it. That's an imaginary mongoose." The
drunk said, "What about the snakes?"

At a summer conference on the novel, at Harvard, one of the
invited speakers gave a rather portentous address on the Responsibilities of the Novelist. Frank O'Connor, on the platform, found
himself giggling at each new solemnity. After the address he
walked to the lectern and said, "All right, if there are any of my
students here I'd like them to remember that writing is fun." On
that point most of these authors would agree. "I have always found
writing pleasant," Forster says, "and don't understand what people
mean by 'throes of creation.'" "I write simply to amuse myself,"
says Moravia. Angus Wilson "started writing as a hobby." Thurber
tells us that the act of writing "is either something the writer
dreads or something he actually likes, and I actually like it. Even
rewriting's fun." At another point he says, "When I'm not writing,
as my wife knows, I'm miserable."

The professional writers who dread writing, as many do, are
usually those whose critical sense is not only strong but unsleeping,
so that it won't allow them to do even a first draft at top speed.
They are in most cases the "bleeders" who write one sentence at
a time, and can't write it until the sentence before has been revised. William Styron, one of the bleeders, is asked if he enjoys
writing. "I certainly don't," he says. "I get a fine warm feeling
when I'm doing well, but that pleasure is pretty much negated
by the pain of getting started each day. Let's face it, writing is
hell." But a moment later he says without any sense of contradiction, "I find that I'm simply the happiest, the placidest, *when*
I'm writing . . . it's the only time that I feel completely self-
possessed, even when the writing itself is not going too well." Not

writing is the genuine hell for Styron and others in his predicament; writing is at worst a purgatory.

Whatever the original impulse that drives them to write—self-
expression, self-discovery, self-aggrandizement, or the pain of not
writing—most authors with a body of work behind them end by
developing new purposes. Simenon, for example, would like to
create the pure novel, without description, exposition, or argument: a book that will do only what a novel can do. "In a pure
novel," he says, "you wouldn't take sixty pages to describe the
South or Arizona or some country in Europe. Just the drama with
only what is absolutely part of this drama . . . almost a translation of the laws of tragedy into the novel. I think the novel is the
tragedy of our day." Critics have always advised him to write a
big novel, one with twenty or thirty characters. His answer is, "I
will never write a big novel. My big novel is the mosaic of all my
small novels."

At this point he suggests still another purpose, or dream, that is
shared by almost all the writers who were interviewed. They want
to write the new book, climb the new mountain, which they hope
will be the highest of all, but still they regard it as only one con-
quest in a chain of mountains. The whole chain, the shelf of
books, the Collected Works, is their ultimate goal. Moravia says,
"In the works of every writer with any body of work to show for
his effort, you will find recurrent themes. I view the novel, a single
novel as well as a writer's entire corpus, as a musical composition
in which the characters are themes." Faulkner says, "With
Soldier's Pay I found out that writing was fun. But I found out
afterward that not only each book had to have a design, but the
whole output or sum of a writer's work had to have a design."
Graham Greene says, in *The Lost Childhood*, "A ruling passion
gives to a shelf of books the unity of a system." Each of these
novelists wants to produce not a random succession of books, like
discrete events for critics to study one by one, without reference
to earlier or later events, but a complete system unified by his

ruling passion, a system of words on paper that is also a world of living persons created in his likeness by the author. This dream must have had a beginning quite early in the author's life; perhaps it goes back to what Thornton Wilder calls "the Nero in the bassinet," the child wanting to be omnipotent in a world he has made for himself; but later it is elaborated with all the wisdom and fire and patient workmanship that the grown man can bring to bear on it. Particle after particle of the living self is transferred into the creation, until at last it is an external world that corresponds to the inner world and has the power of outlasting the author's life.

I suspect that some such dream is shared by many authors, but among those interviewed it is Faulkner who has come closest to achieving it, and he is also the author who reveals it most candidly. "Beginning with *Sartoris*," he says, "I discovered that my own little postage stamp of native soil was worth writing about and that I would never live long enough to exhaust it, and that by sublimating the actual into the apocryphal I would have complete liberty to use whatever talent I might have to its absolute top. It opened up a mine of other people, so I created a cosmos of my own. I can move these people around like God, not only in space but in time." And then he says, looking back on his work as if on the seventh day, "I like to think of the world I created as being a kind of keystone in the universe; that, small as that keystone is, if it were ever taken away the universe itself would collapse. My last book will be the Doomsday Book, the Golden Book, of Yoknapatawpha County. Then I shall break the pencil and I'll have to stop."

That is a good place for me to stop too. I only have to add that thanks for this book are due to three groups of persons. First they are due to the interviewers, all amateurs in the field, who read the authors' works, asked them the right questions, and, at a sacrifice of vanity, kept themselves in the background when writing their reports. Then they are due to the editorial staff of *The*

Paris Review, and notably to George Plimpton, its editor, and Marion Capron, for their work in putting the series together. Finally, and most of all, thanks are due to the authors who gave so much of their time, revealed so much of their working methods, and incidentally told so many good stories. It's a shame that the book couldn't be big enough to contain all the interviews that have so far appeared; not one is without interest; but the series is being continued in the magazine, and I hope the other interviews, new and old, can be included in a later volume.

MALCOLM COWLEY

1. E. M. Forster

E. M. Forster was born on New Year's Day, 1879. He was educated at Tonbridge and at King's College, Cambridge, where he enjoyed the stimulating company of what would later be called the Bloomsbury Group. By 1903, as a political liberal, he was an ardent contributor to the newly formed *Independent Review*. He traveled extensively and in 1910 made his first visit to India, which was to be the setting of his greatest novel.

In 1905, at the age of twenty-six, Forster published his first novel, *Where Angels Fear to Tread*, which he followed with a succession of others: *The Longest Journey* (1907), *A Room with a View* (1908), and *Howards End* (1911). He spent the First World War in Egypt as a civilian war worker, later compiling some of his observations in a guidebook to Alexandria.

In 1924 he finished his fifth and most famous work, *A Passage to India*. It was his last novel. But his reputation was established, and on the basis of his published work his stature as a novelist continued to grow. "His reputation," it was said, "goes up with every book he doesn't write." Actually, Forster continued to produce brilliant work, all of it nonfiction: *Abinger Harvest* (1926), *Aspects of the Novel* (1927), *Two Cheers for Democracy* (1951), and *The Hill of Devi* (1953). In 1951 he produced a libretto for Benjamin Britten's opera *Billy Budd*.

Bombed out of his country home at Abinger during World War II, Forster has lived for the past years in Cambridge, where he is an honorary fellow of King's College.

I

"Gentlemen! Gentlemen!!" Basle station echoed to the colossal word. "If only other people would behave like gentlemen." It was early on an August morning, and the passengers from the Bologna train, who were mostly English, were trying to decant themselves into the train for Lucerne and the south. Difficult, for the Lucerne train was smaller, and they were beginning to fight. They did not want to fight, but by degrees they could not avoid it; there was nothing else to do. Without losing their tempers, they screamed and wedged and hit one another behind the knee with suit cases, and smashed at the brass bars of the train as it backed itself to a standstill. Some had ladies with them, and claimed prior treatment on that account. "Steady on, sir, you might consider the ladies!" Others cried "Bother the ladies!" One tourist was pushed beneath the oncoming wheels, another rescued him, and still the appeal for gentle manliness arose [that password into a city whose gates are barred for ever.]

The station, immense and modern, paid no great heed. Not even the daily passage of the Island Race was an event to her, she was the changing house of Europe. Trains ran into her from four or five countries, washed and slewed themselves, ate in her refreshment rooms, and relooked when necessary; she thought in terms of trains. Behind her lay a town and a swift green river, but she only served the town as an afterthought. Its needs were little to her, its memories of a Mediaeval Council nothing: she was indifferent to Cardinals and Kings, and to all but officials.

Now Martin had managed rather well. He had spied the Lucerne train reposing at a distant platform, had measured it with his eye, and had calculated where the end of the carriage would be when it drew up. Telling Venetia (his wife) and Lady Borlase (his mother in law) to keep out of the crowd, he had slipped past the other tourists, and laid a gloved hand on the door. The rush followed. He was swept sideways by the train and off his legs by the crowd, and it was he who was nearly killed. The man who saved him had the look and gesture of a warrior. He impressed Martin very much, and when the train had started he set out down the corridor to find him and to thank him.

The battle was over now. Every one had found a seat, for there was plenty of room after all, and many every one had forgotten the fright

William Pène du Bois

E. M. Forster

"That is not all 'Arctic Summer'—there is almost half as much of it again—but that's all I want to read, because now it goes off, or at least I think so, and I do not want my voice to go out into the air while my heart is sinking. It will be more interesting to consider what the problems before me were, and why I was un-likely to solve them. I should like to do this, though it may involve us a little in fiction-technicalities . . ."

So said E. M. Forster, addressing an audience at the Aldeburgh Festival of 1951. He had been reading part of an unfinished novel called "Arctic Summer." At the end of the reading, he went on to explain why he had not finished the novel, which led him to mention what he called "fiction-technicalities."

Following up on Mr. Forster's Aldeburgh remarks, we have tried

Opposite: The first page of E. M. Forster's unfinished novel "Arctic Summer"

to record his views on such matters as he gave them in an interview at King's College, Cambridge, on the evening of June 20,
1952.

A spacious and high-ceilinged room, furnished in the Edwardian
taste. One's attention is caught by a massive carved wooden man-
telpiece of elaborate structure holding blue china in its niches.
Large gilt-framed portrait-drawings on the walls (his Thornton
ancestors and others), a "Turner" by his great-uncle, and some
modern pictures. Books of all sorts, handsome and otherwise, in
English and French; armchairs decked in little shawls; a piano, a
solitaire-board, and the box of a Zoe-trope; profusion of opened
letters; slippers neatly arranged in waste-paper basket.

In reading what follows the reader must imagine Mr. Forster's
manner, which though of extreme amenity is a firm one: precise,
yet none the less elusive, administering a series of tiny surprises.
He makes a perpetual slight displacement of the expected emphasis. His habit was to answer our questions by brief statements, followed by decorative asides, often of great interest, but very difficult
to reproduce.

INTERVIEWERS: To begin with, may we ask you again, why did
you never finish "Arctic Summer"?

FORSTER: I have really answered this question in the foreword I
wrote for the reading. The crucial passage was this:

". . . whether these problems are solved or not, there remains
a still graver one. What is going to happen? I had got my antithesis all right, the antithesis between the civilized man, who hopes
for an Arctic Summer in which there is time to get things done,
and the heroic man. But I had not settled what is going to happen,
and that is why the novel remains a fragment. The novelist should,
I think, always settle when he starts what is going to happen, what
his major event is to be. He may alter this event as he approaches
it, indeed he probably will, indeed he probably had better, or the
novel becomes tied up and tight. But the sense of a solid mass

ahead, a mountain round or over or through which (*he interposed,* "in this case it would be *through*") the story must somehow go, is most valuable and, for the novels I've tried to write, essential."

INTERVIEWERS: How much is involved in this "solid mass"? Does it mean that all the important steps in the plot must also be present in the original conception?

FORSTER: Certainly not all the steps. But there must be something, some major object towards which one is to approach. When I began A *Passage to India* I knew that something important happened in the Malabar Caves, and that it would have a central place in the novel—but I didn't know what it would be.

INTERVIEWERS: But if you didn't know what was going to happen to the characters in either instance, why was the case of A *Passage to India* so different from that of "Arctic Summer"? . . . In both cases you had your antithesis.

FORSTER: The atmosphere of "Arctic Summer" did not approach the density of what I had in A *Passage to India.* Let me see how to explain. The Malabar Caves represented an area in which concentration can take place. A cavity. (*We noticed that he always spoke of the caves quite literally—as for instance when he interrupted himself earlier to say that the characters had to pass* "through" *them.*) They were something to focus everything up: they were to engender an event like an egg. What I had in "Arctic Summer" was thinner, a background and color only.

INTERVIEWERS: You spoke of antitheses in your novels. Do you regard these as essential to any novel you might write?

FORSTER: Let me think. . . . There was one in *Howards End.* Perhaps a rather subtler one in *The Longest Journey.*

INTERVIEWERS: Would you agree that all your novels not only deal with some dilemma but are intended to be both true and useful in regard to it—so that if you felt a certain dilemma was too extreme, its incompatibles too impossible to reconcile, you wouldn't write about it?

FORSTER: True and lovable would be my antithesis. I don't think useful comes into it. I'm not sure that I would be put off simply because a dilemma that I wanted to treat was insoluble; at least, I don't think I should be.

INTERVIEWERS: While we are on the subject of the planning of novels, has a novel ever taken an unexpected direction?

FORSTER: Of course, that wonderful thing, a character running away with you—which happens to everyone—that's happened to me, I'm afraid.

INTERVIEWERS: Can you describe any technical problem that especially bothered you in one of the published novels?

FORSTER: I had trouble with the junction of Rickie and Stephen. [The hero of *The Longest Journey* and his half-brother.] How to make them intimate, I mean. I fumbled about a good deal. It is all right once they are together. . . . I didn't know how to get Helen to Howards End. That part is all contrived. There are too many letters. And again, it is all right once she is there. But ends always give me trouble.

INTERVIEWERS: Why is that?

FORSTER: It is partly what I was talking about a moment ago. Characters run away with you, and so won't fit on to what is coming.

INTERVIEWERS: Another question of detail. What was the exact function of the long description of the Hindu festival in *A Passage to India?*

FORSTER: It was architecturally necessary. I needed a lump, or a Hindu temple if you like—a mountain standing up. It is well placed; and it gathers up some strings. But there ought to be more after it. The lump sticks out a little too much.

INTERVIEWERS: To leave technical questions for a moment, have you ever described any type of situation of which you have had no personal knowledge?

FORSTER: The home-life of Leonard and Jacky in *Howards End* is one case. I knew nothing about that. I believe I brought it off.

INTERVIEWERS: How far removed in time do you have to be from an experience in order to describe it?

FORSTER: Place is more important than time in this matter. Let me tell you a little more about A *Passage to India*. I had a great deal of difficulty with the novel, and thought I would never finish it. I began it in 1912, and then came the war. I took it with me when I returned to India in 1921, but found what I had written wasn't India at all. It was like sticking a photograph on a picture. However, I couldn't *write* it when I was in India. When I got away, I could get on with it.

INTERVIEWERS: Some critics have objected to your way of handling incidents of violence. Do you agree with their objections?

FORSTER: I think I solved the problem satisfactorily in *Where Angels Fear to Tread*. In other cases, I don't know. The scene in the Malabar Caves is a good substitute for violence. Which were the incidents you didn't like?

INTERVIEWERS: I have always been worried by the suddenness of Gerald's death in *The Longest Journey*.[1] Why did you treat it in that way?

FORSTER: It had to be passed by. But perhaps it was passed by in the wrong way.

INTERVIEWERS: I have also never felt comfortable about Leonard Bast's seduction of Helen in *Howards End*. It is such a sudden affair. It seems as though we are not told enough about it for it to be convincing. One might say that it came off allegorically but not realistically.

FORSTER: I think you may be right. I did it like that out of a wish to have surprises. It has to be a surprise for Margaret, and this was best done by making it a surprise for the reader too. Too much may have been sacrificed to this.

INTERVIEWERS: A more general question. Would you admit to there being any symbolism in your novels? Lionel Trilling rather seems to imply that there is, in his book on you—symbolism, that is, as distinct from allegory or parable. "Mrs. Moore," he says, "will act with a bad temper to Adela, but her actions will some-

---

[1] The famous fifth chapter of *The Longest Journey* begins "Gerald died that afternoon."

how have a good echo; and her children will be her further echo. . . ."

FORSTER: No, I didn't think of that. But mightn't there be some of it elsewhere? Can you try me with some more examples?

INTERVIEWERS: The tree at Howards End? [A wych-elm, frequently referred to in the novel.]

FORSTER: Yes, that was symbolical; it was the genius of the house.

INTERVIEWERS: What was the significance of Mrs. Wilcox's influence on the other characters after her death?

FORSTER: I was interested in the imaginative effect of someone alive, but in a different way from other characters—living in other lives.

INTERVIEWERS: Were you influenced by Samuel Butler in this? I mean, by his theories of vicarious immortality?

FORSTER: No. (*Pause.*) I think I have a more poetical mind than Butler's.

INTERVIEWERS: Now can we ask you a few questions about the immediate business of writing? Do you keep a notebook?

FORSTER: No, I should feel it improper.

INTERVIEWERS: But you would refer to diaries and letters?

FORSTER: Yes, that's different.

INTERVIEWERS: When you go, say, to the circus, would you ever feel, "How nice it would be to put that in a novel"?

FORSTER: No, I should feel it improper. I never say "that might be useful." I don't think it is right for an author to do so. (*He spoke firmly.*) However I have been inspired on the spot. "The Story of a Panic" is the simplest example; "The Road from Colonus" is another. Sense of a place also inspired me to write a short story called "The Rock," but the inspiration was poor in quality, and the editors wouldn't take the story. But I have talked about this in the introduction to my short stories.

INTERVIEWERS: Do you pre-figure a shape to your novels?

FORSTER: No, I am too unvisual to do so. (*We found this sur-*

prising in view of his explanation of the Hindu festival scene, above.)

INTERVIEWERS: Does this come out in any other way?

FORSTER: I find it difficult to recognize people when I meet them, though I remember about them. I remember their voices.

INTERVIEWERS: Do you have any Wagnerian leitmotiv system to help you keep so many themes going at the same time?

FORSTER: Yes, in a way, and I'm certainly interested in music and musical methods. Though I shouldn't call it a system.

INTERVIEWERS: Do you write every day, or only under inspiration?

FORSTER: The latter. But the act of writing inspires me. It is a nice feeling . . . (*indulgently*). Of course, I had a very literary childhood. I was the author of a number of works between the ages of six and ten. There were "Ear-rings through the Keyhole" and "Scuffles in a Wardrobe."

INTERVIEWERS: Which of your novels came first to your mind?

FORSTER: Half of *A Room with a View*. I got that far, and then there must have been a hitch.

INTERVIEWERS: Did you ever attempt a novel of an entirely different sort from the ones you have published?

FORSTER: For some time I had the idea of an historical novel. The setting was to have been a Renaissance one. Reading *Thaïs* (by Anatole France) finally decided me to try it. But nothing came of it in the end.

INTERVIEWERS: How do you name your characters?

FORSTER: I usually find the name at the start, but not always. Rickie's brother had several names. (*He showed us some early manuscript portions of* The Longest Journey *in which Stephen Wonham appeared as Siegfried; also an omitted chapter, which he described as "extremely romantic."*) Wonham is a country name and so is Quested. (*We looked at an early draft of* A Passage to India *in which to his surprise the heroine was found going under the name of Edith. This was later changed to Janet, before becoming Adela.*) Herriton I made up. Munt was the name of my first governess in the house in Hertfordshire. There really was a family called Howard who once owned the real Howards End. *Where Angels Fear to Tread* should have been called "Monteriano," but the publisher thought this wouldn't sell. It was Dent [Professor E. J. Dent] who gave me the present title.

INTERVIEWERS: How much do you admit to modeling your characters on real people?

FORSTER: We all like to pretend we don't use real people, but one does actually. I used some of my family. Miss Bartlett was my Aunt Emily—they all read the book but they none of them saw it. Uncle Willie turned into Mrs. Failing. He was a bluff and simple character (*correcting himself*)—bluff without being simple. Miss Lavish was actually a Miss Spender. Mrs. Honeychurch was my grandmother. The three Miss Dickinsons condensed into two Miss Schlegels. Philip Herriton I modeled on Professor Dent. He knew this, and took an interest in his own progress. I have used several tourists.

INTERVIEWERS: Do all your characters have real life models?

FORSTER: In no book have I got down more than the people I like, the person I think I am, and the people who irritate me. This puts me among the large body of authors who are not really novelists, and have to get on as best they can with these three categories. We have not the power of observing the variety of life and describing it dispassionately. There are a few who have done this. Tolstoi was one, wasn't he?

INTERVIEWERS: Can you say anything about the process of turning a real person into a fictional one?

FORSTER: A useful trick is to look back upon such a person with half-closed eyes, fully describing certain characteristics. I am left with about two-thirds of a human being and can get to work. A likeness isn't aimed at and couldn't be obtained, because a man's only himself amidst the particular circumstances of his life and not amid other circumstances. So that to refer back to Dent when

Philip was in difficulties with Gino, or to ask one and one-half Miss Dickinsons how Helen should comport herself with an illegitimate baby would have ruined the atmosphere and the book. When all goes well, the original material soon disappears, and a character who belongs to the book and nowhere else emerges.

INTERVIEWERS: Do any of your characters represent yourself at all?

FORSTER: Rickie more than any. Also Philip. And Cecil [in A *Room with a View*] has got something of Philip in him.

INTERVIEWERS: What degree of reality do your characters have for you after you have finished writing about them?

FORSTER: Very variable. There are some I like thinking about. Rickie and Stephen, and Margaret Schlegel—they are characters whose fortunes I have been interested to follow. It doesn't matter if they died in the novel or not.

INTERVIEWERS: We have got a few more questions about your work as a whole. First, to what degree is each novel an entirely fresh experiment?

FORSTER: To quite a large extent. But I wonder if experiment is the word?

INTERVIEWERS: Is there a hidden pattern behind the whole of an author's work, what Henry James called "a figure in the carpet"? (*He looked dubious.*) Well, do you like having secrets from the reader?

FORSTER (*brightening*): Ah now, that's a different question. . . . I was pleased when Peter Burra [1] noticed that the wasp upon which Godbole meditates during the festival in A *Passage to India* had already appeared earlier in the novel.

INTERVIEWERS: Had the wasps any esoteric meaning?

FORSTER: Only in the sense that there is something esoteric in India about all animals. I was just putting it in; and afterwards I saw it was something that might return non-logically in the story later.

---

[1] Burra was the author of the preface to the "Everyman" Edition of A *Passage to India*.

INTERVIEWERS: How far aware are you of your own technical
clevernesses in general?

FORSTER: We keep coming back to that. People will not realize
how little conscious one is of these things; how one flounders
about. They want us to be so much better informed than we are.
If critics could only have a course on writers' *not* thinking things
out—a course of lectures . . . (*He smiled.*)

INTERVIEWERS: You have said elsewhere that the authors you
have learned most from were Jane Austen and Proust. What did
you learn from Jane Austen technically?

FORSTER: I learned the possibilities of domestic humor. I was
more ambitious than she was, of course; I tried to hitch it on to
other things.

INTERVIEWERS: And from Proust?

FORSTER: I learned ways of looking at character from him. The
modern subconscious way. He gave me as much of the modern
way as I could take. I couldn't read Freud or Jung myself; it had
to be filtered to me.

INTERVIEWERS: Did any other novelists influence you technically? What about Meredith?

FORSTER: I admired him—*The Egoist* and the better constructed
bits of the other novels; but then that's not the same as his in-
fluencing me. I don't know if he did that. He did things I couldn't
do. What I admired was the sense of one thing opening into
another. You go into a room with him, and then that opens into
another room, and that into a further one.

INTERVIEWERS: What led you to make the remark quoted by
Lionel Trilling, that the older you got the less it seemed to you to
matter that an artist should "develop."

FORSTER: I am more interested in achievement than in advance
on it and decline from it. And I am more interested in works
than in authors. The paternal wish of critics to show how a writer
dropped off or picked up as he went along seems to me misplaced.
I am only interested in myself as a producer. What was it Mahler
said?—"anyone will sufficiently understand me who will trace my

development through my nine symphonies." This seems odd to me; I couldn't imagine myself making such a remark; it seems too uncasual. Other authors find themselves much more an object of study. I am conceited, but not interested in myself in this particular way. Of course I like reading my own work, and often do it. I go gently over the bits that I think are bad.

INTERVIEWERS: But you think highly of your own work?

FORSTER: That was implicit, yes. My regret is that I haven't written a bit more—that the body, the corpus, isn't bigger. I think I am different from other writers; they profess much more worry (I don't know if it is genuine). I have always found writing pleasant, and don't understand what people mean by "throes of creation." I've enjoyed it, but believe that in some ways it is good. Whether it will last, I have no idea.

P. N. FURBANK
F. J. H. HASKELL

2. François Mauriac

François Mauriac has defined himself as a writer in these words: "I am a metaphysician working on the concrete. I try to make the Catholic universe of evil perceptible, tangible, odorous. The theologians give us an abstract idea of the sinner. I give him flesh and blood."

The author was born of a middle-class family in Bordeaux in 1885 and began his education at a school run by Jesuits. Afterward he attended a *lycée*, the University of Bordeaux, and, very briefly, the University of Paris. In 1909 he published a book of poems, the first of a large body of work preoccupied with themes of conflict between human emotions and religious principle and obligation.

In a dozen years, starting in 1920, he wrote the ten novels which established his reputation as France's leading Catholic novelist. Notable among them were: *Le Baiser au lépreux* (*A Kiss for the Leper*) in 1922, *Génitrix* in 1923, *Thérèse Desqueyroux* (*Therese*) in 1927, and *Le Noeud de vipères* (*Vipers' Tangle*) in 1932. In 1934 he was elected to the French Academy. Shortly afterward, he commenced publication of his *Journals*, volumes of personal reflection and frequently controversial comment on the contemporary French scene. Mauriac has also written lives of Racine (1928) and Jesus (1936); he is the author of four plays, and of many books of stories, literary criticism, and essays. In 1952 he was awarded the Nobel Prize for Literature.

For the last three years he has contributed to the weekly *l'Express* an influential weekly column called "Bloc Notes," which continues the outspoken style of the *Journals*. Mauriac now divides his time between Paris and his estate called Malagar in the Guyenne country near Bordeaux, the setting of many of his novels.

(de Sud)

fatal lieutenant Wiczewsky)? Je sais bien
que l'homme ~~par~~ réduit à lui-même ne peut tendre qu'au
mal ; il m'empêche qu'il y a quelque chose
dans Naaman qui attire la grâce comme
la foudre... Quelle chose ? Je serais tenté de
~~vous~~ répondre : une rupture, un brisement de
cœur. ~~xxxxx xxxx xxxx~~ Il est écrit dans le psaume 50
« Le sacrifice selon Dieu, c'est un esprit brisé » : le
cœur contrit et brisé, o Dieu, vous ne le méprisez
jamais... » Vous répondrez que ce brisement est
déjà un effet de la grâce, une miséricorde toute
gratuite. Mais ~~ne~~ peut-on penser que Dieu sait
de toute éternité, au sein de son présent éternel, que cette grâce sera accueillie ?
~~xxxx~~ Rien n'est ni vain que ces sortes de débats...
~~xxxxxxxxx~~ Disons seulement qu'au départ ~~xx~~ une certaine
disposition intérieure dépend (peut-être) de nous ~~xx xxxx~~
~~xxxxxxxxx xx xxxxxxx xxx~~ à l'égard de l'
~~xx~~ amour, qui est le vrai Nom de Dieu...

An extract from "Bloc-Notes," a series of articles by François Mauriac on
contemporary subjects, in this case a discussion of Julien Green's *Sud*

Guy Pène du Bois

François Mauriac

"Every novelist ought to invent his own technique, that is the fact of the matter. Every novel worthy of the name is like another planet, whether large or small, which has its own laws just as it has its own flora and fauna. Thus, Faulkner's technique is certainly the best one with which to paint Faulkner's world, and Kafka's nightmare has produced its own myths that make it communicable. Benjamin Constant, Stendhal, Eugène Fromentin, Jacques Rivière, Radiguet, all used different techniques, took different liberties, and set themselves different tasks. The work of art itself, whether its title is Adolphe, Lucien Leuwen, Dominique, Le Diable au corps *or* A la Recherche du temps perdu, *is the solution to the problem of technique."*

With these words François Mauriac, discussing the novel in the French literary magazine La Table Ronde of August 1949, described his own position. In March 1953, he was interviewed

on the same subject for The Paris Review *by Jean le Marchand,
Secrétaire Générale of* La Table Ronde. *M. le Marchand began
by asking him about his earlier statement.*

MAURIAC: My opinion hasn't changed. I believe that my
younger fellow novelists are greatly preoccupied with technique.
They seem to think a good novel ought to follow certain rules
imposed from outside. In fact, however, this preoccupation ham-
pers them and embarrasses them in their creation. The great
novelist doesn't depend on anyone but himself. Proust resembled
none of his predecessors and he did not have, he could not have,
any successors. The great novelist breaks his mold; he alone can
use it. Balzac created the "Balzacian" novel; its style was suitable
only for Balzac.

There is a close tie between a novelist's originality in general
and the personal quality of his style. A borrowed style is a bad
style. American novelists from Faulkner to Hemingway invented
a style to express what they wanted to say—and it is a style that
can't be passed on to their followers.

INTERVIEWER: You have said that every novelist should invent
his style for himself—how would you describe your own?

MAURIAC: In all the time I have been writing novels I have
very seldom asked myself about the technique I was using. When
I begin to write I don't stop and wonder if I am interfering too
directly in the story, or if I know too much about my characters,
or whether or not I ought to judge them. I write with complete
naïveté, spontaneously. I've never had any preconceived notion of
what I could or could not do.

If today I sometimes ask myself these questions it's because they
are asked of me—because they are asked all around me.

Really there is no problem of this type whose solution is not
found in the completed work, whether good or bad. The preoccupation with these questions is a stumbling block for the French
novel. The crisis in French novel writing that people talk about so
much will be solved as soon as our young writers succeed in

getting rid of the naïve idea that Joyce, Kafka, and Faulkner hold the Tables of the Law of fictional technique. I'm convinced that a man with the real novelist's temperament would transcend these taboos, these imaginary rules.

INTERVIEWER: All the same, haven't you ever deliberately made use of definite techniques in novel writing?

MAURIAC: A novelist spontaneously works out the techniques that fit his own nature. Thus in *Thérèse Desqueyroux* I used some devices that came from the silent films: lack of preparation, the sudden opening, flashbacks. They were methods that were new and surprising at that time. I simply resorted to the techniques that my instinct suggested to me. My novel *Destins* [*Lines of Life*] was likewise composed with an eye to film techniques.

INTERVIEWER: When you begin to write, are all the important points of the plot already established?

MAURIAC: That depends on the novel. In general they aren't. There is a point of departure, and there are some characters. It often happens that the first characters don't go any further and, on the other hand, vaguer, more inconsistent characters show new possibilities as the story goes on and assume a place we hadn't foreseen. To take an example from one of my plays, *Asmodie*, I had no idea at the outset how M. Coutûre was going to develop, and how important he was going to become in the play.

INTERVIEWER: In writing your novels, has any one problem given you particular trouble?

MAURIAC: Not yet. Today, however, I cannot remain unaware of the comments made on my work from the standpoint of technique. That's why the novel I just finished won't be published this year. I want to look over it again in that light.

INTERVIEWER: Have you ever described a situation of which you had no personal experience?

MAURIAC: That goes without saying—for example, I've never poisoned anyone! Certainly a novelist more or less comprehends all his characters; but I have also described situations of which I had no direct experience.

INTERVIEWER: How distant in time do you have to be before you can describe your own experiences, or things you have seen?

MAURIAC: One cannot be a true novelist before one has attained a certain age, and that is why a young author has almost no chance of writing successfully about any other period of his life than his childhood or adolescence. A certain distance in time is absolutely necessary for a novelist, unless he is writing a journal.

All my novels take place in the period contemporary with my adolescence and my youth. They are all a "remembrance of things past." But if Proust's case helped me to understand my own, it was without any conscious imitation on my part.

INTERVIEWER: Do you make notes for future use? When you see something of interest in the course of life do you think, "That will be something I can use"?

MAURIAC: Never; for the reason I have just given. I don't observe and I don't describe; I rediscover. I rediscover the narrow Jansenist world of my devout, unhappy, and introverted childhood. It is as though when I was twenty a door within me had closed forever on that which was going to become the material of my work.

INTERVIEWER: To what extent is your writing dominated by sense-perceptions—hearing, sound, and sight?

MAURIAC: Very largely—the critics have all commented on the importance of the sense of smell in my novels. Before beginning a novel I recreate inside myself its places, its *milieu*, its colors and smells. I revive within myself the atmosphere of my childhood and my youth—I *am* my characters and their world.

INTERVIEWER: Do you write every day, or only when you feel inspired?

MAURIAC: I write whenever it suits me. During a creative period I write every day; a novel should not be interrupted. When I cease to be carried along, when I no longer feel as though I were taking down dictation, I stop.

INTERVIEWER: Have you ever tried to write a novel entirely different from those you have written?

MAURIAC: Sometimes I've thought of writing a detective story, but I've never done it.

INTERVIEWER: How do you hit on the names of your characters?

MAURIAC: I have been unwise enough to use names that are very well known in my part of the country, around Bordeaux. So far, I have been able to avoid the great embarrassments that this system could have caused me.

INTERVIEWER: To what extent are your characters based on real people?

MAURIAC: There is almost always a real person in the beginning, but then he changes so that sometimes he no longer bears the slightest resemblance to the original. In general it is only the secondary characters who are taken directly from life.

INTERVIEWER: Have you a special system for changing a real person into an imaginary one?

MAURIAC: There is no system . . . it is simply the art of the novel. What takes place is a sort of crystallization around the person. It is quite indescribable. For a true novelist this transformation is a part of one's inner life. If I used some trick of prefabrication the result would not be a living character.

INTERVIEWER: Do you describe yourself in any of your characters?

MAURIAC: To some degree in all of them. I particularly described myself in *L'Enfant chargé de chaines* and in *La Robe prétexte*. Ives Frontenac in *Le Mystère Frontenac* is both me and not me: there are strong resemblances, very strong, but at the same time a considerable deformation.

INTERVIEWER: From the standpoint of technique, what writers influenced you most?

MAURIAC: I can't tell. As far as technique goes I have been influenced by nobody, or again by all the authors I have read. One is always the product of a culture. We are sometimes influenced by humble writers whom we have forgotten—perhaps I was influenced only by those books I was steeped in for so long, the books I read in childhood. I don't think I have been influenced by any other novelist. I am a novelist of atmosphere, and poets have been very important for me: Racine, Baudelaire, Rimbaud, Maurice de Guérin, and François Jammes, for example.

INTERVIEWER: Do you think a novelist should "renew himself"?

MAURIAC: I feel that a writer's first duty is to be himself, to accept his limitations. The effort of self-expression should affect the manner of expression.

I have never begun a novel without hoping that it would be the one that would make it unnecessary for me to write another. I have had to start again from scratch with each one. What had gone before didn't count. . . . I was not adding to a fresco. Like a man who has decided to start his life over again, I have told myself that I had so far accomplished nothing: for I have always believed that my *chef d'œuvre* would be the novel I was working on at the time.

INTERVIEWER: Once a novel is finished do you remain attached to your characters? Do you maintain contact with them?

MAURIAC: My characters exist for me only when someone talks to me about them, or writes an article about them. I wrote a sequel to *Thérèse Desqueyroux* because I was induced to do so from outside. Once a book is written and has left me it exists only through others. Night before last I listened on the radio to an adaptation of *Désert de l'Amour*. Distorted as it was, I recognized Dr. Courrèges, his son Raymond, Marie Cross, the kept woman. This little world was speaking, suffering before me, this world that had left me thirty years before. I recognized it, slightly distorted by the mirror that reflected it.

We put the most of ourselves into certain novels, which perhaps are not the best. For example in *Le Mystère Frontenac* I sought to record my adolescence, to bring to life my mother and my father's brother, who was our tutor. Quite apart from any merits or defects it might possess, this book has for me a heart-rending tone. Actually I don't reread it any more than the others: I only reread my books when I have to in correcting proofs. The publication of my complete works condemned me to this: it is as painful as rereading old letters. It is thus that death emerges from abstraction, thus we touch it like a thing: a handful of ashes, of dust.

INTERVIEWER: Do you still read novels?

MAURIAC: I read very few. Every day I find that age asphyxiates the characters inside of me. I was once a passionate reader, I might say insatiable, but now . . . When I was young, my own future assured to the Madame Bovarys, the Anna Kareninas, the characters from Balzac, the atmosphere that made them, for me, living creatures. They spread out before me all that I dreamed of for myself. My destiny was prefigured by theirs. Then, as I lived longer, they closed around me like rivals. A kind of competition obliged me to measure myself against them, above all against the characters of Balzac. Now, however, they have become part of that which has been completed.

On the other hand, I can still reread a novel by Bernanos, or even Huysmans, because it has a metaphysical extension. As for my younger contemporaries, it is their technique, more than anything else, that interests me.

It is because novels no longer have any hold on me that I am given over more to history, to history in the making.

INTERVIEWER: Do you believe this attitude is peculiar to yourself? Don't you find, rather, that at a time when the impact of events such as those in Algeria is very heavy, the world has detached itself somewhat from fiction? Perhaps the *distance* is no longer there that is necessary for the reception of the novel.

MAURIAC: Every period in history has been more or less tragic. The events we are living through would not suffice to explain what is loosely called the crisis of the novel, which is not, I might add, a crisis of readership, inasmuch as the public does read novels today, and printings are much larger today than they were in my youth.

No, the crisis of the novel, in my opinion, is of a metaphysical nature, and is connected with a certain conception of man. The argument against the psychological novel derives essentially from the conception of man held by the present generation: a conception that is totally negative. This altered view of the individual began a long time ago. The works of Proust show it. Between *Swann's Way* (the perfect novel) and *The Past Recaptured* we watch the characters dissolve. As the novel advances, the characters decay.

Today, along with nonrepresentational art we have the nonrepresentational novel—the characters simply have no distinguishing features.

I believe that the crisis of the novel, if it exists, is right there, essentially, in the domain of technique. The novel has lost its purpose. That is the most serious difficulty, and it is from there that we must begin. The younger generation believes, after Joyce and Proust, that it has discovered the "purpose" of the old novel to have been prefabricated and unrelated to reality.

INTERVIEWER: Doesn't talking about the characters' dissolving put too much emphasis on the experimental novel? After all, there are still characters in the novels of Proust and Kafka. They have changed, of course, as compared to those of Balzac, but you remember them, you know them by name, they exist for the reader.

MAURIAC: I am going to shock you. I scarcely know the names of Kafka's characters, and yet at the same time I know him well, because he himself fascinates me. I have read his diary, his letters, everything about him. But as for his novels, I cannot read them.

In Proust, I have mentioned that one is struck by the slow decay of each character. After *The Captive* the novel turns into a long meditation on jealousy: Albertine no longer exists in the flesh; characters who seem to exist, at the beginning of the novel, such as Charlus, become confused with the vice which devours them.

The crisis of the novel, then, is metaphysical. The generation that preceded ours was no longer Christian, but it believed in the individual, which comes to the same thing as believing in the soul. What each of us understands by the word "soul" is different; but in any case it is the fixed point around which the individual is constructed.

Faith in God was lost for many, but not the values this faith postulates. The good was not bad, and the bad was not good. The collapse of the novel is due to the destruction of this fundamental concept: the awareness of good and evil. The language itself has been devalued and emptied of its meaning by this attack on conscience.

Observe that for the novelist who has remained Christian, like myself, man is someone creating himself or destroying himself. He is not an immobile being, fixed, cast in a mold once and for all. This is what makes the traditional psychological novel so different from what I did or thought I was doing. The human being as I conceive him in the novel is a being caught up in the drama of salvation, even if he doesn't know it.

And yet, I admire in the young novelists their "search for the absolute," their hatred of false appearances and illusions. They made me think of what Alain and Simone Weil said of a "purifying atheism." . . . But let's not go into that—I'm no philosopher.

INTERVIEWER: That's what everyone says you are. Besides, why deny it?

MAURIAC: Each time literary talent decreases, the philosophers gain. I am not saying that's against them, but little by little they have taken over. The present generation is terribly intelligent. In the old days one could have talent and still be a little stupid; today, no. . . . Insofar as the young are philosophers, they probably have much less need of fiction than we did.

It is very important, all the same, that the master who has most influenced our period in literature should be a philosopher. Jean-Paul Sartre has, moreover, great talent, without which he would not have taken the position he has now occupied. Compare his influence to that of Bergson, who stayed in the domain of ideas and only affected literature indirectly, through his influence on the literary men themselves.

INTERVIEWER: Do you believe that literature has been turned over to the philosophers by accident?

MAURIAC: There is a historical reason for it: the tragedy of

France. Sartre expressed the despair of this generation. He did not create it, but he gave it a justification and a style.

INTERVIEWER: You said that you were more interested in the man Kafka than in his work. In the *Figaro littéraire,* you wrote that throughout *Wuthering Heights* it is the figure of Emily Brontë which attracted you. In a word, when the characters disappear, the author steps into the foreground and little by little takes over the scene.

MAURIAC: Almost all the works die while the men remain. We seldom read any more of Rousseau than his *Confessions,* or of Chateaubriand than his *Mémoires d'outre-tombe.* They alone interest us. I have always been and still remain a great admirer of Gide. It already appears, however, that only his journal and *Si le grain ne meurt,* the story of his childhood, have any chance of lasting. The rarest thing in literature, and the only success, is when the author disappears and his work remains. We don't know who Shakespeare was, or Homer. People have worn themselves out writing about the life of Racine without being able to establish anything. He is lost in the radiance of his creation. That is quite rare.

There are almost no writers who disappear into their work. The opposite almost always comes about. Even the great characters that have survived in novels are found now more in handbooks and histories, as though in a museum. As living creatures they get worn out, and they grow feeble. Sometimes we even see them die. Madame Bovary seems to me to be in poorer health than she used to be. . . .

INTERVIEWER: You think so?

MAURIAC: Yes, and even Anna Karenina, even the Karamazovs. First, because they need readers in order to live and the new generations are less and less capable of providing them with the air they need to breathe.

INTERVIEWER: In one place you speak of the greatness of the novel as the perfect literary form, the king of the arts.

MAURIAC: I was praising my merchandise . . . no art is more

royal than another. It is the artist who counts. Tolstoi and Dickens and Balzac are great, not the literary form they demonstrated.

INTERVIEWER: Has Christianity lived so intensely as yours created problems for you as a novelist?

MAURIAC: All the time. It seems comical today, but I was regarded in Catholic circles almost as a pornographic writer. That held me down somewhat.

If I were asked, "Do you believe your faith has hampered or enriched your literary life?" I would answer yes to both parts of the question. My Christian faith has enriched me. It has also hampered me, in that my books are not what they might have been had I let myself go. Today I know that God pays no attention to what we write; He uses it.

I am a Christian, though, and I would like to end my life not in violence and anger, but in peace. For the greatest temptation at the close of a Christian's life is retreat, silence. Even to the music I love most I now prefer silence, because there is no silence with God.

My enemies believe I want to remain on stage at any price— that I make use of politics in order to survive. They would be astounded indeed if they knew that my greatest happiness is to be alone on my terrace, trying to guess the direction of the wind from the odors it carries. What I fear is not being forgotten after my death, but, rather, not being enough forgotten. As we were saying, it is not our books that survive, but our poor lives that linger in the histories.

TRANSLATED BY JOHN TRAIN
AND LYDIA MOFFAT

Additional material courtesy of *L'Express*

3. Joyce Cary

Joyce Cary's success as a novelist came after years of seeming failure. He was born in 1888 in County Donegal, Ireland, of Anglo-Irish parentage. He studied painting at Edinburgh and Paris and then took his degree at Oxford, before setting off to the Balkan War in 1912 to serve with the British Red Cross. In the First World War he fought in the Cameroons, where he was wounded. After the war he served in a long series of remote colonial posts in the West African bush country. He returned to England in 1920 to write novels. He was forty-four when the first was published (*Aissa Saved*, 1932). His first critical success came with *Mister Johnson* (1939), and financial success with the best-selling *The Horse's Mouth* (1944), published in Cary's fifty-sixth year.

Cary is best-known for the novels of his two trilogies: *Herself Surprised* (1941), *To Be a Pilgrim* (1942), *The Horse's Mouth* (1944); and *A Prisoner of Grace* (1952), *Except the Lord* (1953), and *Not Honour More* (1955). The large scope of the trilogy perfectly suited Cary's talent. V. S. Pritchett described him as "the chameleon among contemporary novelists. Put him down in any environment or any class, rich, middling, or poor, English, Irish, or foreign, and he changes color and becomes whatever his subject is from an English cook to an African delinquent."

Never in good health, Cary kept on writing at his home in Oxford even after he learned in 1955 that he was the victim of incurable progressive paralysis. Besides articles and short stories, he had completed a book of critical lectures, *Art and Reality*, before he died in March 1957.

Pincomb ?

day, the eighth, I had information that (Jones) would hold a mass meeting
at the centre.   And a phone call from the police at Lilmouth to look

out for trouble. The Lilmouth gang was on the way to East Tarbiton works
centre.   Jones was going to talk.   This was a gang that had made trouble
in Lilmouth - the only trouble they had.

The unemployment centre was a scheme by the Emergency Committee.
i.e. Nimmo.   He had started it some months before, a plan for workshops,
recreation *rooms for unemployed, clothes mending*

~~rooms for unemployed, old clothes distribution~~, canteens and nurseries,
scattered about in a lot of odd spots around East Tarbiton and Lilmouth.
An old chapel in Tarbiton and a sixteen-room villa just outside,
a half-ruined cloth factory at Batwell and the ~~Manor House~~ *iced Hall* at Ferryport.
Lady Gould, chairman General Welfare Committee; ~~Countess of Lilmouth,~~ *Countess of Lilmouth, & other tournaments   Mrs. James Latter*
chairman Canteen Committee; Mrs. William (Jones) chairman Chi~~l~~dren's *Mrs*
Care.   Nimmo's usual game, hang a nosebag on everyone, keep 'em quiet.

Feeding their own fancies and ~~getting their~~ *feeling their own*
own ~~own~~ importance. But trouble, a lot of fun
the start. Mrs. Pincomb wanted to put Bolshies
in all the nurseries, Lady Gould Red liberal
candidates full of high ideals, and ~~too~~ few
suspicions and the canteens had a string of
colonels widows quite ready to fight the mob
from the chief of the ~~look~~ for of their Cat. ? *Pincomb*

~~a string of colonels' widows.~~ Then Jones came in on the Workshop
Committee and appointed a Bolshy manager. One of Potter's old men,
carpentry instructor, ordered to get out first day. Next morning
Potters manager in the workshop shop, very well,
~~young Wall~~ came down with a crowd of young fellows bringing the old
boy with them, and said if they wanted to put him out they'd have to

---

The extract above is part of the manuscript of Not Honour More, *the work
on which Joyce Cary was engaged at the time of the interview*

Guy Pène du Bois

Joyce Cary

Joyce Cary, a sprightly man with an impish crown of gray hair set at a jaunty angle on the back of his head, lives in a high and rather gloomy house in North Oxford. Extremely animated, Mr. Cary's movements are decisive, uncompromising, and retain some of the brisk alertness of his military career. His speech is overwhelming: voluminous and without hesitation or effort. His rather high voice commands attention, but is expressive and emphatic enough to be a little hard to follow. He is a compactly built, angular man with a keen, determined face, sharp, humorous eyes, and well-defined features. His quick and energetic expressions and bearing create the feeling that it is easier for him to move about than to sit still, and easier to talk than to be silent, even though, like most good talkers, he is a creative and intelligent listener.

His house, a Victorian building with pointed Gothic windows and dark prominent gables, stands opposite the University cricket ground, and just by Keble College. It is a characteristically North Oxford house, contriving to form part of a row without any appearance of being aware of its neighbors. It lies only a little back from the road, behind a small overgrown garden, thick with bushes. The house and garden have all the air of being obstinately "property," self-contained and a little severe. So we weren't really surprised at having to wait on the porch and ring away at the bell three or four times; or to learn, when Mr. Cary himself eventually opened the door, that his housekeeper was deaf. A very large grand piano half fills the comfortable room into which we were led. It has one lamp for the treble, another for the bass The standard of comfort is that of a successful member of the professional class; the atmosphere a little Edwardian, solid, comfortable, unpretentious, with no obtrusive bric-a-brac. Along one wall is a group of representational paintings done by Cary himself in the past. He has, he says, no time for painting now. He is the kind of man who knows exactly what he has time for. So we got down to the questions right away.

INTERVIEWERS: Have you by any chance been shown a copy of Barbara Hardy's essay on your novels in the latest number of *Essays in Criticism?*

CARY: On "Form." Yes I saw it. Quite good, I thought.

INTERVIEWERS: Well, setting the matter of form aside for the moment, we were interested in her attempt to relate you to the tradition of the family chronicle. Is it in fact your conscious intention to re-create what she calls the pseudo-saga?

CARY: Did she say that? Must have skipped that bit.

INTERVIEWERS: Well, she didn't say "consciously," but we were interested to know whether this was your intention.

CARY: You mean, did I intend to follow up Galsworthy and Walpole? Oh, no, no, no. Family life, no. Family life just goes on. Toughest thing in the world. But of course it is also the microcosm of a world. You get everything there—birth, life, death, love and jealousy, conflict of wills, of authority and freedom, the new and the old. And I always choose the biggest stage possible for my theme.

INTERVIEWERS: What about the eighteenth-century novelists? Someone vaguely suggested that you recaptured their spirit, or something of that kind.

CARY: Vaguely is the word. I don't know who I'm like. I've been called a metaphysical novelist, and if that means I have a fairly clear and comprehensive idea of the world I'm writing about, I suppose that's true.

INTERVIEWERS: You mean an idea about the nature of the world which guides the actions of the characters you are creating?

CARY: Not so much the ideas as their background. I don't care for philosophers in books. They are always bores. A novel should be an experience and convey an emotional truth rather than arguments.

INTERVIEWERS: Background—you said background.

CARY: The whole set-up—character—of the world as we know it. Roughly, for me, the principal fact of life is the free mind. For good and evil, man is a free creative spirit. This produces the very queer world we live in, a world in continuous creation and therefore continuous change and insecurity. A perpetually new and lively world, but a dangerous one, full of tragedy and injustice. A world in everlasting conflict between the new idea and the old allegiances, new arts and new inventions against the old establishment.

INTERVIEWERS: Miss Hardy complains that the form shows too clearly in your novels.

CARY: Others complain that I don't make the fundamental idea plain enough. This is every writer's dilemma. Your form is your meaning, and your meaning dictates the form. But what you try to convey is reality—the fact plus the feeling, a total complex experience of a real world. If you make your scheme too explicit the framework shows and the book dies. If you hide it too thoroughly, the book has no meaning and therefore no form. It is a mess.

INTERVIEWERS: How does this problem apply in *The Moonlight?*

CARY: I was dealing there with the contrast between conventional systems in different centuries—systems created by man's imagination to secure their lives and give them what they seek from life.

INTERVIEWERS: Didn't the critics call Rose a tyrant?

CARY: Oh, they were completely wrong about Rose. She was a Victorian accepting the religion and the conventions of her time and sacrificing her own happiness to carry them out. A fine woman. And no more of a tyrant than any parent who tries to guide a child in the right path. That religion, that system, has gone, but it was thoroughly good and efficient in its own time. I mean, it gave people good lives and probably all the happiness that can be achieved for anybody in this world.

INTERVIEWERS: Are the political aspects of your work controlled by the same ideas?

CARY: Religion is organized to satisfy and guide the soul—politics does the same thing for the body. Of course they overlap—this is a very rough description. But the politician is responsible for law, for physical security, and in a world of tumult, of perpetual conflict, he has the alternatives, roughly again, of persuading people or shooting them. In the democracies, we persuade. And this gives great power to the spellbinder, the artist in words, the preacher, the demagogue, whatever you call him. Rousseau, Marx, Tolstoi, these were great spellbinders—as well as Lacordaire. My Nimmo is a typical spellbinder. Bonser was a spellbinder in business, the man of imagination. He was also a crook, but so are many spellbinders. Poets have started most of the revolutions, especially nationalist revolutions. On the other hand, life would die without poets, and democracy must have its spellbinders.

INTERVIEWERS: Roosevelt?

CARY: Yes, look what he did—and compare him with Wilson. Wilson was a good man, but he hadn't the genius of the spellbinder—the art of getting at people and moving the crowd.

INTERVIEWERS: Is Nimmo based on Roosevelt?

CARY: No, he belongs to the type of all of them—Juarez, Lloyd George, Bevan, Sankey and Moody, Billy Graham.

INTERVIEWERS: Do you base your characters on people you know?

CARY: Never, you can't. You may get single hints. But real people are too complex and too disorganized for books. They aren't simple enough. Look at all the great heroes and heroines, Tom Jones, Madame Bovary, Anna Karenina, Baron Charlus, Catherine Linton: they are essentially characters from fable, and so they must be to take their place in a formal construction which is to have a meaning. A musician does not write music by trying to fit chords into his whole. The chords arise from the development of his motives.

INTERVIEWERS: In one of your prefaces you said, didn't you, that Jimson's father came from life?

CARY: I met an old man, an artist who had been in the Academy and a success, and was then ruined by the change of taste when the impressionists created their new symbolic school. But I didn't use him in my book, I don't know anything about his character, only his tragedy. A very common one in this world. (*Suddenly*) The French seem to take me for an existentialist in Sartre's sense of the word. But I'm not. I am influenced by the solitude of men's minds, but equally by the unity of their fundamental character and feelings, their sympathies which bring them together. I believe that there is such a thing as unselfish love and beauty. I am obliged to believe in God as a person. I don't suppose any church would accept me, but I believe in God and His grace with an absolute confidence. It is by His grace that we know beauty and love, that we have all that makes life worth living in a tough, dangerous, and unjust world. Without that belief I could not make sense of the world and I could not write. Of course, if you say I am an existentialist in the school of Kierkegaard, that is more reasonable. But existentialism without a god is nonsense—

it atomizes a world which is plainly a unity. It produces merely frustration and defeat. How can one explain the existence of personal feelings, love and beauty, in nature, unless a person, God, is there? He's there as much as hydrogen gas. He is a fact of experience. And one must not run away from experience. I don't believe in miracles. I'm not talking here of faith cures—but some breach in the fundamental consistency of the world character which is absolutely impossible. I mean absolutely. (*With emphasis*) God is a character, a real and consistent being, or He is nothing. If God did a miracle He would deny His own nature and the universe would simply blow up, vanish, become nothing. And we can't even conceive nothingness. The world is a definite character. It *is*, and therefore it is *something*. And it can't be any other thing. Aquinas tells you all the things that God can't do without contradicting himself.

INTERVIEWERS: But about existentialism.

CARY: Kierkegaard states the uniqueness of the individual and I stand by that.

INTERVIEWERS: That's what you meant, then, when you said that what makes men tick should be the main concern of the novelist? The character's principle of unity?

CARY: And action, their beliefs. You've got to find out what people *believe*, what is pushing them on. . . . And of course it's a matter, too, of the simpler emotional drives—like ambition and love. These are the real stuff of the novel, and you can't have any sort of real form unless you've got an ordered attitude towards them.

INTERVIEWERS: But the fundamental beliefs are not always the most apparent, or, it seems to us, the most successful of the achievements in the novel. We were expecting, for instance, a much closer analysis of the religious beliefs of Brown in *To Be a Pilgrim*. But we felt, in fact, that what came across most successfully were the emotional responses of people to people—compelling, for instance, Lucy to follow Brown.

CARY: The details were there once. That is, Brown's arguments were there, and Lucy's response. But Lucy was only one character, one motive in the symphony. And also I was up against the problem of explicit statement. I may have cut too much, but the book is long and packed already. The essence of Lucy was her deep faith. She wasn't the kind of person who can float along from day to day like a piece of newspaper or a banana skin in the gutter. And in the book, I had her feelings expressed. But I cut them somewhere in the rewriting. I rewrite a great deal and I work over the whole book and cut out anything that does not belong to the emotional development, the texture of feeling. I left too much of the religious argument in *Except the Lord* and people criticize it as too explicit or dull.

INTERVIEWERS: Do you find in those later stages that you're primarily concerned with the more technical side of "form"? With, for example, managing the flashback? And do you think, incidentally, that you owe that particular trick to the films? I believe that you worked on a film in Africa.

CARY: No, I don't really think it has anything to do with films. The flashback in my novels is not just a trick. In, for example, *The Moonlight*, I used it in order to make my theme possible. It was essential to compare two generations. You can't do that without a flashback contrast; the chronological run-through by itself is no good.

INTERVIEWERS: In the preface to *Herself Surprised* you mentioned a technical difficulty you found yourself in. You wanted to show everything through the eyes of Sara, but found that to make her see everything diluted her character. This was the soliloquy as flashback. This struck us as the same dilemma that James found himself in when writing *What Maisie Knew*. Is this a just parallel? Do you read James?

CARY: Yes, but James is not very remarkable technically. He's one of our very greatest novelists, but you will not learn much by studying his technique. *What Maisie Knew*, that was one of the packed ones, wasn't it? Almost too packed. I enjoyed its intense appreciation of the child's nature, and the cruel imbecility of the world in which she was thrown about. But on the whole I prefer the beautifully clear atmosphere of a book like *The Europeans* or *Daisy Miller*—all James is in *Daisy Miller*.

INTERVIEWERS: Have you read *The Bostonians?* There was the spellbinder.

CARY: No, I haven't read that.

INTERVIEWERS: *The Princess Casamassima?*

CARY: I'm afraid I haven't read that either. Cecil is always telling me to read her and I must. But I read James a good deal. There are times you need James, just as there are times when you must have Proust—in his very different world of change. The essential thing about James is that he came into a different, a highly organized, a hieratic society, and for him it was not only a very good and highly civilized society, but static. It was the best the world could do. But it was already subject to corruption. This was the center of James' moral idea—that everything good was, for that reason, specially liable to corruption. Any kind of goodness, integrity of character, exposed that person to ruin. And the whole civilization, because it was a real civilization, cultivated and sensitive, was fearfully exposed to frauds and go-getters, brutes and grabbers. This was his tragic theme. But my world is quite different—it is intensely dynamic, a world in creation. In this world, politics is like navigation in a sea without charts and wise men live the lives of pilgrims.

INTERVIEWERS: Have you sympathy with those who most uncompromisingly pursue their own free idea whatever the opposition?

CARY: I don't put a premium on aggression. Oh, no, no, no. I'm no life-force man. Critics write about my vitality. What is vitality? As a principle it is a lot of balls. The life force is rubbish, an abstraction, an idea without character. Shaw's tale of life force is either ˙senseless rubbish or he really means Shaw—Shaw as God's mind. The life force doesn't exist. Show me some in a bottle. The life of the world is the nature of God, and God is as real as the trees.

INTERVIEWERS: Which novelists do you think have most influenced you?

CARY: Influenced? Oh, lots. Hundreds. Conrad had a great deal at one point. I've got a novel upstairs I wrote forty years ago in Africa, under his influence. But I read very few novels nowadays. I read memoirs and history. And the classics. I've got them at my fingertips and I can turn up the points I want. I don't read many modern novels, I haven't time, but those I do read are often very good. There is plenty of good work being done, and in Britain the public for good work has enormously increased in my lifetime—especially in the last thirty years.

INTERVIEWERS: Do you find, then, that conversation with the novelists of today helps?

CARY: Conversation?

INTERVIEWERS: I mean apart from the personal stimulus, do you find that what they have to say helps to resolve technical problems?

CARY: Oh, no. Not particularly. We chatter. But you have to work problems out for yourself, on paper. Put the stuff down and read it—to see if it works. Construction is a complicated job—later I'll show you my apparatus.

INTERVIEWERS: Is there only one way to get a thing right? How close is form?

CARY: That's a difficult question. Often you have very little room for maneuver. See Proust's letter to Mme. Schiff about Swann, saying he had to make Swann ridiculous. A novelist is often in Proust's jam.

INTERVIEWERS: You are a determinist—you think even novelists are pushed by circumstances?

CARY: Everyone but a lunatic has reason for what he does. Yes, in that sense I am a determinist. But I believe, with Kant, that the mind is self-determined. That is, I believe intensely in the creative freedom of the mind. That is indeed absolutely essential to man's security in a chaotic world of change. He is faced all the time with unique complex problems. To sum them up for action is an act of creative imagination. He fits the different elements together in a coherent whole and invents a rational act to deal with it. He requires to be free, he requires his independence and solitude of mind, he requires his freedom of mind and imagination. Free will is another matter—it is a term, or rather a contradiction in terms, which leads to continual trouble. The will is never free— it is always attached to an object, a purpose. It is simply the engine in the car—it can't steer. It is the mind, the reason, the imagination that steers.

Of course, anyone can deny the freedom of the mind. He can argue that our ideas are conditioned. But anyone who argues so must not stop there. He must deny all freedom and say that the world is simply an elaborate kind of clock. He must be a behaviorist. There is no alternative, in logic, between behaviorism, mechanism, and the personal God who is the soul of beauty, love, and truth. And if you believe in behaviorism, none of these things has any real existence. They are cogwheels in the clock, and you yourself do not exist as a person. You are a delusion. So take your choice. Either it is personal or it is a delusion—a delusion rather difficult to explain.

INTERVIEWERS: How do you fit poetry into this? I once heard you describe it as "prose cut up into lines." Would you stick to that?

CARY: Did I say that? I must have been annoying someone. No, I wouldn't stick to it.

INTERVIEWERS: Anyway, at what stage of your career did you decide to write novels rather than anything else?

CARY: What stage? Oh, I've been telling stories ever since I was very small. I'm telling stories now to the children of a friend of mine. I always tell stories. And I've been writing them from childhood. I told them to other children when I was a child. I told them at school. I told them to my own children and I tell them now to the children of a friend.

INTERVIEWERS: *Aissa Saved* was the first one you published?

CARY: Yes, and that was not until I was forty. I'd written many before, but I was never satisfied with them. They raised political and religious questions I found I could not answer. I have three or four of them up there in the attic, still in manuscript.

INTERVIEWERS: Was this what made you feel that you needed a "new education"?

CARY: At twenty-six I'd knocked about the world a good bit and I thought I knew the answers, but I didn't know. I couldn't finish the novels. The best novel I ever wrote—at least it contained some of my best stuff—there's about a million words of it upstairs, I couldn't finish it. I found that I was faking things all the time, dodging issues and letting my characters dodge them.

INTERVIEWERS: Could you tell us something about your working methods?

CARY: Well—I write the big scenes first, that is, the scenes that carry the meaning of the book, the emotional experience. The first scene in *Prisoner of Grace* was that at the railway station, when Nimmo stops his wife from running away by purely moral pressure. That is, she became the prisoner of grace. When I have the big scenes sketched I have to devise a plot into which they'll fit. Of course often they don't quite fit. Sometimes I have to throw them out. But they have defined my meaning, given form to the book. Lastly I work over the whole surface.

INTERVIEWERS: When does the process, the book, start?

CARY: Possibly years ago—in a note, a piece of dialogue. Often I don't know the real origin. I had an odd experience lately which gave me a glimpse of the process, something I hadn't suspected. I was going round Manhattan—do you know it?

INTERVIEWERS: Not yet.

CARY: It's an island and I went round on a steamer with an American friend, Elizabeth Lawrence, of Harper's. And I noticed a girl sitting all by herself on the other side of the deck—a girl of about thirty, wearing a shabby skirt. She was enjoying herself. A nice expression, with a wrinkled forehead, a good many wrinkles. I said to my friend, "I could write about that girl—what do you think she is?" Elizabeth said that she might be a schoolteacher

taking a holiday, and asked me why I wanted to write about her.
I said I didn't really know—I imagined her as sensitive and intelligent, and up against it. Having a hard life but making something of it, too. In such a case I often make a note. But I didn't
—and I forgot the whole episode. Then, about three weeks later,
in San Francisco, I woke up one night at four—I am not so much
a bad sleeper as a short sleeper—I woke up, I say, with a story
in my head. I sketched the story at once—it was about an English
girl in England, a purely English tale. Next day an appointment
fell through and I had a whole day on my hands. I found my notes
and wrote the story—that is, the chief scenes and some connecting tissue. Some days later, in a plane—ideal for writing—I began
to work it over, clean it up, and I thought, Why all these wrinkles?
that's the third time they come in. And I suddenly realized that
my English heroine was the girl on the Manhattan boat. Somehow she had gone down into my subconscious, and came up again
with a full-sized story. And I imagine that has happened before.
I notice some person because he or she exemplifies some part of
my feeling about things. The Manhattan girl was a motive. And
she brought up a little piece of counterpoint. But the wrinkles
were the first crude impression—a note, but one that counted too
much in the final writing.

INTERVIEWERS: A note—

CARY: I was thinking in terms of music. My short stories are
written with the same kind of economy—and no one would publish them. Some of them, now being published, are twenty years
old. Because each note has to count and it must not be super-
fluous. A son of mine, a composer, wrote some music for the
BBC lately. The orchestra was small, and the Musicians' Union
wouldn't let him conduct. He heard one of the players ask the
conductor what the stuff was like. The conductor, no doubt in-
tending to warn the player, answered, "It's good, but the trouble
is that every note counts." I suppose the editors who rejected me
felt like that. They wanted a little more fluff.

INTERVIEWERS: You can depend around here on practically everyone's having read *The Horse's Mouth*. Do you think that's because it's less philosophical? Or just because it's a Penguin?

CARY: *The Horse's Mouth* is a very heavy piece of metaphysical writing. No, they like it because it's funny. The French have detected the metaphysics and are fussing about the title. I want *Le Tuyau increvable*—the unbustable tip. They say this is unworthy of a philosophical work and too like a *roman policier*. I say *tant mieux*. But they are unconvinced.

INTERVIEWERS: A metaphysical work—

CARY: A study of the creative imagination working in symbols. And symbols are highly uncertain—they also die.

INTERVIEWERS: Gully's picture on the wall then, which is demolished, is in its turn a symbol of the instability of the symbol?

CARY: That's what Mrs. Hardy seems to think. But that would be allegory. I hate allegory. The trouble is that if your books mean anything, the critic is apt to work allegory in. The last scene of Gully is a real conflict, not an allegorical one. And it was necessary to cap the development. It was the catastrophe in a Greek sense.

INTERVIEWERS: *The Horse's Mouth* was part of a trilogy. You're doing this again now, aren't you, in A *Prisoner of Grace, Except the Lord*, and the third yet to come?

CARY: I was dissatisfied with the first trilogy. I've set out this time with the intention of doing better. I think I am doing better. The contrasts between the different worlds are much sharper. When I'd finished A *Prisoner of Grace* I planned a second book on political religion, but contemporary religion. And I found myself bored with the prospect. I nearly threw in the whole plan. Then one of my children urged me to go on. And I had the idea of writing Nimmo's religion as a young man. This appeared to me as opening a new world of explanation, and also giving a strong contrast to the last book. So I got to work. And tried to get at the roots of left-wing English politics in evangelical religion.

INTERVIEWERS: And the third?

CARY: It's going to be called *Not Honour More*. In it, I deal with Jim—the lover in A *Prisoner of Grace*. He is the man of honor, of duty, of service, reacting against the politician. But I'll show it to you in its present state. Upstairs.

We followed Mr. Cary upstairs two stories to his workshop. It was a room with a low ceiling. A window at the far end looked out onto trees. Where the walls downstairs had been covered with pictures, up here it was all bookcases, containing, it seemed, more files than books. Mr. Cary went straight to his desk, pulling out sheaves of paper from the shelves over it. They were, one instantly observed, meticulously organized. The sheaves were numbered and titled, each chapter in its own envelope. Mr. Cary explained that these were the "big scenes." Clipped on the front of each envelope was a sheet of memoranda indicating what still remained to be done within the chapter, what would be required to give the finished scene a more convincing build-up. These were the chapters of the embryonic Not Honour More.

Mr. Cary explained that he was now "plotting" the book. There was research yet to be done. Research, he explained, was sometimes a bore; but it was necessary for getting the political and social background of his work right. He had a secretary who did useful work for him in the Bodleian, the University library. He was at the moment, for example, wanting facts on the General Strike, and had given his secretary a list of questions to work on.

We asked him if what we had heard was true—that often, as he worked, his writing would generate another unrelated idea and he would thus be led to write out a block of about twenty thousand words before returning to the work at hand. Mr. Cary confirmed this account; and it was confirmed too by the large bookcase containing nothing but files and boxes of unfinished work. It was an impressive proliferation of novels and short stories, with the titles on the spines, unfamiliar titles like The Facts of Life. *One file contained "recent short stories."*

The over-all impression of the room in which he worked, as of the novelist himself, was of a man who, much as he himself might eschew the word, radiated "vitality." He rose, he said, early, and was always at his desk by nine. We had already used up more than the period of time he had agreed to give us. As we went downstairs and made again for the sitting room, he looked anxiously at his watch; but we were there only to dig quickly among the deep cushions for the belongings that had spilled from our pockets as we lounged.

JOHN BURROWS
ALEX HAMILTON

4. Dorothy Parker

Dorothy Parker was born Dorothy Rothschild in West End, New Jersey, in 1893, and was educated partly in a convent school. In 1916 she worked for *Vogue* at ten dollars a week; then she became drama critic for *Vanity Fair*. Her first collection of verse, *Enough Rope*, appeared in 1927. That same year she accepted a book-reviewing stint for *The New Yorker*, her columns appearing over the signature "Constant Reader." She was becoming famous as a wit among the group that met at the Round Table in the Hotel Algonquin. There was a time when everything bright or malicious said in New York was ascribed to Dorothy Parker.

In 1929 she won the O. Henry Prize for "Big Blonde," a story which was included in her first collection, *Laments for the Living* (1930). A second collection of stories was *After Such Pleasures* (1933). *Here Lies* (1939) included all her fiction published to that time. She has written three plays: *Close Harmony* (with Elmer Rice, 1924), *The Coast of Illyria* (1949), and *The Ladies of the Corridor* (with Arnaud d'Usseau, 1953). Although she prefers the dramatic form, her plays have never achieved the popularity of her verse and her short stories. Her collections of verse were all best-sellers, a rare occurrence in American publishing. They include *Sunset Gun* (1928), *Death and Taxes* (1931), and *Not So Deep as a Well*, her collected poems (1936).

The Portable Dorothy Parker (1944), including both verse and fiction complete, has been one of the most popular volumes in a famous series. Alexander Woollcott said of her work that it was "so potent a distillation of nectar and wormwood, of ambrosia and deadly night-shade, as might suggest to the rest of us that we write far too much."

and, on consoles and desk and table, photographs of himself at two
and a half and five and seven and nine, framed in broad mirror
bands. Whenever his mother settled in a new domicile, and she
removed often, those photographs were the first things out of the
luggage. The boy hated them. He had had to pass his fifteenth
birthday before his body had caught up with his head; there was that head ~ in those
presentments of his former selves, that pale, enormous blob.
Once he had asked his mother to put the pictures somewhere else -
preferably some small, dark place that could be locked. But he
had had the bad fortune to make his request on one of the occasions
when she was given to weeping suddenly and long. So the photographs stood out on parade, with their frames twinkling away.

There were twinkings, too, to the silver top of the
fat crystal cocktail shaker, but the liquid low within the crystal
was pale and dull. There was no shine, either, to the glass his
mother held.ᵻₙₓₖₘₓₓₕₓₙₔₓ It was cloudy from the clutch of her
hand, and on the inside there were oily dribbles/ₓₕₓₜ of what it had
contained.

His mother shut the door by which she had admitted him
and followed him into the room. She looked at him with her head
tilted to the side.

"Well, aren't you going to kiss me?" she said in a
charming, wheedling voice, the voice of a little, little girl.
"Aren't you, you beautiful big ox, you?"

"Sure," he said. He bent down toward her, but she
stepped suddenly away. A sharp change came over her. She drew
herself tall, with her shoulders back and her head flung high.
Her upper lip lifted over her teeth, and her gaze came cold beneath

---

A manuscript page from a short story by Dorothy Parker. Copyright 1955 by
The New Yorker *Magazine Inc.*

Dorothy Parker

Dorothy Parker lives in a midtown New York hotel. She shares her small apartment with a youthful poodle which has run of the place and has caused it to look, as Mrs. Parker says apologetically, somewhat "Hogarthian": newspapers spread about the floor, picked lamb chops here and there, and a rubber doll—its throat torn from ear to ear—which Mrs. Parker lobs left-handed from her chair into corners of the room for the poodle to retrieve—as it does, never tiring of the opportunity. The room is sparsely decorated, its one overpowering fixture being a large dog portrait, not of the poodle, but of a sheepdog owned by the author Philip Wylie and painted by his wife. The portrait indicates a dog of such size that in real life it must dwarf Mrs. Parker. She is a small woman, her voice gentle, her tone often apologetic, but occasionally, given the opportunity to comment on matters she feels strongly about, her voice rises almost harshly, and her sentences are punctuated with observations phrased with lethal force. Hers is still the wit which made her a legend as a member of the Round Table of the Algonquin—a humor whose particular quality seems a coupling of a brilliant social commentary with a mind of devastating inventiveness. She seems able to produce the well-turned phrase for any occasion. A friend remembers sitting next to her at the theater when the news was announced of the death of the stolid Calvin Coolidge. "How do they know?" whispered Mrs. Parker.

Readers of this interview, however, will find that Mrs. Parker has only contempt for the eager reception accorded her wit. "Why it got so bad," she has said bitterly, "that they began to laugh before I opened my mouth." And she has a similar attitude toward her value as a serious writer.

But Mrs. Parker is her own worst critic. Her three books of poetry may have established her reputation as a master of light verse, but her short stories are essentially serious in tone—serious in that they reflect her own life, which has been in many ways an unhappy one—and also serious in their intention. Franklin P. Adams has described them in an introduction to her work: "Nobody can write such ironic things unless he has a deep sense of injustice—injustice to those members of the race who are the victims of the stupid, the pretentious and the hypocritical."

INTERVIEWER: Your first job was on *Vogue*, wasn't it? How did you go about getting hired, and why *Vogue*?

PARKER: After my father died there wasn't any money. I had to work, you see, and Mr. Crowninshield, God rest his soul, paid twelve dollars for a small verse of mine and gave me a job at ten dollars a week. Well, I thought I was Edith Sitwell. I lived in a boarding house at 103rd and Broadway, paying eight dollars a week for my room and two meals, breakfast and dinner. Thorne Smith was there, and another man. We used to sit around in the evening and talk. There was no money, but Jesus we had fun.

INTERVIEWER: What kind of work did you do at *Vogue*?

PARKER: I wrote captions. "This little pink dress will win you a beau," that sort of thing. Funny, they were plain women working at *Vogue*, not chic. They were decent, nice women—the nicest women I ever met—but they had no business on such a magazine. They wore funny little bonnets and in the pages of their magazine they virginized the models from tough babes into exquisite little loves. Now the editors are what they should be: all chic and worldly; most of the models are out of the mind of a Bram Stoker, and as for the caption writers—*my* old job—they're recommending mink covers at seventy-five dollars apiece for the wooden ends of golf clubs "—for the friend who has everything." Civilization is coming to an end, you understand.

INTERVIEWER: Why did you change to *Vanity Fair?*

PARKER: Mr. Crowninshield wanted me to. Mr. Sherwood and Mr. Benchley—we always called each other by our last names— were there. Our office was across from the Hippodrome. The midgets would come out and frighten Mr. Sherwood. He was about seven feet tall and they were always sneaking up behind him and asking him how the weather was up there. "Walk down the street with me," he'd ask, and Mr. Benchley and I would leave our jobs and guide him down the street. I can't tell you, we had more fun. Both Mr. Benchley and I subscribed to two undertaking magazines: *The Casket* and *Sunnyside*. Steel yourself: *Sunnyside* had a joke column called "From Grave to Gay." I cut a picture out of one of them, in color, of how and where to inject embalming fluid, and had it hung over my desk until Mr. Crowninshield asked me if I could possibly take it down. Mr. Crowninshield was a lovely man, but puzzled. I must say we behaved extremely badly. Albert Lee, one of the editors, had a map over *his* desk with little flags on it to show where our troops were fighting during the First World War. Every day he would get the news and move the flags around. I was married, my husband was overseas, and since I didn't have anything better to do I'd get up half an hour early and go down and change his flags. Later on,

Lee would come in, look at his map, and he'd get very serious about spies—shout, and spend his morning moving his little pins back into position.

INTERVIEWER: How long did you stay at *Vanity Fair?*

PARKER: Four years. I'd taken over the drama criticism from P. G. Wodehouse. Then I fixed three plays—one of them *Caesar's Wife,* with Billie Burke in it—and as a result I was fired.

INTERVIEWER: You *fixed* three plays?

PARKER: Well, *panned.* The plays closed and the producers, who were the big boys—Dillingham, Ziegfeld, and Belasco—didn't like it, you know. *Vanity Fair* was a magazine of no opinion, but *I* had opinions. So I was fired. And Mr. Sherwood and Mr. Benchley resigned their jobs. It was all right for Mr. Sherwood, but Mr. Benchley had a family—two children. It was the greatest act of friendship I'd known. Mr. Benchley did a sign, "Contributions for Miss Billie Burke," and on our way out we left it in the hall of *Vanity Fair.* We behaved very badly. We made ourselves discharge chevrons and wore them.

INTERVIEWER: Where did you all go after *Vanity Fair?*

PARKER: Mr. Sherwood became the motion-picture critic for the old *Life.* Mr. Benchley did the drama reviews. He and I had an office so tiny that an inch smaller and it would have been adultery. We had *Parkbench* for a cable address, but no one ever sent us one. It was so long ago—before you were a gleam in someone's eyes—that I doubt there *was* a cable.

INTERVIEWER: It's a popular supposition that there was much more communication between writers in the twenties. The Round Table discussions in the Algonquin, for example.

PARKER: I wasn't there very often—it cost too much. Others went. Kaufman was there. I guess he was sort of funny. Mr. Benchley and Mr. Sherwood went when they had a nickel. Franklin P. Adams, whose column was widely read by people who wanted to write, would sit in occasionally. And Harold Ross, the *New Yorker* editor. He was a professional lunatic, but I don't know if he was a great man. He had a profound ignorance. On one of Mr. Benchley's manuscripts he wrote in the margin opposite "Andromache," "Who he?" Mr. Benchley wrote back, "You keep out of this." The only one with stature who came to the Round Table was Heywood Broun.

INTERVIEWER: What was it about the twenties that inspired people like yourself and Broun?

PARKER: Gertrude Stein did us the most harm when she said, "You're all a lost generation." That got around to certain people and we all said, "Whee! We're lost." Perhaps it suddenly brought to us the sense of change. Or irresponsibility. But don't forget that, though the people in the twenties seemed like flops, they weren't. Fitzgerald, the rest of them, reckless as they were, drinkers as they were, they worked damn hard and all the time.

INTERVIEWER: Did the "lost generation" attitude you speak of have a detrimental effect on your own work?

PARKER: Silly of me to blame it on dates, but so it happened to be. Dammit, it *was* the twenties and we had to be smarty. I *wanted* to be cute. That's the terrible thing. I should have had more sense.

INTERVIEWER: And during this time you were writing poems?

PARKER: My verses. I cannot say poems. Like everybody was then, I was following in the exquisite footsteps of Miss Millay, unhappily in my own horrible sneakers. My verses are no damn good. Let's face it, honey, my verse is terribly dated—as anything once fashionable is dreadful now. I gave it up, knowing it wasn't getting any better, but nobody seemed to notice my magnificent gesture.

INTERVIEWER: Do you think your verse writing has been of any benefit to your prose?

PARKER: Franklin P. Adams once gave me a book of French verse forms and told me to copy their design, that by copying them I would get precision in prose. The men you imitate in verse influence your prose, and what I got out of it was precision, all I realize I've ever had in prose writing.

INTERVIEWER: How did you get started in writing?

PARKER: I fell into writing, I suppose, being one of those awful children who wrote verses. I went to a convent in New York— The Blessed Sacrament. Convents do the same things progressive schools do, only they don't know it. They don't teach you how to read; you have to find out for yourself. At my convent we *did* have a textbook, one that devoted a page and a half to Adelaide Ann Proctor; but we couldn't read Dickens; he was vulgar, you know. But *I* read him and Thackeray, and I'm the one woman you'll ever know who's read every word of Charles Reade, the author of *The Cloister and the Hearth*. But as for helping me in the outside world, the convent taught me only that if you spit on a pencil eraser it will erase ink. And I remember the smell of oilcloth, the smell of nuns' garb. I was fired from there, finally, for a lot of things, among them my insistence that the Immaculate Conception was spontaneous combustion.

INTERVIEWER: Have you ever drawn from those years for story material?

PARKER: All those writers who write about their childhood! Gentle God, if I wrote about mine you wouldn't sit in the same room with me.

INTERVIEWER: What, then, would you say is the source of most of your work?

PARKER: Need of money, dear.

INTERVIEWER: And besides that?

PARKER: It's easier to write about those you hate—just as it's easier to criticize a bad play or a bad book.

INTERVIEWER: What about "Big Blonde"? Where did the idea for that come from?

PARKER: I knew a lady—a friend of mine who went through holy hell. Just say I knew a woman once. The purpose of the writer is to say what he feels and sees. To those who write fantasies— the Misses Baldwin, Ferber, Norris—I am not at home.

INTERVIEWER: That's not showing much respect for your fellow women, at least not the writers.

PARKER: As artists they're rot, but as providers they're oil wells;

they gush. Norris said she never wrote a story unless it was fun to do. I understand Ferber whistles at her typewriter. And there was that poor sucker Flaubert rolling around on his floor for three days looking for the right word. I'm a feminist, and God knows I'm loyal to my sex, and you must remember that from my very early days, when this city was scarcely safe from buffaloes, I was in the struggle for equal rights for women. But when we paraded through the catcalls of men and when we chained ourselves to lamp posts to try to get our equality—dear child, we didn't foresee *those* female writers. Or Clare Boothe Luce, or Perle Mesta, or Oveta Culp Hobby.

INTERVIEWER: You have an extensive reputation as a wit. Has this interfered, do you think, with your acceptance as a serious writer?

PARKER: I don't want to be classed as a humorist. It makes me feel guilty. I've never read a good tough quotable female humorist, and I never was one myself. I couldn't do it. A "smartcracker" they called me, and that makes me sick and unhappy. There's a hell of a distance between wisecracking and wit. Wit has truth in it; wisecracking is simply calisthenics with words. I didn't mind so much when they were good, but for a long time anything that was called a crack was attributed to me—and then they got the shaggy dogs.

INTERVIEWER: How about satire?

PARKER: Ah, satire. That's another matter. They're the big boys. If I'd been called a satirist there'd be no living with me. But by satirist I mean those boys in the other centuries. The people we call satirists now are those who make cracks at topical topics and consider themselves satirists—creatures like George S. Kaufman and such who don't even know what satire is. Lord knows, a writer should show his times, but not show them in wisecracks. Their stuff is not satire; it's as dull as yesterday's newspaper. Successful satire has got to be pretty good the day after tomorrow.

INTERVIEWER: And how about contemporary humorists? Do you feel about them as you do about satirists?

PARKER: You get to a certain age and only the tried writers are funny. I read my verses now and I ain't funny. I haven't been funny for twenty years. But anyway there aren't any humorists any more, except for Perelman. There's no need for them. Perelman must be very lonely.

INTERVIEWER: Why is there no need for the humorist?

PARKER: It's a question of supply and demand. If we needed them, we'd have them. The new crop of would-be humorists doesn't count. They're like the would-be satirists. They write about topical topics. Not like Thurber and Mr. Benchley. Those two were damn well read and, though I hate the word, they were cultured. What sets them apart is that they both had a point of view to express. That is important to all good writing. It's the difference between Paddy Chayefsky, who just puts down lines, and Clifford Odets, who in his early plays not only sees but has a point of view. The writer must be aware of life around him. Carson McCullers is good, or she used to be, but now she's withdrawn from life and writes about freaks. Her characters are grotesques.

INTERVIEWER: Speaking of Chayefsky and McCullers, do you read much of your own, or the present generation of writers?

PARKER: I will say of the writers of today that some of them, thank God, have the sense to adapt to their times. Mailer's *The Naked and the Dead* is a great book. And I thought William Styron's *Lie Down in Darkness* an extraordinary thing. The start of it took your heart and flung it over there. He writes like a god. But for most of my reading I go back to the old ones—for comfort. As you get older you go much farther back. I read *Vanity Fair* about a dozen times a year. I was a woman of eleven when I first read it—the thrill of that line "George Osborne lay dead with a bullet through his head." Sometimes I read, as an elegant friend of mine calls them, "who-did-its." I love Sherlock Holmes. My life is so untidy and he's so neat. But as for living novelists, I suppose E. M. Forster is the best, not knowing what that is, but at least he's a semi-finalist, wouldn't you think? Somerset Maugham once said to me, "We have a novelist over here, E. M. Forster, though I don't suppose he's familiar to you." Well, I could have kicked him. Did he think I carried a papoose on my back? Why, I'd go on my hands and knees to get to Forster. He once wrote something I've always remembered: "It has never happened to me that I've had to choose between betraying a friend and betraying my country, but if it ever does so happen I hope I have the guts to betray my country." Now doesn't that make the Fifth Amendment look like a bum?

INTERVIEWER: Could I ask you some technical questions? How do you actually write out a story? Do you write out a draft and then go over it or what?

PARKER: It takes me six months to do a story. I think it out and then write it sentence by sentence—no first draft. I can't write five words but that I change seven.

INTERVIEWER: How do you name your characters?

PARKER: The telephone book and from the obituary columns.

INTERVIEWER: Do you keep a notebook?

PARKER: I tried to keep one, but I never could remember where I put the damn thing. I always say I'm going to keep one tomorrow.

INTERVIEWER: How do you get the story down on paper?

PARKER: I wrote in longhand at first, but I've lost it. I use two fingers on the typewriter. I think it's unkind of you to ask. I know so little about the typewriter that once I bought a new one because I couldn't change the ribbon on the one I had.

INTERVIEWER: You're working on a play now, aren't you?

PARKER: Yes, collaborating with Arnaud d'Usseau. I'd like to do a play more than anything. First night is the most exciting thing in the world. It's wonderful to hear your words spoken. Unhappily, our first play, *The Ladies of the Corridor*, was not a success, but writing that play was the best time I ever had, both for the privilege and the stimulation of working with Mr. d'Usseau and because that play was the only thing I have ever done in which I had great pride.

INTERVIEWER: How about the novel? Have you ever tried that form?

PARKER: I wish to God I could do one, but I haven't got the nerve.

INTERVIEWER: And short stories? Are you still doing them?

PARKER: I'm trying now to do a story that's purely narrative. I think narrative stories are the best, though my past stories make themselves stories by telling themselves through what people say. I haven't got a visual mind. I hear things. But I'm not going to do those *he-said she-said* things any more, they're over, honey, they're over. I want to do the story that can only be told in the narrative form, and though they're going to scream about the rent, I'm going to do it.

INTERVIEWER: Do you think economic security an advantage to the writer?

PARKER: Yes. Being in a garret doesn't do you any good unless you're some sort of a Keats. The people who lived and wrote well in the twenties were comfortable and easy-living. They were able to find stories and novels, and good ones, in conflicts that came out of two million dollars a year, not a garret. As for me, I'd like to have money. And I'd like to be a good writer. These two can come together, and I hope they will, but if that's too adorable, I'd rather have money. I hate almost all rich people, but I think I'd be darling at it. At the moment, however, I like to think of Maurice Baring's remark: "If you would know what the Lord God thinks of money, you have only to look at those to whom he gives it." I realize that's not much help when the wolf comes scratching at the door, but it's a comfort.

INTERVIEWER: What do you think about the artist being supported by the state?

PARKER: Naturally, when penniless, I think it's superb. I think that the art of the country so immeasurably adds to its prestige that if you want the country to have writers and artists—persons who live precariously in our country—the state must help. I do not think that any kind of artist thrives under charity, by which

I mean one person or organization giving him money. Here and there, this and that—that's no good. The difference between the state giving and the individual patron is that one is charity and the other isn't. Charity is murder and you know it. But I do think that if the government supports its artists, they need have no feeling of gratitude—the meanest and most sniveling attribute in the world—or baskets being brought to them, or apple-polishing. Working for the state—for Christ's sake, are you grateful to your employers? Let the state see what its artists are trying to do—like France with the Academie Française. The artists are a part of their country and their country should recognize this, so both it and the artists can take pride in their efforts. Now I mean that, my dear.

INTERVIEWER: How about Hollywood as provider for the artist?

PARKER: Hollywood money isn't money. It's congealed snow, melts in your hand, and there you are. I can't talk about Hollywood. It was a horror to me when I was there and it's a horror to look back on. I can't imagine how I did it. When I got away from it I couldn't even refer to the place by name. "Out there," I called it. You want to know what "out there" means to me? Once I was coming down a street in Beverly Hills and I saw a Cadillac about a block long, and out of the side window was a wonderfully slinky mink, and an arm, and at the end of the arm a hand in a white suede glove wrinkled around the wrist, and in the hand was a bagel with a bite out of it.

INTERVIEWER: Do you think Hollywood destroys the artist's talent?

PARKER: No, no, no. I think nobody on earth writes down. Garbage though they turn out, Hollywood writers aren't writing down. That is their best. If you're going to write, don't pretend to write down. It's going to be the best you can do, and it's the fact that it's the best you can do that kills you. I want so much to write well, though I know I don't, and that I didn't make it. But during and at the end of my life, I will adore those who have.

INTERVIEWER: Then what is it that's the evil in Hollywood?

PARKER: It's the people. Like the director who put his finger in Scott Fitzgerald's face and complained, "Pay *you*. Why, you ought to pay us." It was terrible about Scott; if you'd seen him you'd have been sick. When he died no one went to the funeral, not a single soul came, or even sent a flower. I said, "Poor son of a bitch," a quote right out of *The Great Gatsby*, and everyone thought it was another wisecrack. But it was said in dead seriousness. Sickening about Scott. And it wasn't only the people, but also the indignity to which your ability was put. There was a picture in which Mr. Benchley had a part. In it Monty Woolley had a scene in which he had to enter a room through a door on which was balanced a bucket of water. He came into the room covered with water and muttered to Mr. Benchley, who had a part in the scene, "Benchley? Benchley of *Harvard?*" "Yes," mumbled Mr. Benchley and he asked, "Woolley? Woolley of *Yale?*"

INTERVIEWER: How about your political views? Have they made any difference to you professionally?

PARKER: Oh, certainly. Though I don't think this "blacklist" business extends to the theater or certain of the magazines, in Hollywood it exists because several gentlemen felt it best to drop names like marbles which bounced back like rubber balls about people they'd seen in the company of what they charmingly called "commies." You can't go back thirty years to Sacco and Vanzetti. I won't do it. Well, well, well, that's the way it is. If all this means something to the good of the movies, I don't know what it is. Sam Goldwyn said, "How'm I gonna do decent pictures when all my good writers are in jail?" Then he added, the infallible Goldwyn, "Don't misunderstand me, they all ought to be hung." Mr. Goldwyn didn't know about "hanged." That's all there is to say. It's not the tragedies that kill us, it's the messes. I can't stand messes. I'm not being a smartcracker. You know I'm not when you meet me—don't you, honey?

MARION CAPRON

5. James Thurber

The second son of a local Republican politician, James Thurber was born in Columbus, Ohio, in 1895. He attended Ohio State, where he edited the campus humor magazine and was elected to the senior honor society. Unable to enlist in the Army because of a childhood eye injury, he served out World War I as a code clerk in the United States Embassy in Paris.

Back in Ohio, Thurber covered city hall for the *Columbus Dispatch*, then returned to Europe, where he started an abortive novel in a Normandy farmhouse. He took a job at twelve dollars a week on the European edition of the *Chicago Tribune*. After returning to New York in 1926 he worked on the *Evening Post*, in his spare time writing sketches for *The New Yorker*, which rejected him twenty times before accepting a short piece on a man caught in a revolving door. Since then it is in *The New Yorker* that the bulk of his work has appeared.

Of the twenty-odd volumes of collected prose and pictures, T. S. Eliot has written: "It is a form of humour which is also a way of saying something serious. Unlike so much humour it is not merely a criticism of manners—that is, of the superficial aspects of society at a given moment—but something more profound. His writing and also his illustrations are capable of surviving the immediate environment and time out of which they spring. To some extent they will be a document of the age they belong to."

Perhaps the best known of Thurber's works are: the fantasies, *The White Deer* (1945), *The Thirteen Clocks* (1950), *The Wonderful O* (1957); his play *The Male Animal* (1939), which he wrote with Elliott Nugent; his cartoon book *Men, Women, and Dogs*; the collections, *The Thurber Carnival* (1945) and *Thurber Country* (1953); and his autobiographical sketches *My Life and Hard Times* (1933) and *The Thurber Album* (1952).

An example, considerably reduced, of a Thurber manuscript page

James Thurber

The Hôtel Continental, just down from the Place Vendôme on the Rue Castiglione. It is from here that Janet Flanner (Genêt) sends her Paris letter to The New Yorker, and it is here that the Thurbers usually stay while in Paris. "We like it because the service is first-rate without being snobbish."

Thurber was standing to greet us in a small salon whose cold European formality had been somewhat softened and warmed by well-placed vases of flowers, by stacks and portable shelves of American novels in bright dust jackets, and by pads of yellow paper and bouquets of yellow pencils on the desk. Thurber impresses one immediately by his physical size. After years of delighting in the shy, trapped little man in the Thurber cartoons and the confused and bewildered man who has fumbled in and out of some of the funniest books written in this century, we, perhaps like many readers, were expecting to find the frightened little man in person.

Not at all. Thurber by his firm handgrasp and confident voice and by the way he lowered himself into his chair gave the impression of outward calmness and assurance. Though his eyesight has almost failed him, it is not a disability which one is aware of for more than the opening minute, and if Thurber seems to be the most nervous person in the room, it is because he has learned to put his visitors so completely at ease.

He talks in a surprisingly boyish voice, which is flat with the accents of the Midwest where he was raised and, though slow in tempo, never dull. He is not an easy man to pin down with questions. He prefers to sidestep them and, rather than instructing, he entertains with a vivid series of anecdotes and reminiscences.

Opening the interview with a long history of the bloodhound, Thurber was only with some difficulty persuaded to shift to a discussion of his craft. Here again his manner was typical—the anecdotes, the reminiscences punctuated with direct quotes and factual data. His powers of memory are astounding. In quoting anyone—perhaps a conversation of a dozen years before—Thurber pauses slightly, his voice changes in tone, and you know what you're hearing is exactly as it was said.

THURBER: Well, you know it's a nuisance—to have memory like mine—as well as an advantage. It's . . . well . . . like a whore's top drawer. There's so much else in there that's junk—costume jewelry, unnecessary telephone numbers whose exchanges no longer exist. For instance, I can remember the birthday of anybody who's ever told me his birthday. Dorothy Parker—August 22, Lewis Gannett—October 3, Andy White—July 9, Mrs. White—September 17. I can go on with about two hundred. So can my mother. She can tell you the birthday of the girl I was in love with in the third grade, in 1903. Offhand, just like that. I got my powers of memory from her. Sometimes it helps out in the most extraordinary way. You remember Robert M. Coates? Bob Coates? He is the author of *The Eater of Darkness*, which Ford Madox Ford called the first true Dadaist novel. Well, the week after Stephen Vincent Benét died—Coates and I had both known him—we were talking about Benét. Coates was trying to remember an argument he had had with Benét some fifteen years before. He couldn't remember. I said, "I can." Coates told me that was impossible since I hadn't been there. "Well," I said, "you happened to mention it in passing about twelve years ago. You were arguing about a play called *Swords.*" I was right, and Coates was able to take it up from there. But it's strange to reach a position where your friends have to be supplied with their own memories. It's bad enough dealing with your own.

INTERVIEWERS: Still, it must be a great advantage for the writer. I don't suppose you have to take notes.

THURBER: No. I don't have to do the sort of thing Fitzgerald did with *The Last Tycoon*—the voluminous, the tiny and meticulous notes, the long descriptions of character. I can keep all these things in my mind. I wouldn't have to write down "three roses in a vase" or something, or a man's middle name. Henry James dictated notes just the way that I write. His note writing was part of the creative act, which is why his prefaces are so good. He dictated notes to see what it was they might come to.

INTERVIEWERS: Then you don't spend much time prefiguring your work?

THURBER: No. I don't bother with charts and so forth. Elliott Nugent, on the other hand, is a careful constructor. When we were working on *The Male Animal* together, he was constantly concerned with plotting the play. He could plot the thing from back to front—what was going to happen here, what sort of situation would end the first-act curtain, and so forth. I can't work that way. Nugent would say, "Well, Thurber, we've got our problem, we've got all these people in the living room. Now what are we going to do with them?" I'd say that I didn't know and couldn't tell him until I'd sat down at the typewriter and found out. I don't believe the writer should know too much where he's going. If he does, he runs into old man blueprint—old man propaganda.

INTERVIEWERS: Is the act of writing easy for you?

THURBER: For me it's mostly a question of rewriting. It's part of a constant attempt on my part to make the finished version smooth, to make it seem effortless. A story I've been working on —"The Train on Track Six," it's called—was rewritten fifteen complete times. There must have been close to 240,000 words in all the manuscripts put together, and I must have spent two thousand hours working at it. Yet the finished version can't be more than twenty thousand words.

INTERVIEWERS: Then it's rare that your work comes out right the first time?

THURBER: Well, my wife took a look at the first version of something I was doing not long ago and said, "Goddamn it, Thurber, that's high-school stuff." I have to tell her to wait until the seventh draft, it'll work out all right. I don't know why that should be so, that the first or second draft of everything I write reads as if it was turned out by a charwoman. I've only written one piece quickly. I wrote a thing called "File and Forget" in one afternoon—but only because it was a series of letters just as one would ordinarily dictate. And I'd have to admit that the last letter of the series, after doing all the others that one afternoon, took me a week. It was the end of the piece and I had to fuss over it.

INTERVIEWERS: Does the fact that you're dealing with humor slow down the production?

THURBER: It's possible. With humor you have to look out for traps. You're likely to be very gleeful with what you've first put down, and you think it's fine, very funny. One reason you go over and over it is to make the piece sound less as if you were having a lot of fun with it yourself. You try to play it down. In fact, if there's such a thing as a *New Yorker* style, that would be it— playing it down.

INTERVIEWERS: Do you envy those who write at high speed, as against your method of constant revision?

THURBER: Oh, no, I don't, though I do admire their luck. Hervey Allen, you know, the author of the big best-seller *Anthony*

Adverse, seriously told a friend of mine who was working on a biographical piece on Allen that he could close his eyes, lie down on a bed, and hear the voices of his ancestors. Furthermore there was some sort of angel-like creature that danced along his pen while he was writing. He wasn't balmy by any means. He just felt he was in communication with some sort of metaphysical recorder. So you see the novelists have all the luck. I never knew a humorist who got any help from his ancestors. Still, the act of writing is either something the writer dreads or actually likes, and I actually like it. Even rewriting's fun. You're getting somewhere, whether it seems to move or not. I remember Elliot Paul and I used to argue about rewriting back in 1925 when we both worked for the *Chicago Tribune* in Paris. It was his conviction you should leave the story as it came out of the typewriter, no changes. Naturally, he worked fast. Three novels he could turn out, each written in three weeks' time. I remember once he came into the office and said that a sixty-thousand-word manuscript had been stolen. No carbons existed, no notes. We were all horrified. But it didn't bother him at all. He'd just get back to the typewriter and bat away again. But for me—writing as fast as that would seem too facile. Like my drawings, which I do very quickly, sometimes so quickly that the result is an accident, something I hadn't intended at all. People in the arts I've run into in France are constantly indignant when I say I'm a writer and not an artist. They tell me I mustn't run down my drawings. I try to explain that I do them for relaxation, and that I do them too fast for them to be called art.

INTERVIEWERS: You say that your drawings often don't come out the way you intended?

THURBER: Well, once I did a drawing for *The New Yorker* of a naked woman on all fours up on top of a bookcase—a big bookcase. She's up there near the ceiling, and in the room are her husband and two other women. The husband is saying to one of the women, obviously a guest, "This is the present Mrs. Harris. That's my first wife up there." Well, when I did the cartoon

originally I meant the naked woman to be at the top of a flight
of stairs, but I lost the sense of perspective and instead of getting
in the stairs when I drew my line down, there she was stuck up
there, naked, on a bookcase.

Incidentally, that cartoon really threw *The New Yorker* editor,
Harold Ross. He approached any humorous piece of writing, or
more particularly a drawing, not only grimly but realistically. He
called me on the phone and asked if the woman up on the bookcase was supposed to be alive, stuffed, or dead. I said, "I don't
know, but I'll let you know in a couple of hours." After a while
I called him back and told him I'd just talked to my taxidermist,
who said you can't stuff a woman, that my doctor had told me
a dead woman couldn't support herself on all fours. "So, Ross,"
I said, "she must be alive." "Well then," he said, "what's she
doing up there naked in the home of her husband's second wife?"
I told him he had me there.

INTERVIEWERS: But he published it.

THURBER: Yes, he published it, growling a bit. He had a fine
understanding of humor, Ross, though he couldn't have told you
about it. When I introduced Ross to the work of Peter de Vries,
he first said, "He won't be good; he won't be funny; he won't
know English." (He was the only successful editor I've known
who approached everything like a ship going on the rocks.) But
when Ross had looked at the work he said, "How can you get this
guy on the phone?" He couldn't have said why, but he had that
bloodhound instinct. The same with editing. He was a wonderful
man at detecting something wrong with a story without knowing
why.

INTERVIEWERS: Could he develop a writer?

THURBER: Not really. It wasn't true what they often said of him
—that he broke up writers like matches—but still he wasn't the
man to develop a writer. He was an unread man. Well, he'd read
Mark Twain's *Life on the Mississippi* and several other books he
told me about—medical books—and he took the Encyclopedia
Britannica to the bathroom with him. I think he was about up to

H when he died. But still his effect on writers was considerable. When you first met him you couldn't believe he was the editor of *The New Yorker* and afterward you couldn't believe that anyone else could have been. The main thing he was interested in was clarity. Someone once said of *The New Yorker* that it never contained a sentence that would puzzle an intelligent fourteen-year-old or in any way affect her morals badly. Ross didn't like that, but nevertheless he was a purist and perfectionist and it had a tremendous effect on all of us: it kept us from being sloppy. When I first met him he asked me if I knew English. I thought he meant French or a foreign language. But he repeated, "Do you know English?" When I said I did he replied, "Goddamn it, nobody knows English." As Andy White mentioned in his obituary, Ross approached the English sentence as though it was an enemy, something that was going to throw him. He used to fuss for an hour over a comma. He'd call me in for lengthy discussions about the Thurber colon. And as for poetic license, he'd say, "Damn any license to get things wrong." In fact, Ross read so carefully that often he didn't get the sense of your story. I once said: "I wish you'd read my stories for pleasure, Ross." He replied he hadn't time for that.

INTERVIEWERS: It's strange that one of the main ingredients of humor—low comedy—has never been accepted for *The New Yorker*.

THURBER: Ross had a neighbor woman's attitude about it. He never got over his Midwestern provincialism. His idea was that sex is an incident. "If you can prove it," I said, "we can get it in a box on the front page of *The New York Times*." Now I don't want to say that in private life Ross was a prude. But as regards the theater or the printed page he certainly was. For example, he once sent an office memorandum to us in a sealed envelope. It was an order: "When you send me a memorandum with four-letter words in it, *seal it*. There are women in this office." I said, "Yah, Ross, and they know a lot more of these words than you do." When women were around he was very conscious of them.

Once my wife and I were in his office and Ross was discussing a man and woman he knew much better than we did. Ross told us, "I have every reason to believe that they're *s-l-e-e-p-i-n-g* together." My wife replied, "Why, Harold Ross, what words you do spell out." But honest to goodness, that was genuine. Women are either good or bad, he once told me, and the good ones must not hear these things.

Incidentally, I'm telling these things to refresh my memory. I'm doing a short book on him called "Ross in Charcoal." I'm putting a lot of this stuff in. People may object, but after all it's a portrait of the man and I see no reason for not putting it in.

INTERVIEWERS: Did he have much direct influence on your own work?

THURBER: After the seven years I spent in newspaper writing, it was more E. B. White who taught me about writing, how to clear up sloppy journalese. He was a strong influence, and for a long time in the beginning I thought he might be too much of one. But at least he got me away from a rather curious style I was starting to perfect—tight journalese laced with heavy doses of Henry James.

INTERVIEWERS: Henry James was a strong influence, then?

THURBER: I have the reputation for having read all of Henry James. Which would argue a misspent youth *and* middle age.

INTERVIEWERS: But there were things to be learned from him?

THURBER: Yes, but again he was an influence you had to get over. Especially if you wrote for *The New Yorker*. Harold Ross wouldn't have understood it. I once wrote a piece called "The Beast in the Dingle" which everybody took as a parody. Actually it was a conscious attempt to write the story as James would have written it. Ross looked at it and said: "Goddamn it, this is too literary; I got only fifteen per cent of the allusions." My wife and I often tried to figure out which were the fifteen per cent he could nave got.

You know, I've occasionally wondered what James would have done with our world. I've just written a piece—"Preface to Old

Friends," it's called—in which James at the age of a hundred and four writes a preface to a novel about our age in which he summarizes the trends and complications, but at the end is so completely lost he doesn't really care enough to read it over to find his way out again.

That's the trouble with James. You get bored with him finally. He lived in the time of four-wheelers, and no bombs, and the problems then seemed a bit special and separate. That's one reason you feel restless reading him. James is like—well, I had a bulldog once who used to drag rails around, enormous ones—six-, eight-, twelve-foot rails. He loved to get them in the middle and you'd hear him growling out there, trying to bring the thing home. Once he brought home a chest of drawers—without the drawers in it Found it on an ash-heap. Well, he'd start to get these things in the garden gate, everything finely balanced, you see, and then *crash*, he'd come up against the gate posts. He'd get it through finally, but I had that feeling in some of the James novels: that he was trying to get that rail through a gate not wide enough for it.

INTERVIEWERS: How about Mark Twain? Pretty much everybody believes him to have been the major influence on American humorists.

THURBER: Everybody wants to know if I've learned from Mark Twain. Actually I've never read much of him. I did buy *Tom Sawyer*, but dammit, I'm sorry, I've not got around to reading it all the way through. I told H. L. Mencken that, and he was shocked. He said America had produced only two fine novels: *Huck Finn* and *Babbitt*. Of course it's always a matter of personal opinion—these lists of the great novels. I can remember calling on Frank Harris—he was about seventy then—when I was on the *Chicago Tribune*'s edition in Nice. In his house he had three portraits on the wall—Mark Twain, Frank Harris, and I think it was Hawthorne. Harris was in the middle. Harris would point up to them and say, "Those three are the best American writers. The one in the middle is the best." Harris really thought he was wonderful. Once he told me he was going to live to be a hundred. When I asked him what the formula was, he told me it was very simple. He said, "I've bought myself a stomach pump and one half-hour after dinner I pump myself out." Can you imagine that? Well, it didn't work. It's a wonder it didn't kill him sooner.

INTERVIEWERS: Could we ask you why you've never attempted a long work?

THURBER: I've never wanted to write a long work. Many writers feel a sense of frustration or something if they haven't, but I don't.

INTERVIEWERS: Perhaps the fact that you're writing humor imposes a limit on the length of a work.

THURBER: Possibly. But brevity in any case—whether the work is supposed to be humorous or not—would seem to me to be desirable. Most of the books I like are short books: *The Red Badge of Courage, The Turn of the Screw*, Conrad's short stories, *A Lost Lady*, Joseph Hergesheimer's *Wild Oranges*, Victoria Lincoln's *February Hill, The Great Gatsby*. . . . You know Fitzgerald once wrote Thomas Wolfe: "You're a putter-inner and I'm a taker-outer." I stick with Fitzgerald. I don't believe, as Wolfe did, that you have to turn out a massive work before being judged a writer. Wolfe once told me at a cocktail party I didn't know what it was to be a writer. My wife, standing next to me, complained about that. "But my husband *is* a writer," she said. Wolfe was genuinely surprised. "He is?" he asked. "Why, all I ever see is that stuff of his in *The New Yorker*." In other words, he felt that prose under five thousand words was certainly not the work of a writer . . . it was some kind of doodling in words. If you said you were a writer, he wanted to know where the books were, the great big long books. He was really genuine about that.

I was interested to see William Faulkner's list not so long ago of the five most important American authors of this century. According to him Wolfe was first, Faulkner second—let's see, now that Wolfe's dead that puts Faulkner up there in the lead, doesn't it?— Dos Passos third, then Hemingway, and finally Steinbeck.

It's interesting that the first three are putter-inners. They write expansive novels.

INTERVIEWERS: Wasn't Faulkner's criterion whether or not the author dared to go out on a limb?

THURBER: It seems to me you're going out on a limb these days to keep a book short.

INTERVIEWERS: Though you've never done a long serious work you have written stories—"The Cane in the Corridor" and "The Whippoorwill" in particular—in which the mood is far from humorous.

THURBER: In anything funny you write that isn't close to serious you've missed something along the line. But in those stories of which you speak there was an element of anger—something I wanted to get off my chest. I wrote "The Whippoorwill" after five eye operations. It came somewhere out of a grim fear in the back of my mind. I've never been able to trace it.

INTERVIEWERS: Some critics think that much of your work can be traced to the depicting of trivia as a basis for humor. In fact, there's been some criticism—

THURBER: Which is trivia—the diamond or the elephant? Any humorist must be interested in trivia, in every little thing that occurs in a household. It's what Robert Benchley did so well— in fact so well that one of the greatest fears of the humorous writer is that he has spent three weeks writing something done faster and better by Benchley in 1919. Incidentally, you never got very far talking to Benchley about humor. He'd do a take-off of Max Eastman's *Enjoyment of Laughter*. "We must understand," he'd say, "that all sentences which begin with W are funny."

INTERVIEWERS: Would you care to define humor in terms of your own work?

THURBER: Well, someone once wrote a definition of the difference between English and American humor. I wish I could remember his name. I thought his definition very good. He said that the English treat the commonplace as if it were remarkable and the Americans treat the remarkable as if it were common-place. I believe that's true of humorous writing. Years ago we did a parody of *Punch* in which Benchley did a short piece depicting a wife bursting into a room and shouting "The primroses are in bloom!"—treating the commonplace as remarkable, you see. In "The Secret Life of Walter Mitty" I tried to treat the remarkable as commonplace.

INTERVIEWERS: Does it bother you to talk about the stories on which you're working? It bothers many writers, though it would seem that particularly the humorous story is polished through retelling.

THURBER: Oh, yes. I often tell them at parties and places. And I write them there too.

INTERVIEWERS: You write them?

THURBER: I never quite know when I'm not writing. Sometimes my wife comes up to me at a party and says, "Dammit, Thurber, stop writing." She usually catches me in the middle of a para-graph. Or my daughter will look up from the dinner table and ask, "Is he sick?" "No," my wife says, "he's writing something." I have to do it that way on account of my eyes. I still write occa-sionally—in the proper sense of the word—using black crayon on yellow paper and getting perhaps twenty words to the page. My usual method, though, is to spend the mornings turning over the text in my mind. Then in the afternoon, between two and five, I call in a secretary and dictate to her. I can do about two thousand words. It took me about ten years to learn.

INTERVIEWERS: How about the new crop of writers? Do you note any good humorists coming along with them?

THURBER: There don't seem to be many coming up. I once had a psychoanalyst tell me that the depression had a considerable effect—much worse than Hitler and the war. It's a tradition for a child to see his father in uniform as something glamorous—not his father coming home from Wall Street in a three-button sack suit saying, "We're ruined," and the mother bursting into tears— a catastrophe that to a child's mind is unexplainable. There's been a great change since the thirties. In those days students used to ask me what Peter Arno did at night. And about Dorothy Parker. Now they want to know what my artistic credo is. An element of interest seems to have gone out of them.

INTERVIEWERS: Has the shift in the mood of the times had any effect on your own work?

THURBER: Well, *The Thurber Album* was written at a time when in America there was a feeling of fear and suspicion. It's quite different from *My Life and Hard Times*, which was written earlier and is a funnier and better book. The *Album* was kind of an escape—going back to the Middle West of the last century and the beginning of this, when there wasn't this fear and hysteria. I wanted to write the story of some solid American characters, more or less as an example of how Americans started out and what they should go back to—to sanity and soundness and away from this jumpiness. It's hard to write humor in the mental weather we've had, and that's likely to take you into reminiscence. Your heart isn't in it to write anything funny. In the years 1950 to 1953 I did very few things, nor did they appear in *The New Yorker*. Now, actually, I think the situation is beginning to change for the better.

INTERVIEWERS: No matter what the "mental climate," though, you would continue writing?

THURBER: Well, the characteristic fear of the American writer is not so much that as it is the process of aging. The writer looks in the mirror and examines his hair and teeth to see if they're still with him. "Oh my God," he says, "I wonder how my writing is. I bet I can't write today." The only time I met Faulkner he told me he wanted to live long enough to do three more novels. He was fifty-three then, and I think he *has* done them. Then Hemingway says, you know, that he doesn't expect to be alive after sixty. But he doesn't look forward *not* to being. When I met Hemingway with John O'Hara in Costello's Bar five or six years ago we sat around and talked about how *old* we were getting. You see it's constantly on the minds of American writers. I've never known a woman who could weep about her age the way the men I know can.

Coupled with this fear of aging is the curious idea that the writer's inventiveness and ability will end in his fifties. And of course it often does. Carl Van Vechten stopped writing. The prolific Joseph Hergesheimer suddenly couldn't write any more. Over here in Europe that's never been the case—Hardy, for instance, who started late and kept going. Of course Keats had good reason to write, "When I have fears that I may cease to be Before my pen has glean'd my teeming brain." That's the great classic statement. But in America the writer is more likely to fear that his brain may cease to teem. I once did a drawing of a man at his typewriter, you see, and all this crumpled paper is on the floor, and he's staring down in discouragement. "What's the matter," his wife is saying, "has your pen gleaned your teeming brain?"

INTERVIEWERS: In your case there wouldn't be much chance of this?

THURBER: No. I write basically because it's so much fun—even though I can't see. When I'm not writing, as my wife knows, I'm miserable. I don't have that fear that suddenly it will all stop. I have enough outlined to last me as long as I live.

GEORGE PLIMPTON
MAX STEELE

6. Thornton Wilder

Born in 1897, in Madison, Wisconsin, Thornton Niven Wilder spent his early years in Hong Kong and Shanghai, where his father was the consul general. He had an extensive and far-flung education. He attended schools in Ojai and Berkeley, California, and Chefoo, China, spent his undergraduate years at Oberlin and Yale, and took graduate work at both the American Academy in Rome and Princeton.

From 1921 to 1928 Wilder taught French at Lawrenceville Academy. Writing in his spare time, he finished *The Cabala* in 1925. In 1927 he won critical recognition and a Pulitzer Prize with his second novel, *The Bridge of San Luis Rey*. Other novels followed: *The Woman of Andros* (1930), *Heaven's My Destination* (1935), and *The Ides of March* (1948).

As a playwright Wilder has matched his success as a novelist. He received Pulitzer Prizes for *Our Town* (1938) and *The Skin of Our Teeth* (1942). More recently, he rewrote and turned one of his few failures, *The Merchant of Yonkers* (1938), into the long-run Broadway success, *The Matchmaker* (1956). He has written a number of one-act plays which have been collected in two volumes, *The Angel That Troubled the Waters* and *The Long Christmas Dinner*.

Many universities, including Harvard, Yale, and Kenyon, have awarded Wilder honorary degrees. His home is in Hamden, Connecticut, but he travels widely and has taught or lectured at cultural centers throughout the world.

Book TWO : chapter Two

~~XXXX~~ ~~BOOK~~ ~~TWO~~ :- ~~PAMPHILUS~~

Under the burden of perplexities and self-reproach Pamphilus decided to ~~seek~~ seek some light on his problem by reviving an old custom. This custom ~~had been~~ ~~there had been a certain custom~~ in frequent use among Greeks of the great age, but ~~which~~ had fallen off at the time of the events of this story. Athletes still observed it several days before a race; brides ~~observed it on~~ on the eve of their wedding ✓ and devout soldiers about to set out upon an expedition ~~and~~ (old ladies who hoped to recover some lost trinket) It ~~XXXX~~ consisted of abstaining from speech and from food from one sunrise to the next and of either passing the night in the temple enclosure or arriving there before the dawn that closed the "watch". There was not thought to be any particular magic in the practice; ~~and the Greek XXXX XXXX XXXX XXXX~~ ~~XXXXX the experience by any further self-denial:~~ it cleared the mind slightly of ~~XXXX~~ fumes, removed it from the commerce of the day, and prepared it perhaps for a significant dream. The Watcher guarded his fast and his silence, but the Greek mind did not approve of heightening the experience by any further self-denial. The Watcher moved about the home as usual; he exercised in the palaestra; ~~if~~ he drew some uninformed person spoke to him, he ~~laid~~ drew his finger across his lips and the situation was understood. ~~XXXX~~ ~~The XXXX of XXXXXX XXXX XXXXX. XXXXXXXXX XXX XXXXX XXXXXXXXXX, XXXXX XXX XXXXX XXXX XXXXXXX XXXXXX XXXXXXX. The XXXX XXX XXXX~~ forbidden ~~XXXX to XXXX XXXXXX nor had he consented. The decision seemed to be left to XXXX and he decided to observe this discipline~~ ~~XX XXX XXX To XXXXX XXX XXXXX~~ It was indeed little short of odd for a full grown man, in the even current of private life to revive this custom, but the Islanders were still sufficiently religious to respect the habits that had expressed the spiritual life of their glorious grandfathers, and now made no comment.

A manuscript page from Thornton Wilder's The Woman of Andros. Reprinted by permission of the Yale University Library

Rosalie Seidler

Thornton Wilder

A national newsmagazine not very long ago in its weekly cover story depicted Thornton Wilder as an amiable, eccentric itinerant schoolmaster who wrote occasional novels and plays which won prizes and enjoyed enormous but somewhat unaccountable success. Wilder himself has said, "I'm almost sixty and look it. I'm the kind of man whom timid old ladies stop on the street to ask about the nearest subway station. News vendors in university towns call me 'professor,' and hotel clerks, 'doctor.'"

Many of those who have viewed him in the classroom, on the speaker's rostrum, on shipboard, or at gatherings have been reminded of Theodore Roosevelt, who was at the top of his form when Wilder was an adolescent, and whom Wilder resembles in his driving energy, his enthusiasms, and his unbounded gregariousness.

It is unlikely that more than a few of his countless friends have

*seen Wilder in repose. Only then does one realize that he wears
a mask. The mask is no figure of speech. It is his eyeglasses. As do
most glasses, they partially conceal his eyes. They also distort his
eyes so that they appear larger: friendly, benevolent, alive with
curiosity and interest. Deliberately or not, he rarely removes his
glasses in the presence of others. When he does remove them,
unmasks himself, so to speak, the sight of his eyes is a shock.
Unobscured, the eyes—cold light blue—reveal an intense severity
and an almost forbidding intelligence. They do not call out a
cheerful "Kinder! Kinder!"; rather, they specify: "I am listening
to what you are saying. Be serious. Be precise."*

*Seeing Wilder unmasked is a sobering and tonic experience.
For his eyes dissipate the atmosphere of indiscriminate amiability
and humbug that collects around celebrated and gifted men; the
eyes remind you that you are confronted by one of the toughest
and most complicated minds in contemporary America.*

*An apartment overlooking the Hudson River in New York City.
During the conversations, which took place on the evening of
December 14, 1956, and the following afternoon, Mr. Wilder
could watch the river lights or the river barges as he meditated
his replies.*

INTERVIEWER: Sir, do you mind if we begin with a few irrelevant
—and possibly impertinent—questions, just for a warm-up?

WILDER: Perfectly all right. Ask whatever comes into your head.

INTERVIEWER: One of our really eminent critics, in writing
about you recently, suggested that among the critics you had made
no enemies. Is that a healthy situation for a serious writer?

WILDER (*after laughing somewhat ironically*): The important
thing is that you make sure that neither the favorable nor the
unfavorable critics move into your head and take part in the composition of your next work.

INTERVIEWER: One of your most celebrated colleagues said recently that about all a writer really needs is a place to work, to-

bacco, some food, and good whisky. Could you explain to the non-drinkers among us how liquor helps things along?

WILDER: Many writers have told me that they have built up mnemonic devices to start them off on each day's writing task. Hemingway once told me he sharpened twenty pencils; Willa Cather that she read a passage from the Bible (not from piety, she was quick to add, but to get in touch with fine prose; she also regretted that she had formed this habit, for the prose rhythms of 1611 were not those she was in search of). My springboard has always been long walks. I drink a great deal, but I do not associate it with writing.

INTERVIEWER: Although military service is a proud tradition among contemporary American writers, I wonder if you would care to comment on the circumstance that you volunteered in 1942, despite the fact that you were a veteran of the First World War. That is to say, do you believe that a seasoned and mature artist is justified in abandoning what he is particularly fitted to do for patriotic motives?

WILDER: I guess everyone speaks for himself in such things. I felt very strongly about it. I was already a rather old man, was fit only for staff work, but I certainly did it with conviction. I have always felt that both enlistments were valuable for a number of reasons.

One of the dangers of the American artist is that he finds himself almost exclusively thrown in with persons more or less in the arts. He lives among them, eats among them, quarrels with them, marries them. I have long felt that portraits of the non-artist in American literature reflect a pattern, because the artist doesn't really frequent. He portrays the man in the street as he remembers him from childhood, or as he copies him out of other books. So one of the benefits of military service, *one* of them, is being thrown into daily contact with non-artists, something a young American writer should consciously seek—his acquaintance should include also those who have read only *Treasure Island* and have forgotten that. Since 1800 many central figures in narratives have been, like their authors, artists or quasi-artists. Can you name three heroes in earlier literature who partook of the artistic temperament?

INTERVIEWER: Did the young Thornton Wilder resemble George Brush, and in what ways?

WILDER: Very much so. I came from a very strict Calvinistic father, was brought up partly among the missionaries of China, and went to that splendid college at Oberlin at a time when the classrooms and student life carried a good deal of the pious didacticism which would now be called narrow Protestantism. And that book [*Heaven's My Destination*] is, as it were, an effort to come to terms with those influences.

The comic spirit is given to us in order that we may analyze, weigh, and clarify things in us which nettle us, or which we are outgrowing, or trying to reshape. That is a very autobiographical book.

INTERVIEWER: Why have you generally avoided contemporary settings in your work?

WILDER: I think you would find that the work is a gradual drawing near to the America I know. I began with the purely fantastic twentieth-century Rome (I did not frequent such circles there); then Peru, then Hellenistic Greece. I began, first with *Heaven's My Destination*, to approach the American scene. Already, in the one-act plays, I had become aware of how difficult it is to invest one's contemporary world with the same kind of imaginative life one has extended to those removed in time and place. But I always feel that the progression is there and visible; I can be seen collecting the practice, the experience and courage, to present my own times.

INTERVIEWER: What is your feeling about "authenticity"? For example, you had never been in Peru when you wrote *The Bridge of San Luis Rey*.

WILDER: The chief answer to that is that the journey of the imagination to a remote place is child's play compared to a journey into another time. I've been often in New York, but it's just as preposterous to write about the New York of 1812 as to write about the Incas.

INTERVIEWER: You have often been cited as a "stylist." As a writer who is obviously concerned with tone and exactness of expression, do you find that the writing of fiction is a painful and exhausting process, or do you write easily, quickly and joyously?

WILDER: Once you catch the idea for an extended narration—drama or novel—and if that idea is firmly within you, then the writing brings you perhaps not so much pleasure as a deep absorption. . . . (*He reflected here for a moment and then continued.*) You see, my waste-paper basket is filled with works that went a quarter through and which turned out to be among those things that failed to engross the whole of me. And then, for a while, there's a very agonizing period of time in which I try to explore whether the work I've rejected cannot be reoriented in such a way as to absorb me. The decision to abandon it is hard.

INTERVIEWER: Do you do much rewriting?

WILDER: I forget which of the great sonneteers said: "One line in the fourteen comes from the ceiling; the others have to be adjusted around it." Well, likewise there are passages in every novel whose first writing is pretty much the last. But it's the joint and cement, between those spontaneous passages, that take a great deal of rewriting.

INTERVIEWER: I don't know exactly how to put the next question, because I realize you have a lot of theories about narration, about how a thing should be told—theories all related to the decline of the novel, and so on. But I wonder if you would say something about the problem of giving a "history" or a summary of your life in relation to your development as a writer.

WILDER: Let's try. The problem of telling you about my past life as a writer is like that of imaginative narration itself; it lies in the effort to employ the past tense in such a way that it does not rob those events of their character of having occurred in freedom. A great deal of writing and talking about the past is unacceptable. It freezes the historical in a determinism. Today's writer smugly passes his last judgment and confers on existing attitudes the lifeless aspect of plaster-cast statues in a museum. He recounts the past as though the characters knew what was going to happen next.

INTERVIEWER: Well, to begin—do you feel that you were born in a place and at a time, and to a family all of which combined favorably to shape you for what you were to do?

WILDER: Comparisons of one's lot with others' teaches us nothing and enfeebles the will. Many born in an environment of poverty, disease, and stupidity, in an age of chaos, have put us in their debt. By the standards of many people, and by my own, these dispositions were favorable—but what are our judgments in such matters? Everyone is born with an array of handicaps—even Mozart, even Sophocles—and acquires new ones. In a famous passage, Shakespeare ruefully complains that he was not endowed with another writer's "scope"! We are all equally distant from the sun, but we all have a share in it. The most valuable thing I inherited was a temperament that does not revolt against Necessity and that is constantly renewed in Hope. (I am alluding to Goethe's great poem about the problem of each man's "lot"—the *Orphische Worte.*)

INTERVIEWER: Did you have a happy childhood?

WILDER: I think I did, but I also think that that's a thing about which people tend to deceive themselves. Gertrude Stein once said, "Communists are people who fancied that they had an unhappy childhood." (I think she meant that the kind of person who can persuade himself that the world would be completely happy if everyone denied himself a vast number of free decisions, is the same kind of person who could persuade himself that in early life he had been thwarted and denied all free decision.) I think of myself as having been—right up to and through my college years—a sort of sleepwalker. I was not a dreamer, but a muser and a self-amuser. I have never been without a whole repertory of absorbing hobbies, curiosities, inquiries, interests. Hence, my head has always seemed to me to be like a brightly lighted room, full of the most delightful objects, or perhaps I should say, filled with tables on which are set up the most engrossing games. I have never been a collector, but the resource that I am describing must be much like that of a collector busying himself with his coins or minerals. Yet collectors are apt to be "avid" and competitive, while I have no ambition and no competitive sense. Gertrude also said, with her wonderful yes-saying laugh, "Oh, I wish I were a miser; being a miser must be so occupying." I have never been unoccupied. That's as near as I can get to a statement about the happiness or unhappiness of my childhood. Yet I am convinced that, except in a few extraordinary cases, one form or another of an unhappy childhood is essential to the formation of exceptional gifts. Perhaps I should have been a better man if I had had an unequivocally unhappy childhood.

INTERVIEWER: Can you see—or analyze, perhaps—tendencies in your early years which led you into writing?

WILDER: I thought we were supposed to talk about the art of the novel. Is it all right to go on talking about myself this way?

INTERVIEWER: I feel that it's all to the point.

WILDER: We often hear the phrase, "a winning child." Winning children (who appear so guileless) are children who have discovered how effective charm and modesty and a delicately calculated spontaneity are in winning what they want. All children, emerging from the egocentric monsterhood of infancy— "Gimme! Gimme!" cries the Nero in the bassinet—are out to win their way—from their parents, playmates, from "life," from all that is bewildering and inexplicable in themselves. They are also out to win some expression of themselves as individuals. Some are early marked to attempt it by assertion, by slam-bang methods; others by a watchful docility; others by guile. The future author is one who discovers that language, the exploration and manipulation of the resources of language, will serve him in winning through to his way. This does not necessarily mean that he is highly articulate in persuading or cajoling or outsmarting his parents and companions, for this type of child is not usually of the "community" type—he is at one remove from the persons around him. (The future scientist is at eight removes.) Language for him is the instrument for digesting experience, for explaining himself to himself. Many great writers have been extraordinarily awkward in daily exchange, but the greatest give the impression that their style was nursed by the closest attention to colloquial speech.

Let me digress for a moment: probably you won't want to use it. For a long time I tried to explain to myself the spell of Madame de Sévigné; she is not devastatingly witty nor wise. She is simply at one with French syntax. Phrase, sentence, and paragraph breathe this effortless at-homeness with how one sees, feels, and says a thing in the French language. What attentive ears little Marie de Rabutin-Chantal must have had! Greater writers than she had such an adjustment to colloquial speech—Montaigne, La Fontaine, Voltaire—but they had things to say: didactic matter; she had merely to exhibit the genius in the language. I have learned to watch the relation to language on the part of young ones— those community-directed toward persuasion, edification, instruction; and those engaged ("merely" engaged) in fixing some image of experience; and those others for whom language is nothing more than a practical convenience—"Oh, Mr. Wilder, tell me how I can get a wider vocabulary."

INTERVIEWER: Well now, inasmuch as you have gone from story-telling to playwriting, would you say the same tendencies which produced the novelist produced the dramatist?

WILDER: I think so, but in stating them I find myself involved in a paradox. A dramatist is one who believes that the pure event, an action involving human beings, is more arresting than any comment that can be made upon it. On the stage it is always *now*; the personages are standing on that razor-edge, between the past and the future, which is the essential character of conscious being; the words are rising to their lips in immediate spontaneity. A novel is what *took place*; no self-effacement on the part of the narrator can hide the fact that we hear his voice recounting, recalling events that are past and over, and which he has selected—from uncountable others—to lay before us from his presiding intelligence. Even the most objective novels are cradled in the authors' emotions and the authors' assumptions about life and mind and the passions. Now the paradox lies not so much in the fact that you and I know that the dramatist equally has selected what he exhibits and what the characters will say—such an operation is inherent in any work of art—but that all the greatest dramatists, except the very greatest *one*, have precisely employed the stage to convey a moral or religious point of view concerning the action. The theater is supremely fitted to say: "Behold! These things are." Yet most dramatists employ it to say: "This moral truth can be learned from beholding this action."

The Greek tragic poets wrote for edification, admonition, and even for our political education. The comic tradition in the theater carries the intention of exposing folly and curbing excess. Only in Shakespeare are we free of hearing axes ground.

INTERVIEWER: How do you get around this difficulty?

WILDER: By what may be an impertinence on my part. By believing that the moralizing intention resided in the authors as a convention of their times—usually, a social convention so deeply buried in the author's mode of thinking that it seemed to him to be inseparable from creation. I reverse a popular judgment: we say that Shaw wrote diverting plays to sugar-coat the pill of a social message. Of these other dramatists, I say they injected a didactic intention in order to justify to themselves and to their audiences the exhibition of pure experience.

INTERVIEWER: Is your implication, then, that drama should be art for art's sake?

WILDER: Experience for experience's sake—rather than for moral improvement's sake. When we say that Vermeer's "Girl Making Lace" is a work of art for art's sake, we are not saying anything contemptuous about it. I regard the theater as the greatest of all art forms, the most immediate way in which a human being can share with another the sense of what it is to be a human being. This supremacy of the theater derives from the fact that it is always "now" on the stage. It is enough that generations have been riveted by the sight of Clytemnestra luring Agamemnon to the fatal bath, and Oedipus searching out the truth which will ruin him; those circumambient tags about "Don't get prideful" and "Don't call anybody happy until he's dead" are incidental concomitants.

INTERVIEWER: Is it your contention that there is no place in the theater for didactic intentions?

WILDER: The theater is so vast and fascinating a realm that there is room in it for preachers and moralists and pamphleteers. As to the highest function of the theater, I rest my case with Shakespeare—*Twelfth Night* as well as *Macbeth*.

INTERVIEWER: If you will forgive me, I'm afraid I've lost track of something we were talking about a while back—we were talking about the tendencies in your childhood which went into the formation of a dramatist.

WILDER: The point I've been leading up to is that a dramatist is one who from his earliest years has found that sheer gazing at the shocks and countershocks among people is quite sufficiently engrossing without having to encase it in comment. It's a form of tact. It's a lack of presumption. That's why so many earnest people have been so exasperated by Shakespeare: they cannot isolate the passages wherein we hear him speaking in his own voice. Somewhere Shaw says that one page of Bunyan, "who plants his standard on the forefront of—I-forget-what—is worth a hundred by such shifting opalescent men."

INTERVIEWER: Are we to infer from what you say that the drama ought to have no social function?

WILDER: Oh, yes—there are at least two. First, the presentation of *what is*, under the direction of those great hands, is important enough. We live in *what is*, but we find a thousand ways not to face it. Great theater strengthens our faculty to face it.

Secondly, to be present at any work of man-made order and harmony and intellectual power—Vermeer's "Lace Maker" or a Haydn quartet or *Twelfth Night*—is to be confirmed and strengthened in our potentialities as man.

INTERVIEWER: I wonder if you don't hammer your point pretty hard because actually you have a considerable element of the didactic in you.

WILDER: Yes, of course. I've spent a large part of my life trying to sit on it, to keep it down. The pages and pages I've had to tear up! I think the struggle with it may have brought a certain kind of objectivity into my work. I've become accustomed to readers' taking widely different views of the intentions in my books and plays. A good example is George Brush, whom we were talking about before. George, the hero of a novel of mine which I wrote when I was nearly forty, is an earnest, humorless, moralizing, preachifying, interfering product of Bible-belt evangelism. I received many letters from writers of the George Brush mentality angrily denouncing me for making fun of sacred things, and a letter from the Mother Superior of a convent in Ohio saying that she regarded the book as an allegory of the stages in the spiritual life.

Many thank me for the "comfort" they found in the last act of *Our Town*; others tell me that it is a desolating picture of our limitation to "realize" life—almost too sad to endure.

Many assured me that *The Bridge of San Luis Rey* was a satisfying demonstration that all the accidents of life were overseen and harmonized in providence; and a society of atheists in New York wrote me that it was the most artful exposure of shallow optimisms since *Candide* and asked me to address them.

A very intelligent woman to whom I offered the dedication of *The Skin of Our Teeth* refused it, saying that the play was so defeatist. ("Man goes stumbling, bumbling down the ages.") *The Happy Journey to Trenton and Camden* received its first performance, an admirable one, at the University of Chicago.

Edna St. Vincent Millay happened to be in the audience. At the close of the play she congratulated me at having so well pictured that "detestable bossy kind of mother."

Most writers firmly guide their readers to "what they should think" about the characters and events. If an author refrains from intruding his point of view, readers will be nettled, but will project into the text their own assumptions and turns of mind. If the work has vitality, it will, however slightly, alter those assumptions.

INTERVIEWER: So that you have *not* eliminated all didactic intentions from your work after all?

WILDER: I suspect that all writers have some didactic intention. That starts the motor. Or let us say: many of the things we eat are cooked over a gas stove, but there is no taste of gas in the food.

INTERVIEWER: In one of your Harvard lectures you spoke of—I don't remember the exact words—a prevailing hiatus between the highbrow and lowbrow reader. Do you think a work could appear at this time which would satisfy both the discriminating reader and the larger public?

WILDER: What we call a great age in literature is an age in which that is completely possible: the whole Athenian audience took part in the flowering of Greek tragedy and Greek comedy. And so in the age of the great Spaniards. So in the age of Elizabeth. We certainly are not, in any sense, in the flowering of a golden age now; and one of the unfortunate things about the situation is this great gulf. It would be a very wonderful thing if we could see more and more works which close that gulf between highbrows and lowbrows.

INTERVIEWER: Someone has said—one of your dramatist colleagues, I believe, I can't remember which one—that a writer deals with only one or two ideas throughout his work. Would you say your work reflects those one or two ideas?

WILDER: Yes, I think so. I have become aware of it myself only recently. Those ideas seem to have prompted my work before I realized it. Now, at my age, I am amused by the circumstance that what is now conscious with me was for a long time latent. One of those ideas is this: an unresting preoccupation with the surprise of the gulf between each tiny occasion of the daily life and the vast stretches of time and place in which every individual plays his role. By that I mean the absurdity of any single person's claim to the importance of his saying, "I love!" "I suffer!" when one thinks of the background of the billions who have lived and died, who are living and dying, and presumably will live and die.

This was particularly developed in me by the almost accidental chance that, having graduated from Yale in 1920, I was sent abroad to study archaeology at the American Academy in Rome. We even took field trips in those days and in a small way took part in diggings. Once you have swung a pickax that will reveal the curve of a street four thousand years covered over which was once an active, much-traveled highway, you are never quite the same again. You look at Times Square as a place about which you imagine some day scholars saying, "There appears to have been some kind of public center here."

This preoccupation came out in my work before I realized it. Even *Our Town*, which I now see is filled with it, was not so consciously directed by me at the time. At first glance, the play appears to be practically a genre study of a village in New Hampshire. On second glance, it appears to be a meditation about the difficulty of, as the play says, "realizing life while you live it." But buried back in the text, from the very commencement of the play, is a constant repetition of the words "hundreds," "thousands," "millions." It's as though the audience—no one has ever mentioned this to me, though—is looking at that town at ever greater distances through a telescope.

I'd like to cite some examples of this. Soon after the play begins, the Stage Manager calls upon the professor from the geology department of the state university, who says how many million years old the ground is they're on. And the Stage Manager talks about putting some objects and reading matter into the cornerstone of a new bank and covering it with a preservative so that it can be read a thousand years from now. Or as minister presiding at the wedding, the Stage Manager muses to himself about all the marriages that have ever taken place—"millions of 'em, millions of 'em . . . Who set out to live two by two . . ." Finally, among the seated dead, one of the dead says, "My son was a sailor and used to sit on the porch. And he says the light from that star took millions of years to arrive." There is still more of this. So that when finally the heartbreak of Emily's unsuccessful return to life again occurs, it is against the background of the almost frightening range of these things.

Then *The Skin of Our Teeth*, which takes five thousand years to go by, is really a way of trying to make sense out of the *multiplicity* of the human race and its affections.

So that I see myself making an effort to find the dignity in the trivial of our daily life, against those preposterous stretches which seem to rob it of any such dignity; and the validity of each individual's emotion.

INTERVIEWER: I feel that there is another important theme running through your work which has to do with the nature of love. For example, there are a number of aphorisms in *The Bridge of San Luis Rey* which are often quoted and which relate to that theme. Do your views on the nature of love change in your later works?

WILDER: My ideas have not greatly changed; but those aphorisms in *The Bridge* represent only one side of them and are limited by their application to what is passing in that novel. In *The Ides of March*, my ideas are more illustrated than stated.

Love started out as a concomitant of reproduction; it is what makes new life and then shelters it. It is therefore an affirmation about existence and a belief in value. Tens of thousands of years have gone by; more complicated forms of society and of consciousness have arisen. Love acquired a wide variety of secondary expressions. It got mixed up with a power conflict between male and female; it got cut off from its primary intention and took its place among the refinements of psychic life, and in the cult of pleasure; it expanded beyond the relations of the couple and the family and reappeared as philanthropy; it attached itself to man's ideas about the order of the universe and was attributed to the gods and God.

I always see beneath it, nevertheless, the urge that strives toward justifying life, harmonizing it—the source of energy on which life must draw in order to better itself. In *The Ides of March* I illustrate its educative power (Caesar toward Cleopatra and toward his wife; the actress toward Marc Antony) and its power to "crystallize" idealization in the lover (Catullus's infatuation for the destructive "drowning" Clodia—he divines in her the great qualities she once possessed). This attitude has so much the character of self-evidence for me that I am unable to weigh or even "hear" any objections to it. I don't know whether I am uttering an accepted platitude or a bit of naïve nonsense.

INTERVIEWER: Your absorbing interest in James Joyce and Gertrude Stein is pretty well known. I wonder if there are any other literary figures who are of particular interest to you.

WILDER: In present-day life?

INTERVIEWER: Well, past or present.

WILDER: I am always, as I said earlier, in the middle of a whole succession of very stormy admirations up and down literature. Every now and then, I lose one; very sad. Among contemporaries, I am deeply indebted to Ezra Pound and Mr. Eliot. In the past, I have these last few years worked a good deal with Lope de Vega, not in the sense of appraisal of his total work, but almost as a curious and very absorbing game—the pure technical business of dating his enormous output of plays. I could go on forever about these successive enthusiasms.

INTERVIEWER: Do you believe that a serious young writer can write for television or the movies without endangering his gifts?

WILDER: Television and Hollywood are a part of show business. If that young writer is to be a dramatist, I believe that he's tackling one of the most difficult of all métiers—far harder than the novel. All excellence is equally difficult, but, considering sheer métier, I would always advise any young writer for the theater to do everything—to adapt plays, to translate plays, to hang around theaters, to paint scenery, to become an actor, if possible. Writing for TV or radio or the movies is all part of it. There's a bottomless pit in the acquisition of how to tell an imagined story to listeners and viewers.

INTERVIEWER: If that young writer has the problem of earning a livelihood, is advertising or journalism or teaching English a suitable vocation?

WILDER: I think all are unfavorable to the writer. If by day you handle the English language either in the conventional forms which are journalism and advertising, or in the analysis which is teaching English in school or college, you will have a double, a quadruple difficulty in finding *your* English language at night and on Sundays. It is proverbial that every newspaper reporter has a half finished novel in his bureau drawer. Reporting—which can be admirable in itself—is poles apart from shaping concepts into imagined actions and requires a totally different ordering of mind and language. When I had to earn my living for many years, I taught French. I should have taught mathematics. By teaching math or biology or physics, you come refreshed to writing.

INTERVIEWER: Mr. Wilder, why do you write?

WILDER: I think I write in order to discover on my shelf a new book which I would enjoy reading, or to see a new play that would engross me.

INTERVIEWER: Do your books and plays fulfill this expectation?
WILDER: No.

INTERVIEWER: They disappoint you?

WILDER: No, I do not repudiate them. I am merely answering your question—they do not fulfill *that* expectation. An author, unfortunately, can never experience the sensation of reading his own work as though it were a book he had never read. Yet with each new work that expectation is prompting me. That is why the first months of work on a new project are so delightful: you see the book already bound, or the play already produced, and you have the illusion that you will read or see it as though it were a work by another that will give you pleasure.

INTERVIEWER: Then all those other motivations to which other writers have confessed play no part in your impulse to write—sharing what experience has taught you, or justifying your life by making a thing which you hope to be good?

WILDER: Yes, I suppose they are present also, but I like to keep them below the level of consciousness. Not because they would seem pretentious, but because they might enter into the work as strain. Unfortunately, good things are not made by the resolve to make a good thing, but by the application to develop fitly the one specific idea or project which presents itself to you. I am always uncomfortable when, in "studio" conversation, I hear young artists talking about "truth" and "humanity" and "what is art," and most happy when I hear them talking about pigments or the timbre of the flute in its lower range or the spelling of dialects or James's "center of consciousness."

INTERVIEWER: Is there some final statement you would wish to make about the novel?

WILDER: I'm afraid that I have made no contribution toward the intention of this series of conversations on the art of the novel. I think of myself as a fabulist, not a critic. I realize that every writer is necessarily a critic—that is, each sentence is a skeleton accompanied by enormous activity of rejection; and each selection is governed by general principles concerning truth, force, beauty, and so on. But, as I have just suggested, I believe that the practice of writing consists in more and more relegating all that schematic operation to the subconscious. The critic that is in every fabulist is like the iceberg—nine-tenths of him is under water. Yeats warned against probing into how and why one writes; he called it "muddying the spring." He quoted Browning's lines:

> *Where the apple reddens never pry—*
> *Lest we lose our Edens, Eve and I.*

I have long kept a journal to which I consign meditations abou.
"the omniscience of the novelist" and thoughts about how time
can be expressed in narration, and so on. But I never reread those
entries. They are like the brief canters that a man would take on
his horse during the days preceding a race. They inform the buried
critic that I know he's there, that I hope he's constantly at work
clarifying his system of principles, helping me when I'm not aware
of it, and that I also hope he will not intrude on the day of the
race.

Gertrude Stein once said laughingly that writing is merely
"telling what you know." Well, that telling is as difficult an
exercise in technique as it is in honesty; but it should emerge as
immediately, as spontaneously, as *undeliberately* as possible.

RICHARD H. GOLDSTONE

7. William Faulkner

William Faulkner was born in 1897 in New Albany, Mississippi, where his father was then working as a conductor on the railroad built by the novelist's great-grandfather Colonel William Falkner (without the "u"), author of *The White Rose of Memphis*. Soon the family moved to Oxford, thirty-five miles away, where young Faulkner, although he was a voracious reader, failed to earn enough credits to be graduated from the local high school. In 1918 he enlisted as a student flyer in the Royal Canadian Air Force. He spent a little more than a year as a special student at the state university, "Ole Miss," and later worked as postmaster at the university station until he was fired for reading on the job.

Encouraged by Sherwood Anderson, he wrote *Soldier's Pay* (1926). His first widely read book was *Sanctuary* (1931), a sensational novel which he says that he wrote for money after his previous books—including *Mosquitoes* (1927), *Sartoris* (1929), *The Sound and the Fury* (1929), and *As I Lay Dying* (1930)—had failed to earn enough royalties to support a family.

A steady succession of novels followed, most of them related to what has come to be called the Yoknapatawpha saga: *Light in August* (1932), *Pylon* (1935), *Absalom, Absalom!* (1936), *The Unvanquished* (1938), *The Wild Palms* (1939), *The Hamlet* (1940), and *Go Down Moses* (1941). Since World War II his principal works have been *Intruder in the Dust* (1948), *A Fable* (1954), and *The Town* (1957). His *Collected Stories* received the National Book Award in 1951, as did *A Fable* in 1955. In 1949 Faulkner was awarded the Nobel Prize for Literature.

Recently, though shy and retiring, Faulkner has traveled widely, lecturing for the United States Information Service.

A *reproduction of the first manuscript page of Faulkner's* As I Lay Dying; *actual size (marginal note has been turned). By courtesy of Saxe Commins of Random House* ol into his wooden face, to reason the ~~brace and putty~~ (lon in 4 strides, with the aured gravely of a apon-sing Indian dressed in painted overalls and enclosed with life from the hips clann, and steps over a single stride than the opposite window and into the porch opens just as I come around the house corner.

In single file and 3 feet apart and level now as level, we go on up the path, ~~up to the trace~~ to the foot of the bluff. ~~At the foot~~.

Tull's

~~At the foot of the bluff.~~ ~~his~~ Dimpins worm stands beside the spring. the box ~~on the~~ instead to the railway, the rains warped about a ~~stanchion~~. In the bed are 2 chains. Jewel stops at the spring and takes the dip from the willow-leaves and drinks I pour him and so up the path, having to have Cash's saw.

When I cross the top he has quit sawing. Standing in a litter of chips he is fitting ~~this~~ two of the boards to-gether ~~this garb~~ Between the shadow-spaces they are yellow as gold, like soft gold, becoming on them Planks in smooth undulations the marks of the adze blade: a good carpenter. B Cash is. He holds the two boards on the trestle, fitted along the edge in the shape of ~~that~~ ~~one of~~ the coffin a quarter of the coffin, the boards and spends along the edge of them. (A good carpenter. Many cannot not want a better one, a better box to lie in. It will give him confidence and comfort. I go on to the house, followed by the ~~slow~~ chuck. Chunk. Chunk of the adze.

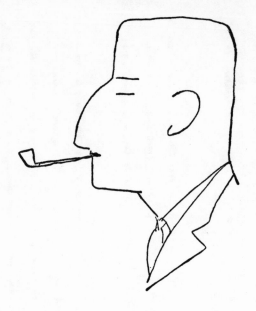

Self-portrait

William Faulkner

This conversation took place in New York City, early in 1956.

INTERVIEWER: Mr. Faulkner, you were saying a while ago that you don't like interviews.

FAULKNER: The reason I don't like interviews is that I seem to react violently to personal questions. If the questions are about the work, I try to answer them. When they are about me, I may answer or I may not, but even if I do, if the same question is asked tomorrow, the answer may be different.

INTERVIEWER: How about yourself as a writer?

FAULKNER: If I had not existed, someone else would have written me, Hemingway, Dostoevski, all of us. Proof of that is that there are about three candidates for the authorship of Shakespeare's plays. But what is important is *Hamlet* and *Midsummer Night's*

Dream, not who wrote them, but that somebody did. The artist is of no importance. Only what he creates is important, since there is nothing new to be said. Shakespeare, Balzac, Homer have all written about the same things, and if they had lived one thousand or two thousand years longer, the publishers wouldn't have needed anyone since.

INTERVIEWER: But even if there seems nothing more to be said, isn't perhaps the individuality of the writer important?

FAULKNER: Very important to himself. Everybody else should be too busy with the work to care about the individuality.

INTERVIEWER: And your contemporaries?

FAULKNER: All of us failed to match our dream of perfection. So I rate us on the basis of our splendid failure to do the impossible. In my opinion, if I could write all my work again, I am convinced that I would do it better, which is the healthiest condition for an artist. That's why he keeps on working, trying again; he believes each time that this time he will do it, bring it off. Of course he won't, which is why this condition is healthy. Once he did it, once he matched the work to the image, the dream, nothing would remain but to cut his throat, jump off the other side of that pinnacle of perfection into suicide. I'm a failed poet. Maybe every novelist wants to write poetry first, finds he can't, and then tries the short story, which is the most demanding form after poetry. And, failing at that, only then does he take up novel writing.

INTERVIEWER: Is there any possible formula to follow in order to be a good novelist?

FAULKNER: Ninety-nine per cent talent . . . 99 per cent discipline . . . 99 per cent work. He must never be satisfied with what he does. It never is as good as it can be done. Always dream and shoot higher than you know you can do. Don't bother just to be better than your contemporaries or predecessors. Try to be better than yourself. An artist is a creature driven by demons. He don't know why they choose him and he's usually too busy to wonder why. He is completely amoral in that he will rob, borrow, beg, or steal from anybody and everybody to get the work done.

INTERVIEWER: Do you mean the writer should be completely ruthless?

FAULKNER:. The writer's only responsibility is to his art. He will be completely ruthless if he is a good one. He has a dream. It anguishes him so much he must get rid of it. He has no peace until then. Everything goes by the board: honor, pride, decency, security, happiness, all, to get the book written. If a writer has to rob his mother, he will not hesitate; the "Ode on a Grecian Urn" is worth any number of old ladies.

INTERVIEWER: Then could the *lack* of security, happiness, honor, be an important factor in the artist's creativity?

FAULKNER: No. They are important only to his peace and contentment, and art has no concern with peace and contentment.

INTERVIEWER: Then what would be the best environment for a writer?

FAULKNER: Art is not concerned with environment either; it doesn't care where it is. If you mean me, the best job that was ever offered to me was to become a landlord in a brothel. In my opinion it's the perfect milieu for an artist to work in. It gives him perfect economic freedom; he's free of fear and hunger; he has a roof over his head and nothing whatever to do except keep a few simple accounts and to go once every month and pay off the local police. The place is quiet during the morning hours, which is the best time of the day to work. There's enough social life in the evening, if he wishes to participate, to keep him from being bored; it gives him a certain standing in his society; he has nothing to do because the madam keeps the books; all the inmates of the house are females and would defer to him and call him "sir." All the bootleggers in the neighborhood would call him "sir." And he could call the police by their first names.

So the only environment the artist needs is whatever peace, whatever solitude, and whatever pleasure he can get at not too high a cost. All the wrong environment will do is run his blood pressure up; he will spend more time being frustrated or outraged.

My own experience has been that the tools I need for my trade are paper, tobacco, food, and a little whisky.

INTERVIEWER: Bourbon, you mean?

FAULKNER: No, I ain't that particular. Between scotch and nothing, I'll take scotch.

INTERVIEWER: You mentioned economic freedom. Does the writer need it?

FAULKNER: No. The writer doesn't need economic freedom. All he needs is a pencil and some paper. I've never known anything good in writing to come from having accepted any free gift of money. The good writer never applies to a foundation. He's too busy writing something. If he isn't first rate he fools himself by saying he hasn't got time or economic freedom. Good art can come out of thieves, bootleggers, or horse swipes. People really are afraid to find out just how much hardship and poverty they can stand. They are afraid to find out how tough they are. Nothing can destroy the good writer. The only thing that can alter the good writer is death. Good ones don't have time to bother with success or getting rich. Success is feminine and like a woman; if you cringe before her, she will override you. So the way to treat her is to show her the back of your hand. Then maybe she will do the crawling.

INTERVIEWER: Can working for the movies hurt your own writing?

FAULKNER: Nothing can injure a man's writing if he's a first-rate writer. If a man is not a first-rate writer, there's not anything can help it much. The problem does not apply if he is not first rate, because he has already sold his soul for a swimming pool.

INTERVIEWER: Does a writer compromise in writing for the movies?

FAULKNER: Always, because a moving picture is by its nature a collaboration, and any collaboration is compromise because that is what the word means—to give and to take.

INTERVIEWER: Which actors do you like to work with most?

FAULKNER: Humphrey Bogart is the one I've worked with best.

He and I worked together in *To Have and Have Not* and *The Big Sleep.*

INTERVIEWER: Would you like to make another movie?

FAULKNER: Yes, I would like to make one of George Orwell's 1984. I have an idea for an ending which would prove the thesis I'm always hammering at: that man is indestructible because of his simple will to freedom.

INTERVIEWER: How do you get the best results in working for the movies?

FAULKNER: The moving-picture work of my own which seemed best to me was done by the actors and the writer throwing the script away and inventing the scene in actual rehearsal just before the camera turned. If I didn't take, or feel I was capable of taking, motion-picture work seriously, out of simple honesty to motion pictures and myself too, I would not have tried. But I know now that I will never be a good motion-picture writer; so that work will never have the urgency for me which my own medium has.

INTERVIEWER: Would you comment on that legendary Hollywood experience you were involved in?

FAULKNER: I had just completed a contract at MGM and was about to return home. The director I had worked with said, "If you would like another job here, just let me know and I will speak to the studio about a new contract." I thanked him and came home. About six months later I wired my director friend that I would like another job. Shortly after that I received a letter from my Hollywood agent enclosing my first week's paycheck. I was surprised because I had expected first to get an official notice or recall and a contract from the studio. I thought to myself the contract is delayed and will arrive in the next mail. Instead, a week later I got another letter from the agent, enclosing my second week's paycheck. That began in November 1932 and continued until May 1933. Then I received a telegram from the studio. It said: *William Faulkner, Oxford, Miss. Where are you? MGM Studio.*

I wrote out a telegram: *MGM Studio, Culver City, California. William Faulkner.*

The young lady operator said, "Where is the message, Mr. Faulkner?" I said, "That's it." She said, "The rule book says that I can't send it without a message, you have to say something." So we went through her samples and selected I forget which one— one of the canned anniversary greeting messages. I sent that. Next was a long-distance telephone call from the studio directing me to get on the first airplane, go to New Orleans, and report to Director Browning. I could have got on a train in Oxford and been in New Orleans eight hours later. But I obeyed the studio and went to Memphis, where an airplane did occasionally go to New Orleans. Three days later one did.

I arrived at Mr. Browning's hotel about six p.m. and reported to him. A party was going on. He told me to get a good night's sleep and be ready for an early start in the morning. I asked him about the story. He said, "Oh, yes. Go to room so and so. That's the continuity writer. He'll tell you what the story is."

I went to the room as directed. The continuity writer was sitting in there alone. I told him who I was and asked him about the story. He said, "When you have written the dialogue I'll let you see the story." I went back to Browning's room and told him what had happened. "Go back," he said, "and tell that so and so —never mind, you get a good night's sleep so we can get an early start in the morning."

So the next morning in a very smart rented launch all of us except the continuity writer sailed down to Grand Isle, about a hundred miles away, where the picture was to be shot, reaching there just in time to eat lunch and have time to run the hundred miles back to New Orleans before dark.

That went on for three weeks. Now and then I would worry a little about the story, but Browning always said, "Stop worrying. Get a good night's sleep so we can get an early start tomorrow morning."

One evening on our return I had barely entered my room when the telephone rang. It was Browning. He told me to come to his room at once. I did so. He had a telegram. It said: *Faulkner is fired. MGM Studio.* "Don't worry," Browning said. "I'll call that so-and-so up this minute and not only make him put you back on the payroll but send you a written apology." There was a knock on the door. It was a page with another telegram. This one said: *Browning is fired. MGM Studio.* So I came back home. I presume Browning went somewhere too. I imagine that continuity writer is still sitting in a room somewhere with his weekly salary check clutched tightly in his hand. They never did finish the film. But they did build a shrimp village—a long platform on piles in the water with sheds built on it something like a wharf. The studio could have bought dozens of them for forty or fifty dollars apiece. Instead, they built one of their own, a false one. That is, a platform with a single wall on it, so that when you opened the door and stepped through it, you stepped right on off to the ocean itself. As they built it, on the first day, the Cajun fisherman paddled up in his narrow tricky pirogue made out of a hollow log. He would sit in it all day long in the broiling sun watching the strange white folks building this strange imitation platform. The next day he was back in the pirogue with his whole family, his wife nursing the baby, the other children, and the mother-in-law, all to sit all that day in the broiling sun to watch this foolish and incomprehensible activity. I was in New Orleans two or three years later and heard that the Cajun people were still coming in for miles to look at that imitation shrimp platform which a lot of white people had rushed in and built and then abandoned.

INTERVIEWER: You say that the writer must compromise in working for the motion pictures. How about his writing? Is he under any obligation to his reader?

FAULKNER: His obligation is to get the work done the best he can do it; whatever obligation he has left over after that he can spend any way he likes. I myself am too busy to care about the public. I have no time to wonder who is reading me. I don't care about John Doe's opinion on my or anyone else's work. Mine is the standard which has to be met, which is when the work makes me feel the way I do when I read *La Tentation de Saint Antoine*, or the Old Testament. They make me feel good. So does watching a bird make me feel good. You know that if I were reincarnated, I'd want to come back a buzzard. Nothing hates him or envies him or wants him or needs him. He is never bothered or in danger, and he can eat anything.

INTERVIEWER: What technique do you use to arrive at your standard?

FAULKNER: Let the writer take up surgery or bricklaying if he is interested in technique. There is no mechanical way to get the writing done, no short cut. The young writer would be a fool to follow a theory. Teach yourself by your own mistakes; people learn only by error. The good artist believes that nobody is good enough to give him advice. He has supreme vanity. No matter how much he admires the old writer, he wants to beat him.

INTERVIEWER: Then would you deny the validity of technique?

FAULKNER: By no means. Sometimes technique charges in and takes command of the dream before the writer himself can get his hands on it. That is *tour de force* and the finished work is simply a matter of fitting bricks neatly together, since the writer knows probably every single word right to the end before he puts the first one down. This happened with *As I Lay Dying*. It was not easy. No honest work is. It was simple in that all the material was already at hand. It took me just about six weeks in the spare time from a twelve-hour-a-day job at manual labor. I simply imagined a group of people and subjected them to the simple universal natural catastrophes, which are flood and fire, with a simple natural motive to give direction to their progress. But then, when technique does not intervene, in another sense writing is easier too. Because with me there is always a point in the book where the characters themselves rise up and take charge and finish the job—say somewhere about page 275. Of course I don't know what would happen if I finished the book on page 274. The quality an artist must have is objectivity in judging his work, plus the honesty and courage not to kid himself about it. Since none of my work has met my own standards, I must judge it on the basis of that one which caused me the most grief and anguish, as the mother loves the child who became the thief or murderer more than the one who became the priest.

INTERVIEWER: What work is that?

FAULKNER: *The Sound and the Fury.* I wrote it five separate times, trying to tell the story, to rid myself of the dream which would continue to anguish me until I did. It's a tragedy of two lost women: Caddy and her daughter. Dilsey is one of my own favorite characters, because she is brave, courageous, generous, gentle, and honest. She's much more brave and honest and generous than me.

INTERVIEWER: How did *The Sound and the Fury* begin?

FAULKNER: It began with a mental picture. I didn't realize at the time it was symbolical. The picture was of the muddy seat of a little girl's drawers in a pear tree, where she could see through a window where her grandmother's funeral was taking place and report what was happening to her brothers on the ground below. By the time I explained who they were and what they were doing and how her pants got muddy, I realized it would be impossible to get all of it into a short story and that it would have to be a book. And then I realized the symbolism of the soiled pants, and that image was replaced by the one of the fatherless and mother-less girl climbing down the rainpipe to escape from the only home she had, where she had never been offered love or affection or understanding.

I had already begun to tell the story through the eyes of the idiot child, since I felt that it would be more effective as told by someone capable only of knowing what happened, but not why. I saw that I had not told the story that time. I tried to tell it again, the same story through the eyes of another brother. That was still not it. I told it for the third time through the eyes of the third brother. That was still not it. I tried to gather the pieces together and fill in the gaps by making myself the spokesman

It was still not complete, not until fifteen years after the book was published, when I wrote as an appendix to another book the final effort to get the story told and off my mind, so that I myself could have some peace from it. It's the book I feel tenderest towards. I couldn't leave it alone, and I never could tell it right, though I tried hard and would like to try again, though I'd probably fail again.

INTERVIEWER: What emotion does Benjy arouse in you?

FAULKNER: The only emotion I can have for Benjy is grief and pity for all mankind. You can't feel anything for Benjy because he doesn't feel anything. The only thing I can feel about him personally is concern as to whether he is believable as I created him. He was a prologue, like the gravedigger in the Elizabethan dramas. He serves his purpose and is gone. Benjy is incapable of good and evil because he had no knowledge of good and evil.

INTERVIEWER: Could Benjy feel love?

FAULKNER: Benjy wasn't rational enough even to be selfish. He was an animal. He recognized tenderness and love though he could not have named them, and it was the threat to tenderness and love that caused him to bellow when he felt the change in Caddy. He no longer had Caddy; being an idiot he was not even aware that Caddy was missing. He knew only that something was wrong, which left a vacuum in which he grieved. He tried to fill that vacuum. The only thing he had was one of Caddy's discarded slippers. The slipper was his tenderness and love which he could not have named, but he knew only that it was missing. He was dirty because he couldn't coordinate and because dirt meant nothing to him. He could no more distinguish between dirt and cleanliness than between good and evil. The slipper gave him comfort even though he no longer remembered the person to whom it had once belonged, any more than he could remember why he grieved. If Caddy had reappeared he probably would not have known her.

INTERVIEWER: Does the narcissus given to Benjy have some significance?

FAULKNER: The narcissus was given to Benjy to distract his attention. It was simply a flower which happened to be handy that fifth of April. It was not deliberate.

INTERVIEWER: Are there any artistic advantages in casting the novel in the form of an allegory, as the Christian allegory you used in A *Fable?*

FAULKNER: Same advantage the carpenter finds in building square corners in order to build a square house. In A *Fable* the Christian allegory was the right allegory to use in that particular story, like an oblong square corner is the right corner with which to build an oblong rectangular house.

INTERVIEWER: Does that mean an artist can use Christianity simply as just another tool, as a carpenter would borrow a hammer?

FAULKNER: The carpenter we are speaking of never lacks that hammer. No one is without Christianity, if we agree on what we mean by the word. It is every individual's individual code of behavior by means of which he makes himself a better human being than his nature wants to be, if he followed his nature only. Whatever its symbol—cross or crescent or whatever—that symbol is man's reminder of his duty inside the human race. Its various allegories are the charts against which he measures himself and learns to know what he is. It cannot teach man to be good as the textbook teaches him mathematics. It shows him how to discover himself, evolve for himself a moral code and standard within his capacities and aspirations, by giving him a matchless example of suffering and sacrifice and the promise of hope. Writers have always drawn, and always will draw, upon the allegories of moral consciousness, for the reason that the allegories are matchless— the three men in *Moby Dick*, who represent the trinity of conscience: knowing nothing, knowing but not caring, knowing and caring. The same trinity is represented in A *Fable* by the young Jewish pilot officer, who said, "This is terrible. I refuse to accept it, even if I must refuse life to do so"; the old French Quartermaster General, who said, "This is terrible, but we can weep and bear it"; and the English battalion runner, who said, "This is terrible, I'm going to do something about it."

INTERVIEWER: Are the two unrelated themes in *The Wild Palms* brought together in one book for any symbolic purpose? Is it as certain critics intimate a kind of esthetic counterpoint, or is it merely haphazard?

FAULKNER: No, no. That was one story—the story of Charlotte Rittenmeyer and Harry Wilbourne, who sacrificed everything for love, and then lost that. I did not know it would be two separate stories until after I had started the book. When I reached the end of what is now the first section of *The Wild Palms*, I realized suddenly that something was missing, it needed emphasis, something to lift it like counterpoint in music. So I wrote on the "Old Man" story until "The Wild Palms" story rose back to pitch. Then I stopped the "Old Man" story at what is now its first section, and took up "The Wild Palms" story until it began again to sag. Then I raised it to pitch again with another section of its antithesis, which is the story of a man who got his love and spent the rest of the book fleeing from it, even to the extent of voluntarily going back to jail where he would be safe. They are only two stories by chance, perhaps necessity. The story is that of Charlotte and Wilbourne.

INTERVIEWER: How much of your writing is based on personal experience?

FAULKNER: I can't say. I never counted up. Because "how much" is not important. A writer needs three things, experience, observation, and imagination, any two of which, at times any one of which, can supply the lack of the others. With me, a story usually begins with a single idea or memory or mental picture. The writing of the story is simply a matter of working up to that moment, to explain why it happened or what it caused to follow. A writer is trying to create believable people in credible moving situations in the most moving way he can. Obviously he must use as one of his tools the environment which he knows. I would say that music is the easiest means in which to express, since it came first in man's experience and history. But since words are my talent, I must try to express clumsily in words what the pure music would have done better. That is, music would express better and simpler, but I prefer to use words, as I prefer to read rather than listen. I prefer silence to sound, and the image produced by words occurs in silence. That is, the thunder and the music of the prose take place in silence.

INTERVIEWER: Some people say they can't understand your writing, even after they read it two or three times. What approach would you suggest for them?

FAULKNER: Read it four times.

INTERVIEWER: You mentioned experience, observation, and imagination as being important for the writer. Would you include inspiration?

FAULKNER: I don't know anything about inspiration, because I don't know what inspiration is—I've heard about it, but I never saw it.

INTERVIEWER: As a writer you are said to be obsessed with violence.

FAULKNER: That's like saying the carpenter is obsessed with his hammer. Violence is simply one of the carpenter's tools. The writer can no more build with one tool than the carpenter can.

INTERVIEWER: Can you say how you started as a writer?

FAULKNER: I was living in New Orleans, doing whatever kind of work was necessary to earn a little money now and then. I met Sherwood Anderson. We would walk about the city in the afternoon and talk to people. In the evenings we would meet again and sit over a bottle or two while he talked and I listened. In the forenoon I would never see him. He was secluded, working. The next day we would repeat. I decided that if that was the life of a writer, then becoming a writer was the thing for me. So I began to write my first book. At once I found that writing was fun. I even forgot that I hadn't seen Mr. Anderson for three weeks until he walked in my door, the first time he ever came to see me, and said, "What's wrong? Are you mad at me?" I told him I was writing a book. He said, "My God," and walked out. When I finished the book—it was *Soldier's Pay*—I met Mrs. Anderson on the street. She asked how the book was going, and I said I'd finished it. She said, "Sherwood says that he will make a trade with you. If he doesn't have to read your manuscript he will tell his publisher to accept it." I said, "Done," and that's how I became a writer.

INTERVIEWER: What were the kinds of work you were doing to earn that "little money now and then"?

FAULKNER: Whatever came up. I could do a little of almost anything—run boats, paint houses, fly airplanes. I never needed much money because living was cheap in New Orleans then, and all I wanted was a place to sleep, a little food, tobacco, and whisky. There were many things I could do for two or three days and earn enough money to live on for the rest of the month. By temperament I'm a vagabond and a tramp. I don't want money badly enough to work for it. In my opinion it's a shame that there is so much work in the world. One of the saddest things is that the only thing a man can do for eight hours a day, day after day, is work. You can't eat eight hours a day nor drink for eight hours a day nor make love for eight hours—all you can do for eight hours is work. Which is the reason why man makes himself and everybody else so miserable and unhappy.

INTERVIEWER: You must feel indebted to Sherwood Anderson, but how do you regard him as a writer?

FAULKNER: He was the father of my generation of American writers and the tradition of American writing which our successors will carry on. He has never received his proper evaluation. Dreiser is his older brother and Mark Twain the father of them both.

INTERVIEWER: What about the European writers of that period?

FAULKNER: The two great men in my time were Mann and Joyce. You should approach Joyce's *Ulysses* as the illiterate Baptist preacher approaches the Old Testament: with faith.

INTERVIEWER: How did you get your background in the Bible?

FAULKNER: My Great-Grandfather Murry was a kind and gentle man, to us children anyway. That is, although he was a Scot, he was (to us) neither especially pious nor stern either: he was simply a man of inflexible principles. One of them was, everybody, children on up through all adults present, had to have a verse from the Bible ready and glib at tongue-tip when we gathered at the table for breakfast each morning; if you didn't have your scripture verse ready, you didn't have any breakfast; you would be excused long enough to leave the room and swot one up (there was a maiden aunt, a kind of sergeant-major for this duty, who retired with the culprit and gave him a brisk breezing which carried him over the jump next time).

It had to be an authentic, correct verse. While we were little, it could be the same one, once you had it down good, morning after morning, until you got a little older and bigger, when one morning (by this time you would be pretty glib at it, galloping through without even listening to yourself since you were already five or ten minutes ahead, already among the ham and steak and fried chicken and grits and sweet potatoes and two or three kinds of hot bread) you would suddenly find his eyes on you—very blue, very kind and gentle, and even now not stern so much as inflexible; and next morning you had a new verse. In a way, that was when you discovered that your childhood was over; you had outgrown it and entered the world.

INTERVIEWER: Do you read your contemporaries?

FAULKNER: No, the books I read are the ones I knew and loved when I was a young man and to which I return as you do to old friends: the Old Testament, Dickens, Conrad, Cervantes—*Don Quixote*. I read that every year, as some do the Bible. Flaubert, Balzac—he created an intact world of his own, a bloodstream running through twenty books—Dostoevski, Tolstoi, Shakespeare. I read Melville occasionally, and of the poets Marlowe, Campion, Jonson, Herrick, Donne, Keats, and Shelley. I still read Housman. I've read these books so often that I don't always begin at page one and read on to the end. I just read one scene, or about one character, just as you'd meet and talk to a friend for a few minutes.

INTERVIEWER: And Freud?

FAULKNER: Everybody talked about Freud when I lived in New Orleans, but I have never read him. Neither did Shakespeare. I doubt if Melville did either, and I'm sure Moby Dick didn't.

INTERVIEWER: Do you ever read mystery stories?

FAULKNER: I read Simenon because he reminds me something of Chekhov.

INTERVIEWER: What about your favorite characters?

FAULKNER: My favorite characters are Sarah Gamp—a cruel, ruthless woman, a drunkard, opportunist, unreliable, most of her character was bad, but at least it was character; Mrs. Harris, Falstaff, Prince Hal, Don Quixote, and Sancho of course. Lady Macbeth I always admire. And Bottom, Ophelia, and Mercutio —both he and Mrs. Gamp coped with life, didn't ask any favors, never whined. Huck Finn, of course, and Jim. Tom Sawyer I never liked much—an awful prig. And then I like Sut Lovingood, from a book written by George Harris about 1840 or '50 in the Tennessee mountains. He had no illusions about himself, did the best he could; at certain times he was a coward and knew it and wasn't ashamed; he never blamed his misfortunes on anyone and never cursed God for them.

INTERVIEWER: Would you comment on the future of the novel?

FAULKNER: I imagine as long as people will continue to read novels, people will continue to write them, or vice versa; unless of course the pictorial magazines and comic strips finally atrophy man's capacity to read, and literature really is on its way back to the picture writing in the Neanderthal cave.

INTERVIEWER: And how about the function of the critics?

FAULKNER: The artist doesn't have time to listen to the critics. The ones who want to be writers read the reviews, the ones who want to write don't have the time to read reviews. The critic too is trying to say "Kilroy was here." His function is not directed toward the artist himself. The artist is a cut above the critic, for the artist is writing something which will move the critic. The critic is writing something which will move everybody but the artist.

INTERVIEWER: So you never feel the need to discuss your work with anyone?

FAULKNER: No, I am too busy writing it. It has got to please me and if it does I don't need to talk about it. If it doesn't please me, talking about it won't improve it, since the only thing to improve it is to work on it some more. I am not a literary man but only a writer. I don't get any pleasure from talking shop.

INTERVIEWER: Critics claim that blood relationships are central in your novels.

FAULKNER: That is an opinion and, as I have said, I don't read critics. I doubt that a man trying to write about people is any more interested in blood relationships than in the shape of their noses, unless they are necessary to help the story move. If the writer concentrates on what he does need to be interested in, which is the truth and the human heart, he won't have much time left for anything else, such as ideas and facts like the shape of noses or blood relationships, since in my opinion ideas and facts have very little connection with truth.

INTERVIEWER: Critics also suggest that your characters never consciously choose between good and evil.

FAULKNER: Life is not interested in good and evil. Don Quixote was constantly choosing between good and evil, but then he was choosing in his dream state. He was mad. He entered reality only when he was so busy trying to cope with people that he had no time to distinguish between good and evil. Since people exist only in life, they must devote their time simply to being alive. Life is motion, and motion is concerned with what makes man move— which is ambition, power, pleasure. What time a man can devote to morality, he must take by force from the motion of which he is a part. He is compelled to make choices between good and evil sooner or later, because moral conscience demands that from him in order that he can live with himself tomorrow. His moral conscience is the curse he had to accept from the gods in order to gain from them the right to dream.

INTERVIEWER: Could you explain more what you mean by motion in relation to the artist?

FAULKNER: The aim of every artist is to arrest motion, which is life, by artificial means and hold it fixed so that a hundred years later, when a stranger looks at it, it moves again since it is life. Since man is mortal, the only immortality possible for him is to leave something behind him that is immortal since it will always move. This is the artist's way of scribbling "Kilroy was here" on the wall of the final and irrevocable oblivion through which he must someday pass.

INTERVIEWER: It has been said by Malcolm Cowley that your characters carry a sense of submission to their fate.

FAULKNER: That is his opinion. I would say that some of them do and some of them don't, like everybody else's characters. I would say that Lena Grove in *Light in August* coped pretty well with hers. It didn't really matter to her in her destiny whether her man was Lucas Birch or not. It was her destiny to have a husband and children and she knew it, and so she went out and attended to it without asking help from anyone. She was the captain of her soul. One of the calmest, sanest speeches I ever heard was when she said to Byron Bunch at the very instant of repulsing his final desperate and despairing attempt at rape, "Ain't you ashamed? You might have woke the baby." She was never for one moment confused, frightened, alarmed. She did not even know that she didn't need pity. Her last speech for example: "Here I ain't been traveling but a month, and I'm already in Tennessee. My, my, a body does get around."

The Bundren family in *As I Lay Dying* pretty well coped with theirs. The father having lost his wife would naturally need another one, so he got one. At one blow he not only replaced the family cook, he acquired a gramophone to give them all pleasure while they were resting. The pregnant daughter failed this time to undo her condition, but she was not discouraged. She intended to try again, and even if they all failed right up to the last, it wasn't anything but just another baby.

INTERVIEWER: And Mr. Cowley says you find it hard to create characters between the ages of twenty and forty who are sympathetic.

FAULKNER: People between twenty and forty are not sympathetic. The child has the capacity to do but it can't know. It only knows when it is no longer able to do—after forty. Between twenty and forty the will of the child to do gets stronger, more dangerous, but it has not begun to learn to know yet. Since his capacity to do is forced into channels of evil through environment and pressures, man is strong before he is moral. The world's anguish is caused by people between twenty and forty. The people around my home who have caused all the interracial tension— the Milams and the Bryants (in the Emmet Till murder) and the gangs of Negroes who grab a white woman and rape her in revenge, the Hitlers, Napoleons, Lenins—all these people are symbols of human suffering and anguish, all of them between twenty and forty.

INTERVIEWER: You gave a statement to the papers at the time of the Emmet Till killing. Have you anything to add to it here?

FAULKNER: No, only to repeat what I said before: that if we Americans are to survive it will have to be because we choose and elect and defend to be first of all Americans; to present to the world one homogeneous and unbroken front, whether of white Americans or black ones or purple or blue or green. Maybe the purpose of this sorry and tragic error committed in my native Mississippi by two white adults on an afflicted Negro child is to prove to us whether or not we deserve to survive. Because if we in America have reached that point in our desperate culture when we must murder children, no matter for what reason or what color, we don't deserve to survive, and probably won't.

INTERVIEWER: What happened to you between *Soldier's Pay* and *Sartoris*—that is, what caused you to begin the Yoknapatawpha saga?

Faulkner: With *Soldier's Pay* I found out writing was fun. But I found out afterward that not only each book had to have a design but the whole output or sum of an artist's work had to have a design. With *Soldier's Pay* and *Mosquitoes* I wrote for the sake of writing because it was fun. Beginning with *Sartoris* I discovered that my own little postage stamp of native soil was worth writing about and that I would never live long enough to exhaust it, and that by sublimating the actual into the apocryphal I would have complete liberty to use whatever talent I might have to its absolute top. It opened up a gold mine of other people, so I created a cosmos of my own. I can move these people around like God, not only in space but in time too. The fact that I have moved my characters around in time successfully, at least in my own estimation, proves to me my own theory that time is a fluid condition which has no existence except in the momentary avatars of individual people. There is no such thing as *was*—only *is*. If *was* existed, there would be no grief or sorrow. I like to think of the world I created as being a kind of keystone in the universe; that, small as that keystone is, if it were ever taken away the universe itself would collapse. My last book will be the Doomsday Book, the Golden Book, of Yoknapatawpha County. Then I shall break the pencil and I'll have to stop.

Jean Stein vanden Heuvel

8. Georges Simenon

André Gide, who at the end of his life was writing a study of Georges Simenon's fiction, called Simenon "perhaps the greatest" novelist of contemporary France.

Simenon published his first novel, *Au Pont des Arches*, at seventeen, and by writing it in ten days began at once his phenomenal practice of rapid production. Using at least sixteen pen-names ranging from Christian Brulls to Gom Gut, he began writing scores of commercial novels—one of them in exactly twenty-five hours —with the intention of training himself for more serious works. He shortened the period of training in commercial novels when he began to write a transitional fiction—his series of books about the detective Maigret. From the Maigrets he moved on rapidly to the tense psychological novel of less than two hundred pages—known to his thousands of European readers as "a simenon"—of which he has now written more than seventy-five.

Today, except for an infrequent Maigret, he publishes only serious novels. These books, which he writes in French, are not only translated widely but continually used for movies and television—in adaptations which Simenon does not supervise, for dramas which he does not see.

Among his novels currently available in English translation are *The Heart of a Man, The Snow Was Black, Four Days in a Lifetime, I Take This Woman, The Girl in His Past, The Brothers Rico*, and recently, in a combined volume, *The Magician* and *The Widow*. In all, he has published more than 150 novels under his own name, besides about 350 under various pseudonyms.

Simenon was born in Belgium in 1903, spent much of his life in France, and came to live in the United States in 1945.

Above, the 11-by-16-inch calendar sheet on which Simenon marked off in black each day of his writing The Brothers Rico, one chapter a day, and in red the three days spent revising it. At right, the two sides of a 7-by-10 brown manila envelope on which Simenon began consciously shaping the characters of The Brothers Rico two days before he began the novel on July 14, 1952

William Marshall

Georges Simenon

Mr. Simenon's study in his rambling white house on the edge of Lakeville, Connecticut, after lunch on a January day of bright sun. The room reflects its owner: cheerful, efficient, hospitable, controlled. On its walls are books of law and medicine, two fields in which he has made himself an expert; the telephone directories from many parts of the world to which he turns in naming his characters; the map of a town where he has just set his forty-ninth Maigret novel; and the calendar on which he has X-ed out in heavy crayon the days spent writing the Maigret—one day to a chapter—and the three days spent revising it, a labor which he has generously interrupted for this interview.

In the adjoining office, having seen that everything is arranged comfortably for her husband and the interviewer. Mme. Simenon returns her attention to the business affairs of a writer whose novels

appear six a year and whose contracts for books, adaptations, and
translations are in more than twenty languages.

With great courtesy and in a rich voice which gives to his state-
ments nuances of meaning much beyond the ordinary range, Mr.
Simenon continues a discussion begun in the dining room.

SIMENON: Just one piece of general advice from a writer has
been very useful to me. It was from Colette. I was writing short
stories for *Le Matin*, and Colette was literary editor at that time.
I remember I gave her two short stories and she returned them
and I tried again and tried again. Finally she said, "Look, it is
too literary, always too literary." So I followed her advice. It's
what I do when I write, the main job when I rewrite.

INTERVIEWER: What do you mean by "too literary"? What do
you cut out, certain kinds of words?

SIMENON: Adjectives, adverbs, and every word which is there
just to make an effect. Every sentence which is there just for the
sentence. You know, you have a beautiful sentence—cut it. Every
time I find such a thing in one of my novels it is to be cut.

INTERVIEWER: Is that the nature of most of your revision?

SIMENON: Almost all of it.

INTERVIEWER: It's not revising the plot pattern?

SIMENON: Oh, I never touch anything of that kind. Sometimes
I've changed the names while writing: a woman will be Helen in
the first chapter and Charlotte in the second, you know; so in revising I straighten this out. And then, cut, cut, cut.

INTERVIEWER: Is there anything else you can say to beginning
writers?

SIMENON: Writing is considered a profession, and I don't think
it is a profession. I think that everyone who does not *need* to be a
writer, who thinks he can do something else, ought to do something else. Writing is not a profession but a vocation of unhappiness. I don't think an artist can ever be happy.

INTERVIEWER: Why?

SIMENON: Because, first, I think that if a man has the urge to be an artist, it is because he needs to find himself. Every writer tries to find himself through his characters, through all his writing.

INTERVIEWER: He is writing for himself?

SIMENON: Yes. Certainly.

INTERVIEWER: Are you conscious there will be readers of the novel?

SIMENON: I know that there are many men who have more or less the same problems I have, with more or less intensity, and who will be happy to read the book to find the answer—if the answer can possibly be found.

INTERVIEWER: Even when the author can't find the answer do the readers profit because the author is meaningfully fumbling for it?

SIMENON: That's it. Certainly. I don't remember whether I have ever spoken to you about the feeling I have had for several years. Because society today is without a very strong religion, without a firm hierarchy of social classes, and people are afraid of the big organization in which they are just a little part, for them reading certain novels is a little like looking through the keyhole to learn what the neighbor is doing and thinking—does he have the same inferiority complex, the same vices, the same temptations? This is what they are looking for in the work of art. I think many more people today are insecure and are in a search for themselves.

There are now so few literary works of the kind Anatole France wrote, for example, you know—very quiet and elegant and reassuring. On the contrary, what people today want are the most complex books, trying to go into every corner of human nature. Do you understand what I mean?

INTERVIEWER: I think so. You mean this is not just because today we think we know more about psychology but because more readers need this kind of fiction?

SIMENON: Yes. An ordinary man fifty years ago—there are many problems today which he did not know. Fifty years ago he had the answers. He doesn't have them any more.

INTERVIEWER: A year or so ago you and I heard a critic ask that the novel today return to the kind of novel written in the nine-teenth century.

SIMENON: It is impossible, completely impossible, I think. (*Pausing*) Because we live in a time when writers do not always have barriers around them, they can try to present characters by the most complete, the most full expression. You may show love in a very nice story, the first ten months of two lovers, as in the literature of a long time ago. Then you have a second kind of story: they begin to be bored; that was the literature of the end of the last century. And then, if you are free to go further, the man is fifty and tries to have another life, the woman gets jealous, and you have children mixed in it; that is the third story. We are the third story now. We don't stop when they marry, we don't stop when they begin to be bored, we go to the end.

INTERVIEWER: In this connection, I often hear people ask about the violence in modern fiction. I'm all for it, but I'd like to ask why you write of it.

SIMENON: We are accustomed to see people driven to their limit.

INTERVIEWER: And violence is associated with this?

SIMENON: More or less. (*Pausing*) We no longer think of a man from the point of view of some philosophers; for a long time man was always observed from the point of view that there was a God and that man was the king of creation. We don't think any more that man is the king of creation. We see man almost face to face. Some readers still would like to read very reassuring novels, novels which give them a comforting view of humanity. It can't be done.

INTERVIEWER: Then if the readers interest you, it is because they want a novel to probe their troubles? Your role is to look into yourself and—

SIMENON: That's it. But it's not only a question of the artist's looking into himself but also of his looking into others with the experience he has of himself. He writes with sympathy because he feels that the other man is like him.

INTERVIEWER: If there were no readers you would still write?

SIMENON: Certainly. When I began to write I didn't have the idea my books would sell. More exactly, when I began to write I did commercial pieces—stories for magazines and things of that kind—to earn my living, but I didn't call it writing. But for myself, every evening, I did some writing without any idea that it would ever be published.

INTERVIEWER: You probably have had as much experience as anybody in the world in doing what you have just called commercial writing. What is the difference between it and noncommercial?

SIMENON: I call "commercial" every work, not only in literature but in music and painting and sculpture—any art—which is done for such-and-such a public or for a certain kind of publication or for a particular collection. Of course, in commercial writing there are different grades. You may have things which are very cheap and some very good. The books of the month, for example, are commercial writing; but some of them are almost perfectly done, almost works of art. Not completely, but almost. And the same with certain magazine pieces; some of them are wonderful. But very seldom can they be works of art, because a work of art can't be done for the purpose of pleasing a certain group of readers.

INTERVIEWER: How does this change the work? As the author you know whether or not you tailored a novel for a market, but, looking at your work from the outside only, what difference would the reader see?

SIMENON: The big difference would be in the concessions. In writing for any commercial purpose you have always to make concessions.

INTERVIEWER: To the idea that life is orderly and sweet, for example?

SIMENON: And the view of morals. Maybe that is the most important. You can't write anything commercial without accepting some code. There is always a code—like the code in Hollywood, and in television and radio. For example, there is now a very good program on television, it is probably the best for plays. The first two acts are always first-class. You have the impression of something completely new and strong, and then at the end the concession comes. Not always a happy end, but something comes to arrange everything from the point of view of a morality or philosophy—you know. All the characters, who were beautifully done, change completely in the last ten minutes.

INTERVIEWER: In your non-commercial novels you feel no need to make concessions of any sort?

SIMENON: I never do that, never, never, never. Otherwise I wouldn't write. It's too painful to do it if it's not to go to the end.

INTERVIEWER: You have shown me the manila envelopes you use in starting novels. Before you actually begin writing, how much have you been working consciously on the plan of that particular novel?

SIMENON: As you suggest, we have to distinguish here between consciously and unconsciously. Unconsciously I probably always have two or three, not novels, not ideas about novels, but themes in my mind. I never even think that they might serve for a novel; more exactly, they are the things about which I worry. Two days before I start writing a novel I consciously take up one of those ideas. But even before I consciously take it up I first find some atmosphere. Today there is a little sunshine here. I might remember such and such a spring, maybe in some small Italian town, or some place in the French provinces or in Arizona, I don't know, and then, little by little, a small world will come into my mind, with a few characters. Those characters will be taken partly from people I have known and partly from pure imagination—you know, it's a complex of both. And then the idea I had before will come and stick around them. They will have the same problem I have in my mind myself. And the problem—with those people —will give me the novel.

INTERVIEWER: This is a couple of days before?

SIMENON: Yes, a couple of days. Because as soon as I have the beginning I can't bear it very long; so the next day I take my envelope, take my telephone book for names, and take my town map—you know, to see exactly where things happen. And two days later I begin writing. And the beginning will be always the same; it is almost a geometrical problem: I have such a man, such a woman, in such surroundings. What can happen to them to oblige them to go to their limit? That's the question. It will be sometimes a very simple incident, anything which will change their lives. Then I write my novel chapter by chapter.

INTERVIEWER: What has gone on the planning envelope? Not an outline of the action?

SIMENON: No, no. I know nothing about the events when I begin the novel. On the envelope I put only the names of the characters, their ages, their families. I know nothing whatever about the events that will occur later. Otherwise it would not be interesting to me.

INTERVIEWER: When do the incidents begin to form?

SIMENON: On the eve of the first day I know what will happen in the first chapter. Then, day after day, chapter after chapter, I find what comes later. After I have started a novel I write a chapter each day, without ever missing a day. Because it is a strain, I have to keep pace with the novel. If, for example, I am ill for forty-eight hours, I have to throw away the previous chapters. And I never return to that novel.

INTERVIEWER: When you did commercial fiction, was your method at all similar?

SIMENON: No. Not at all. When I did a commercial novel I didn't think about that novel except in the hours of writing it. But when I am doing a novel now I don't see anybody, I don't speak to anybody, I don't take a phone call—I live just like a monk. All the day I am one of my characters. I feel what he feels.

INTERVIEWER: You are the same character all the way through the writing of that novel?

SIMENON: Always, because most of my novels show what happens around one character. The other characters are always seen by him. So it is in this character's skin I have to be. And it's almost unbearable after five or six days. That is one of the reasons my novels are so short; after eleven days I can't—it's impossible. I have to— It's physical. I am too tired.

INTERVIEWER: I should think so. Especially if you drive the main character to his limit.

SIMENON: Yes, yes.

INTERVIEWER: And you are playing this role with him, you are—

SIMENON: Yes. And it's awful. That is why, before I start a novel—this may sound foolish here, but it is the truth—generally a few days before the start of a novel I look to see that I don't have any appointments for eleven days. Then I call the doctor. He takes my blood pressure, he checks everything. And he says, "Okay."

INTERVIEWER: Cleared for action.

SIMENON: Exactly. Because I have to be sure that I am good for the eleven days.

INTERVIEWER: Does he come again at the end of the eleven days?

SIMENON: Usually.

INTERVIEWER: His idea or yours?

SIMENON: It's his idea.

INTERVIEWER: What does he find?

SIMENON: The blood pressure is usually down.

INTERVIEWER: What does he think of this? Is it all right?

SIMENON: He thinks it is all right but unhealthy to do it too often.

INTERVIEWER: Does he ration you?

SIMENON: Yes. Sometimes he will say, "Look, after this novel take two months off." For example, yesterday he said, "Okay, but how many novels do you want to do before you go away for the summer?" I said, "Two." "Okay," he said.

INTERVIEWER: Fine. I'd like to ask now whether you see any pattern in the development of your views as they have worked out in your novels.

SIMENON: I am not the one who discovered it, but some critics in France did. All my life, my literary life, if I may say so, I have taken several problems for my novels, and about every ten years I have taken up the same problems from another point of view. I have the impression that I will never, probably, find the answer. I know of certain problems I have taken more than five times.

INTERVIEWER: And do you know that you will take those up again?

SIMENON: Yes, I will. And then there are a few problems—if I may call them problems—that I know I will never take again, because I have the impression that I went to the end of them. I don't any more care about them.

INTERVIEWER: What are some of the problems you have dealt with often and expect to deal with in future?

SIMENON: One of them, for example, which will probably haunt me more than any other is the problem of communication. I mean communication between two people. The fact that we are I don't know how many millions of people, yet communication, complete communication, is completely impossible between two of those people, is to me one of the biggest tragic themes in the world. When I was a young boy I was afraid of it. I would almost scream because of it. It gave me such a sensation of solitude, of loneliness. That is a theme I have taken I don't know how many times. But I know it will come again. Certainly it will come again.

INTERVIEWER: And another?

SIMENON: Another seems to be the theme of escape. Between two days changing your life completely: without caring at all what has happened before, just go. You know what I mean?

INTERVIEWER: Starting over?

SIMENON: Not even starting over. Going to nothing.

INTERVIEWER: I see. Is either of these themes or another not far in the offing as a subject, do you suppose? Or is it harmful to ask this?

SIMENON: One is not very far away, probably. It is something on the theme of father and child, of two generations, man coming and man going. That's not completely it, but I don't see it neatly enough just yet to speak about it.

INTERVIEWER: This theme could be associated with the theme of lack of communication?

SIMENON: That's it; it is another branch of the same problem.

INTERVIEWER: What themes do you feel rather certain you will not deal with again?

SIMENON: One, I think, is the theme of the disintegration of a unit, and the unit was generally a family.

INTERVIEWER: Have you treated this theme often?

SIMENON: Two or three times, maybe more.

INTERVIEWER: In the novel *Pedigree?*

SIMENON: In *Pedigree* you have it, yes. If I had to choose one of my books to live and not the others, I would never choose *Pedigree*.

INTERVIEWER: What one might you choose?

SIMENON: The next one.

INTERVIEWER: And the next one after that?

SIMENON: That's it. It's always the next one. You see, even technically I have the feeling now that I am very far away from the goal.

INTERVIEWER: Apart from the next ones, would you be willing to nominate a published novel to survive?

SIMENON: Not one. Because when a novel is finished I have always the impression that I have not succeeded. I am not discouraged, but I see—I want to try again.

But one thing—I consider my novels about all on the same level, yet there are steps. After a group of five or six novels I have a kind of—I don't like the word "progress"—but there seems to be a progress. There is a jump in quality, I think. So every five or six novels there is one I prefer to the others.

INTERVIEWER: Of the novels now available, which one would you say was one of these?

SIMENON: *The Brothers Rico.* The story might be the same if instead of a gangster you had the cashier of one of our banks or a teacher we might know.

INTERVIEWER: A man's position is threatened and so he will do anything to keep it?

SIMENON: That's it. A man who always wants to be on top with the small group where he lives. And who will sacrifice anything to stay there. And he may be a very good man, but he made such an effort to be where he is that he will never accept not being there any more.

INTERVIEWER: I like the simple way that novel does so much.

SIMENON: I tried to do it very simply, simply. And there is not a single "literary" sentence there, you know? It's written as if by a child.

INTERVIEWER: You spoke earlier about thinking of atmosphere when you first think of a novel.

SIMENON: What I mean by atmosphere might be translated by "the poetic line." You understand what I mean?

INTERVIEWER: Is "mood" close enough?

SIMENON: Yes. And with the mood goes the season, goes the detail—at first it is almost like a musical theme.

INTERVIEWER: And so far in no way geographically located?

SIMENON: Not at all. That's the atmosphere for me, because I try—and I don't think I have done it, for otherwise the critics would have discovered it—I try to do with prose, with the novel, what generally is done with poetry. I mean I try to go beyond the real, and the explainable ideas, and to explore the man—not doing it by the sound of the words as the poetical novels of the beginning of the century tried to do. I can't explain technically but—I try to put in my novels some things which you can't explain, to give some message which does not exist practically. You understand what I mean? I read a few days ago that T. S. Eliot, whom I admire very much, wrote that poetry is necessary in plays having one kind of story and not in plays having another, that it depends on the subject you treat. I don't think so. I think you may have the same secret message to give with any kind of subject. If your vision of the world is of a certain kind you will put poetry in everything, necessarily.

But I am probably the only one who thinks there is something of this kind in my books.

INTERVIEWER: One time you spoke about your wish to write the "pure" novel. Is this what you were speaking of a while ago—about cutting out the "literary" words and sentences—or does it also include the poetry you have just spoken of?

SIMENON: The "pure" novel will do only what the novel can do. I mean that it doesn't have to do any teaching or any work of journalism. In a pure novel you wouldn't take sixty pages to describe the South or Arizona or some country in Europe. Just the drama, with only what is absolutely part of this drama. What I think about novels today is almost a translation of the rules of tragedy into the novel. I think the novel is the tragedy for our day.

INTERVIEWER: Is length important? Is it part of your definition of the pure novel?

SIMENON: Yes. That sounds like a practical question, but I think it is important, for the same reason you can't see a tragedy in more than one sitting. I think that the pure novel is too tense for the reader to stop in the middle and take it up the next day.

INTERVIEWER: Because television and movies and magazines are under the codes you have spoken of, I take it you feel the writer of the pure novel is almost obligated to write freely.

SIMENON: Yes. And there is a second reason why he should be. I think that now, for reasons probably political, propagandists are trying to create a type of man. I think the novelist has to show man as he is and not the man of propaganda. And I do not mean only political propaganda; I mean the man they teach in the third grade of school, a man who has nothing to do with man as he really is.

INTERVIEWER: What is your experience with conversion of your books for movies and radio?

SIMENON: These are very important for the writer today. For they are probably the way the writer may still be independent. You asked me before whether I ever change anything in one of my novels commercially. I said, "No." But I would have to do it without the radio, television, and movies.

INTERVIEWER: You once told me Gide made a helpful practical suggestion about one of your novels. Did he influence your work in any more general way?

SIMENON: I don't think so. But with Gide it was funny. In 1936 my publisher said he wanted to give a cocktail party so we could meet, for Gide had said he had read my novels and would like to meet me. So I went, and Gide asked me questions for more than two hours. After that I saw him many times, and he wrote me almost every month and sometimes oftener until he died—always to ask questions. When I went to visit him I always saw my books with so many notes in the margins that they were almost more Gide than Simenon. I never asked him about them; I was very shy about it. So now I will never know.

INTERVIEWER: Did he ask you any special kinds of questions?

SIMENON: Everything, but especially about the mechanism of my—may I use the word? it seems pretentious—creation. And I think I know why he was interested. I think Gide all his life had the dream of being the creator instead of the moralist, the philosopher. I was exactly his opposite, and I think that is why he was interested.

I had the same experience five years before with Count Keyserling. He wrote me exactly the same way Gide did. He asked me to visit him at Darmstadt. I went there and he asked me questions for three days and three nights. He came to see me in Paris and asked me more questions and gave me a commentary on each of my books. For the same reason.

Keyserling called me an *"imbécile de génie."*

INTERVIEWER: I remember you once told me that in your commercial novels you would sometimes insert a non-commercial passage or chapter.

SIMENON: Yes, to train myself.

INTERVIEWER: How did that part differ from the rest of the novel?

SIMENON: Instead of writing just the story, in this chapter I tried to give a third dimension, not necessarily to the whole chapter, perhaps to a room, to a chair, to some object. It would be easier to explain it in the terms of painting.

INTERVIEWER: How?

SIMENON: To give the weight. A commercial painter paints flat; you can put your finger through. But a painter—for example, an apple by Cézanne has weight. And it has juice, everything, with just three strokes. I tried to give to my words just the weight that a stroke of Cézanne's gave to an apple. That is why most of the time I use concrete words. I try to avoid abstract words, or poetical words, you know, like "crepuscule," for example. It is very nice, but it gives nothing. Do you understand? To avoid every stroke which does not give something to this third dimension.

On this point, I think that what the critics call my "atmosphere" is nothing but the impressionism of the painter adapted to literature. My childhood was spent at the time of the impressionists and I was always in the museums and exhibitions. That gave me a kind of sense of it. I was haunted by it.

INTERVIEWER: Have you ever dictated fiction, commercial or any other?

SIMENON: No. I am an artisan; I need to work with my hands. I would like to carve my novel in a piece of wood. My characters —I would like to have them heavier, more three-dimensional. And I would like to make a man so that everybody, looking at him, would find his own problems in this man. That's why I spoke about poetry, because this goal looks more like a poet's goal than the goal of a novelist. My characters have a profession, have characteristics; you know their age, their family situation, and everything. But I try to make each one of those characters heavy, like a statue, and to be the brother of everybody in the world. (*Pausing*) And what makes me happy is the letters I get. They never speak

about my beautiful style; they are the letters a man would write
to his doctor or his psychoanalyst. They say, "You are one who
understands me. So many times I find myself in your novels."
Then there are pages of their confidences; and they are not crazy
people. There are crazy people too, of course; but many are on
the contrary people who—even important people. I am surprised.

INTERVIEWER: Early in your life did any particular book or
author especially impress you?

SIMENON: Probably the one who impressed me most was Gogol.
And certainly Dostoevski, but less than Gogol.

INTERVIEWER: Why do you think Gogol interested you?

SIMENON: Maybe because he makes characters who are just like
everyday people but at the same time have what I called a few
minutes ago the third dimension I am looking for. All of them
have this poetic aura. But not the Oscar Wilde kind—a poetry
which comes naturally, which is there, the kind Conrad has. Each
character has the weight of sculpture, it is so heavy, so dense.

INTERVIEWER: Dostoevski said of himself and some of his fellow
writers that they came out from Gogol's *Overcoat*, and now you
feel you do too.

SIMENON: Yes. Gogol. And Dostoevski.

INTERVIEWER: When you and I were discussing a particular trial
while it was going on a year or two ago, you said you often followed such newspaper accounts with interest. Do you ever in
following them say to yourself, "This is something I might some
day work into a novel"?

SIMENON: Yes.

INTERVIEWER: Do you consciously file it away?

SIMENON: No. I just forget I said it might be useful some day,
and three or four or ten years later it comes. I don't keep a file.

INTERVIEWER: Speaking of trials, what would you say is the
fundamental difference, if there is any, between your detective
fiction—such as the Maigret which you finished a few days ago—
and your more serious novels?

SIMENON: Exactly the same difference that exists between the painting of a painter and the sketch he will make for his pleasure or for his friends or to study something.

INTERVIEWER: In the Maigrets you look at the character only from the point of view of the detective?

SIMENON: Yes. Maigret can't go inside a character. He will see, explain, and understand; but he does not give the character the weight the character should have in another of my novels.

INTERVIEWER: So in the eleven days spent writing a Maigret novel your blood pressure does not change much?

SIMENON: No. Very little.

INTERVIEWER: You are not driving the detective to the limit of his endurance.

SIMENON: That's it. So I only have the natural fatigue of being so many hours at the typewriter. But otherwise, no.

INTERVIEWER: One more question, if I may. Has published general criticism ever in any way made you consciously change the way you write? From what you say I should imagine not.

SIMENON: Never. (*Pausing, and looking down*) I have a very, very strong will about my writing, and I will go my way. For instance, all the critics for twenty years have said the same thing: "It is time for Simenon to give us a big novel, a novel with twenty or thirty characters." They do not understand. I will never write a big novel. My big novel is the mosaic of all my small novels. (*Looking up*) You understand?

CARVEL COLLINS

9. Frank O'Connor

Frank O'Connor was born Michael Francis O'Donovan in 1903, in Cork, Ireland. His family was too poor to afford his education beyond the fourth grade. But by the time he was twelve he had learned Gaelic from his grandmother, was puzzling out Goethe with the aid of a dictionary, and had written enough to form a collected edition of his own work.

His writing continued through years spent as a traveling teacher of Gaelic, librarian in Dublin, manager of the Abbey Theatre, and even during an eighteen-month imprisonment for involvement in the Free State agitation of 1921–25. He has written poetry, plays, and a book on Shakespeare, but he is primarily known for his short stories. In praising them, William Butler Yeats spoke of their author as "doing for Ireland what Chekhov did for Russia."

Since the publication of "Guests of the Nation" in the *Atlantic Monthly* in 1931, over one hundred of O'Connor's short stories have been published in the United States. Six book-length collections have appeared, of which *Domestic Relations* is the last, published in 1957. Among his best-known stories are "The Long Road to Ummera," "The Holy Door," "First Confession," and "Don Juan's Temptation."

O'Connor has lived in the United States since 1952, often absent from his Brooklyn home on extensive lecture tours across the nation.

EXPECTATION OF LIFE.

[handwritten: And let be she is a virgin ~ Leslie]

When Shiela Hennessey married Jim Gaffney, a man twenty years older
than herself, wexx were all pleased and rather surprised. Because by the
time she married him we were certain she would never marry at all. Her
father was a small builder and one of the town jokers put it down to a
hereditary distaste for contracts.

At the same time she had been keeping company with a fellow called
Matt Sheridan off and on for ten years. Matt, who was a quiet fellow, let
on it was because he was interested in the bit of money her father left her,
but he was really very much in love with her, and, to give her her due,
she had been in love with him as well whenever time and other young men
permitted. Shiela had to a pronounced extent the usual feminine weakness
for second strings. She would suddenly scare off the prospect of a long
life with a quiet fellow like Matt and run a wild line with some intellectual bloke that lasted for six months or so. At first Matt resented
it quietly, but then he grew resigned: he realised that the girl couldn't
help it; it was the way she was made; she always had to have a spare part
there in case the car broke down on a lonely bit of road. And she did
get something out of each of those affairs. A fellow called Magennis left
her with a really sound appreciation of Jane Austen and Bach, and another
fellow, who went heavy on his sexual life, taught her to admire Henry
James. But all of them had some grave fault, and Matt in his quiet
determined way knew if only he sat tight and didn't seem to be jealous
and encouraged her to talk about the/drawbacks of the other fellows, she
would be bound eventually to talk herself out of them. Until the next
time, of course, but Matt had the hope that one of those days she'd tire
of her wanderings and turn to him for good. He realised, of course, like
the rest of us that she mightn't marry at all. She was the type of well-
courted, dissatisfied girl that as often as not ends up in a convent; but
he was in no hurry; she was worth waiting for and worth taking a chance
on. Unless she has gone into a convent

And no doubt she would have married him eventually if she hadn't got
the crazy notion of marrying Jim Gaffney instead. Jim was a man in his
early fifties, small and stout and good-natured, a nice fellow, if not remarkable
grown son in Dublin, a little business on the Grand Parade and a queer
old house on Fair Hill. Jim didn't even know was it right for him to
marry her at all. He had the Gaffney expectation of life worked out over
three generations, and according to this he had at the most eight years
to live. But when Matt asked her bitterly what she proposed to do then
As if these were not drawback enough he was a man without
religion while Shiela was the last word in piety

---

*A page from the manuscript of Frank O'Connor's short story "Expectation
of Life"*

Bee W. Dabney

Frank O'Connor

Frank O'Connor is of medium height and build; he has heavy silver hair, brushed back; dark, heavy eyebrows; and a mustache. His voice is bass-baritone in pitch and very resonant—what has been described as juke-box bass. His accent is Irish, but with no suggestion of the "flannel-mouth," his intonation musical. He enjoys talk and needed no urging regarding the subject of the interview. His clothes tend toward the tweedy and casual: desert boots, corduroy jacket, rough tweed topcoat; and a bit of California touch evident in a heavy silver ornament hung on a cord around his neck in place of a tie.

Although a friendly and approachable man, O'Connor has a way of appraising you on early meetings which suggests the Irishman who would just as soon knock you down as look at you if he doesn't like what he sees. His wife provides a description of an encounter with a group of loitering teen-agers while the two of

*them were out for a walk. A remark of some sort was made,
O'Connor whipped over to them and told them to get home if
they knew what was good for them. The boys took him in, silvery
hair and all, and moved off.*

*O'Connor's apartment is in Brooklyn, where he lives with his
pretty young American wife. The large white-walled modern living
room has a wide corner view of lower Manhattan and New York
Harbor. The Brooklyn Bridge sweeps away across the river from a
point close at hand. On his table, just under the window looking
out on the harbor, are a typewriter, a small litter of papers, and a
pair of binoculars. The binoculars are for watching liners "on
their way to Ireland," to which he returns once a year. He says
he'd die if he didn't.*

INTERVIEWER: What determined you to become a writer?

O'CONNOR: I've never been anything else. From the time I was
nine or ten, it was a toss-up whether I was goin' to be a writer or
a painter, and I discovered by the time I was sixteen or seventeen
that paints cost too much money, so I became a writer because
you could be a writer with a pencil and a penny notebook. I did
at one time get a scholarship to Paris, but I couldn't afford to take
it up because of the family. That's where my life changed its
course; otherwise I'd have been a painter. I have a very strongly
developed imitative instinct, which I notice is shared by some of
my children. I always wrote down bits of music that impressed
me in staff notation, though I couldn't read staff notation—I
didn't learn to read it until I was thirty-five—but this always gave
me the air of being a musician. And in the same way, I painted.
I remember a friend of mine who painted in water colors and he
was rather shy. He was painting in the city, so he used to get up
at six in the morning when there was nobody to observe him and
go out and paint. And one day he was going in to work at nine
o'clock and he saw a little girl sitting where he had sat, with a can
of water and an old stick, pretending to paint a picture—she'd
obviously been watching him from an upstairs window. That's

what I mean by the imitative instinct, and I've always had that strongly developed. So I always play at knowing things until, in fact, I find I've learned them almost by accident.

INTERVIEWER: Why do you prefer the short story for your medium?

O'CONNOR: Because it's the nearest thing I know to lyric poetry —I wrote lyric poetry for a long time, then discovered that God had not intended me to be a lyric poet, and the nearest thing to that is the short story. A novel actually requires far more logic and far more knowledge of circumstances, whereas a short story can have the sort of detachment from circumstances that lyric poetry has.

INTERVIEWER: Faulkner has said, "Maybe every novelist wants to write poetry first, finds he can't, and then tries the short story, which is the most demanding form after poetry. And, failing at that, only then does he take up novel writing." What do you think about this?

O'CONNOR: I'd love to console myself, it's that neat—it sounds absolutely perfect except that it implies, as from a short-story writer, that the novel is just an easy sort of thing that you slide gently into, whereas, in fact, my own experience with the novel is that it was always too difficult for me to do. At least to do a novel like *Pride and Prejudice* requires something more than to be a failed B. A. or a failed poet or a failed short-story writer, or a failed anything else. Creating in the novel a sense of continuing life is the thing. We don't have that problem in the short story, where you merely suggest continuing life. In the novel, you have to create it, and that explains one of my quarrels with modern novels. Even a novel like *As I Lay Dying*, which I admire enormously, is not a novel at all, it's a short story. To me a novel is something that's built around the character of time, the nature of time, and the effects that time has on events and characters. When I see a novel that's supposed to take place in twenty-four hours, I just wonder why the man padded out the short story.

INTERVIEWER: Yeats said, "O'Connor is doing for Ireland what

Chekhov did for Russia." What do you think of Chekhov?

O'Connor: Oh, naturally I admire Chekhov extravagantly, I think every short-story writer does. He's inimitable, a person to read and admire and worship—but never, never, never to imitate. He's got all the most extraordinary technical devices, and the moment you start imitating him without those technical devices, you fall into a sort of rambling narrative, as I think even a good story writer like Katherine Mansfield did. She sees that Chekhov apparently constructs a story without episodic interest, so she decides that if she constructs a story without episodic interest it will be equally good. It isn't. What she forgets is that Chekhov had a long career as a journalist, as a writer for comic magazines, writing squibs, writing vaudevilles, and he had learned the art very, very early of maintaining interest, of creating a bony structure. It's only concealed in the later work. They think they can do without that bony structure, but they're all wrong.

Interviewer: What about your experiences in the Irish Republican Army?

O'Connor: My soldiering was rather like my efforts at being a musician; it was an imitation of the behavior of soldiers rather than soldiering. I was completely incapable of remembering anything for ten minutes. And I always got alarmed the moment people started shooting at me, so I was a wretchedly bad soldier, but that doesn't prevent you from picking up the atmosphere of the period. I really got into it when I was about fifteen as a sort of Boy Scout, doing odd jobs, for the I. R. A., and then continued on with it until finally I was captured and interned for a year. Nearly all the writers went with the extreme Republican group. People like O'Faolain, myself, Francis Stuart, Peadar O'Donnell, all the young writers of our generation went Republican. Why we did it, the Lord knows, except that young writers are never capable of getting the facts of anything correctly.

Interviewer: And after that, you were with the Abbey?

O'Connor: Yes, for a few years. Yeats said, "I looked around me and saw all the successful businesses were being run by ex-gunmen, so I said, 'I must have gunmen,' and now the theater's on its feet again." Again, Yeats was a romantic man who romanticized me as a gunman, whereas in fact I was very much a student—I always have been a student masquerading as a gunman. I'd been a director for a number of years and then I was managing director for a period—the only other managing director before me had been Yeats. So I said to him, "What do I do as managing director of this theater?" And he said, "Well, that's the question I asked Lady Gregory when I was named managing director, and she said, 'Give very few orders, but see they're obeyed.'" It must have been about a year after I became a director of the board, when we had at last got the thing organized properly, which it hadn't been for years, that the secretary submitted his report and read out that the balance for the year was one and sixpence—about thirty cents—and there was great applause. It was the first time in years the theater had paid its way.

INTERVIEWER: What writers do you feel have influenced you in your own work?

O'CONNOR: It's very hard to say. The man who has influenced me most, I suppose, is really Isaak Babel, and again with that natural enthusiasm of mine for imitating everybody, "Guests of the Nation" and a couple of the other stories in that book are really imitations of Babel's stories in *The Red Cavalry* [*Konarmia*].

INTERVIEWER: What about working habits? How do you start a story?

O'CONNOR: "Get black on white" used to be Maupassant's advice—that's what I always do. I don't give a hoot what the writing's like, I write any sort of rubbish which will cover the main outlines of the story, then I can begin to see it. When I write, when I draft a story, I never think of writing nice sentences about, "It was a nice August evening when Elizabeth Jane Moriarty was coming down the road." I just write roughly what happened, and then I'm able to see what the construction looks like. It's the design of the story which to me is most important, the thing that tells you there's a bad gap in the narrative here and you really ought to fill that up in some way or another. I'm always looking at the design of a story, not the treatment. Yesterday I was finishing off a piece about my friend A. E. Coppard, the greatest of all the English storytellers, who died about a fortnight ago. I was describing the way Coppard must have written these stories, going around with a notebook, recording what the lighting looked like, what that house looked like, and all the time using metaphor to suggest it to himself, "The road looked like a mad serpent going up the hill," or something of the kind, and, "She said so-and-so, and the man in the pub said something else." After he had written them all out, he must have got the outline of his story, and he'd start working in all the details. Now, I could never do that at all. I've got to see what these people did, first of all, and *then* I start thinking of whether it was a nice August evening or a spring evening. I have to wait for the theme before I can do anything.

INTERVIEWER: Do you rewrite?

O'CONNOR: Endlessly, endlessly, endlessly. And keep on rewriting, and after it's published, and then after it's published in book form, I usually rewrite it again. I've rewritten versions of most of my early stories and one of these days, God help, I'll publish these as well.

INTERVIEWER: Do you keep notes as a source of supply for future stories?

O'CONNOR: Just notes of themes. If somebody tells me a good story, I'll write it down in my four lines; that is the secret of the theme. If you make the subject of a story twelve or fourteen lines, that's a treatment. You've already committed yourself to the sort of character, the sort of surroundings, and the moment you've committed yourself, the story is already written. It has ceased to be fluid, you can't design it any longer, you can't model it. So I always confine myself to my four lines. If it won't go into four, that means you haven't reduced it to its ultimate simplicity, reduced it to the fable.

INTERVIEWER: I have noticed in your stories a spareness of physical description of people and places. Why this apparent rejection of sense impressions?

O'Connor: I thoroughly agree, it's one of the things I know I do, and sometimes when I'm reading Coppard I feel that it's entirely wrong. I'd love to be able to describe people as he describes them, and landscapes as he describes them, but I begin the story in the man's head and it never gets out of the man's head. And in fact, in real life, when you meet somebody in the street you don't start recording that she had this sort of nose—at least a man doesn't. I mean, if you're the sort of person that meets a girl in the street and instantly notices the color of her eyes and of her hair and the sort of dress she's wearing, then you're not in the least like me. I just notice a feeling from people. I notice particularly the cadence of their voices, the sort of phrases they'll use, and that's what I'm all the time trying to hear in my head, how people word things—because everybody speaks an entirely different language, that's really what it amounts to. I have terribly sensitive hearing and I'm terribly aware of voices. If I remember somebody, for instance, that I was very fond of, I don't remember what he or she looked like, but I can absolutely take off the voice. I'm a good mimic; I've a bit of the actor in me, I suppose, that's really what it amounts to. I cannot pass a story as finished unless I connect it myself, unless I know how everybody in it spoke, which, as I say, can go quite well with the fact that I couldn't tell you in the least what they looked like. If I use the right phrase and the reader hears the phrase in his head, he sees the individual. It's like writing for the theater, you see. A bad playwright will "pull" an actor because he'll tell him what to do, but a really good playwright will give you a part that you can do what you like with. It's transferring to the reader the responsibility for acting those scenes. I've given him all the information I have and put it into his own life.

Interviewer: What about adapting your own work to another medium—say, movies?

O'Connor: Well, I've tried it here and there and generally it's pretty awful. First of all, I've never been really allowed to follow through with a movie as I'd like to do it. One of my sad experiences with the movies is with the film I did for the Lifeboat Society. I was told that my story mustn't sink anything larger than a tiny fishing boat because that was all the money they had, so I wrote the story about the fishing boat—two brothers who wouldn't have anything to do with each other, one commanding the lifeboat, the other, skipper of the fishing boat. When the director came down to the location, a magnificent American ship had gone on the sands, and he decided to shift the story and bring in the American ship, so he brought it in. The producer saw the film and said, "But this isn't the story you were told to film!" So, the producer then canned the beautiful thing about the ship, all the money was gone, and they couldn't give me my little boat, and all the thing you had was somebody telling the story. It wasn't the same. What I really enjoy doing is transferring stories to the air. Again, my sort of story is suitable for that. The ones I've seen on television, they don't impress me. Again, they become too precise. Also, of course, there is this awful business in television, even, certainly with the cinema, of the amount of money involved, so that everything has to be tested again, and again, and again; this thing's got to be submitted to So-and-so, and So-and-so, and they all lay down different laws and your script is being changed all the time. Finally, what comes over is nobody's job—it's a sort of accident, and sometimes, by accident, you'll get a fairly decent movie or a fairly decent television show. But you never have that feeling you have in the theater, or in the story, above all (that's the reason I like writing short stories) that you're your own theater. You can control every bloomin' thing—if you say it's going to be twilight, it's going to be twilight and you're not askin' the advice of a lighting man who will say to you, "Well, you can't have a second twilight, you had twilight ten minutes ago, you can't have another one." You can do what you please and you're ultimately the only person responsible. To tell you the truth, I don't think any of these mass media is a satisfactory art form. The real trouble is, the

moment you get a mass audience, commercial interests become
involved. They say, "Oh, boy! There's big money in this! Now
we've got to consider what the audiences like." And then they tell
you, "Now you mustn't offend the Catholics, you mustn't offend
the Jews, you mustn't offend the Salvation Army, you mustn't
offend the mayors of cities." They make a list of taboos a mile
long, and then they say, "Now, inside this, you can say what you
like"—and it's maniac. The moment big money's involved and
the pressures are put on, that is going to happen. And they're the
most wonderful artists in the world. I mean, it's all damn well to
talk, but Hollywood has the finest brains in the world out there.
But they're up against all these vested interests, and vested interests are the very devil for the artist. In the Abbey, the government
voted to give us a hundred thousand dollars to build a new theater,
and instantly the intrigues began: who was going to be the
manager of this theater? "This is going to be a really worth-while
job; big money in this, boys." And as long as it was a question of
who was going to lose money in accepting this job, you got service.
But that is true and that's the really frightening thing about it.
The people who want to exploit the forty million are the danger.
And they don't want to exploit 'em too far—bless 'em, they're so
nice, they're so decent—"I mean, between ourselves, you don't
really want to hurt the feelin's of this old Jew down here"—and
you don't, you don't! All you know perfectly well is you're not
saying anything to hurt his feelings. But somebody is interpreting
for him, he's not being allowed to give his own views at all. You
get the smart commercial boy who is going to tell you, "Well,
what they really like now is a little bit of sadism. Couldn't you
introduce just a lit-tle sadistic scene here?" And he'll introduce it,
all right. Again, the forty million, left to their own decent devices,
would probably reject the sadistic thing. They're being told, "Now
this is what you like." No, no, you can only do works of art with
an audience that you know, with all commercial people left out
of it. The great theater is a theater like the Abbey, which was
really run by a few people in their spare time, and where the

actors were working in their spare time. They worked in their offices until five, had a sandwich, came along to the theater, and the most any of them ever got was six pounds a week, about fifteen dollars, which was the highest salary ever paid while I was there, even for the people on contract. And then you get real works of art. But the moment Hollywood pops in on the Abbey and says, "Oh, well, we can fix those up, we can give him twenty thousand dollars," then they begin screaming against one another, they begin competing.

INTERVIEWER: How do you feel about the academic approach to the novel as compared to the natural approach?

O'CONNOR: To me, the novel is so human, the only thing I'm interested in—I can't imagine anything better in the world than people. A novel is about people, it's written for people, and the moment it starts getting so intellectual that it gets beyond the range of people and reduces them to academic formulae, I'm not interested in it any longer. I really got into this row, big, at the novel conference at Harvard, when I had a couple of people talking about the various types of novel—analyzing them—and then we had a novelist get up and speak about the responsibilities of the novelist. I was with Anthony West on the stage and I was gradually getting into hysterics. It's never happened to me before in public; I was giggling, I couldn't stop myself. And, "All right," I said at the end of it, "if there are any of my students here I'd like them to remember that writing is fun." That's the reason you do it, because you enjoy it, and you read it because you enjoy it. You don't read it because of the serious moral responsibility to read, and you don't write it because it's a serious moral responsibility. You do it for exactly the same reason that you paint pictures or play with the kids. It's a creative activity.

Take Faulkner; you mentioned him earlier. Faulkner tries to be serious, tries to use all sorts of devices, technical devices, which don't come natural to him, which he really isn't interested in, and gives everybody the impression that he's pompous. Well, he's not pompous, he's naïve—and humorous. And what a humorist! There's nobody else to touch him.

The man really is ingenuous. Joyce was not ingenuous. Joyce was a university man. Paris Review's interview with Faulkner reminded me strongly of the description that Robert Greene gives of Shakespeare. All the university men of Shakespeare's day thought he was a simpleton, a bit of an idiot. He hadn't been educated, he just didn't know how to write. And I can see Faulkner approaching Joyce in exactly the way that Shakespeare approached Ben Jonson. Ben Jonson had been to a university, Ben Jonson knew Greek and Latin, and it never occurred to Faulkner that he was greater than Joyce as it never occurred to Shakespeare that he was greater than Ben Jonson. Look at the way he imitates Ben Jonson in Twelfth Night—just a typical Jonson play—doing the best he can to be like Jonson and all he succeeds in doing is to be brittle. I'm really thinking of the time he came under Ben Jonson's influence—that would have been about the time Julius Caesar was produced. Jonson has a crack somewhere or other about Shakespeare's being so uneducated that he didn't even know that Bohemia didn't have a seacoast, and he mentions how he used to talk to the players about the horrible errors in Shakespeare's plays. He quotes from Julius Caesar—"Caesar doth never wrong, but with just cause"—and he says, "I told the players this was an absurd line." Shakespeare cut it out of Julius Caesar, it's no longer there. As a natural writer, Faulkner is a fellow who's got to accept himself for what he is, and he's got to realize that the plain people in Mississippi know a damn sight more about the business of literature than the dons at Cambridge.

INTERVIEWER: How important an ingredient do you consider technique in writing?

O'CONNOR: I was cursed at birth with a passion for techniques, but that's a different thing entirely. I don't think I'm ever fool enough to imagine that a novel like Anglo-Saxon Attitudes, by Angus Wilson, is a good novel merely because it exploits every known form of technique in the modern novel. It takes advantage of the cinema; it goes off from *Point Counter Point*, which itself is full of technical devices, and it's all unnecessary. If you've got a story to tell about people and tell it in the way in which it comes chronologically, you've got the best thing you can get in fiction. But, you see, one of the troubles about the modern novel is this idea that the novel has to be concentrated into twenty-four hours, forty-eight hours, a week, a month, and you must cut out everything that goes before. The classical novel realized that you begin with the conception of the hero and move on from there—you demonstrate him through all his phases. That's where the death of the hero really appears in modern fiction, because the hero doesn't matter any longer, the circumstances are what matter—those twenty-four hours. It used to be twenty-four hours in my youth, but there hasn't been a twenty-four-hour novel for at least twenty years, as far as I can remember.

INTERVIEWER: Can't you overcome the limits of a time frame with such things as flashbacks and recollections?

O'CONNOR: That's what the cinema has done to the novel. Here, in *Anglo-Saxon Attitudes*, you get a novel which would have been a good novel if it had begun twenty years earlier. A certain crime, a fraud, had been committed on archaeology, and if you traced the people from the fraud on, you'd have had a good novel. What happens? You get the crisis—the old gentleman who suspects a fraud has been committed—what are his moral problems in the last few weeks before he decides he's going to reveal the fraud? And that's the cinema. This thing, the twenty-four-hour novel, began in the twenties—you get *Ulysses*, you get Virginia Woolf—everybody was publishing twenty-four-hour novels at the time, and the unities had at last been brought back into literature. As though the unities mattered a damn, one way or the other, as though what you wanted in the novel wasn't the organic feeling of life, the feeling, "This is the way it happens"—"If it happened at all, it happened this way."

INTERVIEWER: Can't you use the unities as a convenient framework in which to carry your story, to provide structure?

O'CONNOR: No, I disagree all along the line. Not in a novel. In flashbacks you describe minor points: at this point, he did this rather than the other thing. You never frequent this man—there's that very good French verb, *fréquenter*, which is the essence of a novel. You've got to be inside that man's head, and you're never inside this man's head if at any moment he's got to observe the unities. That's all right in the theater, which is a craft as much as an art.

INTERVIEWER: Of course you have the time and space limitations of the theater.

O'CONNOR: And your audience, which is the biggest limitation of all—the number of things you can do to that audience. It's no use referring that audience to something they've never heard of—you take an audience of Louis XIV's time and you refer to some mythological figure, they knew perfectly well what you were talking about, but no use doing that nowadays—nobody'd know what you were talking about.

This construct novel, *Anglo-Saxon Attitudes*, falsifies the novel from the word go. Having been a librarian, I understand it perfectly, because your job when you're making a catalogue is to provide all the cross-references you're ever likely to need. So this is a book about Irish archaeology, but it's got an awful lot about modern American history, and consequently you give a cross-reference to American history and if you're a really good cataloguer, that thing is a set of cross-references so that anybody who wants to find out about modern American history can find it out in Irish archaeology. False surprise, I think, is the real basis of it.

INTERVIEWER: As Edmund Wilson said, "Who cares who killed Roger Ackroyd?"

O'CONNOR: I care, passionately. That's a different thing entirely. I'm fascinated by detective stories. There you get a real form—you don't get this fake form imposed. At least it's a passionate, logical structure. Somebody killed this guy. Who killed him? And if you have a real writer on the job, you can get wonderful effects.

INTERVIEWER: But they haven't much in the way of characterization, have they?

O'CONNOR: Gosh, some of the good ones have. And very good characterization, too. Even Erle Stanley Gardner. Perry Mason, when he began, was a real character—he's become a prototype now—he was a real person and you could feel him striding into a room. I could see that man.

INTERVIEWER: Did you know James Joyce?

O'CONNOR: As well as one can know a man one has met a couple of times and corresponded with. He was shy in a different way from Faulkner—he was arrogant in a way that Faulkner is not arrogant.

INTERVIEWER: Joyce's looks were sort of against him, don't you think?

O'CONNOR: An extraordinarily handsome man! He gave the impression of being a great surgeon, but not a writer at all. And he was a surgeon, he was not a writer. He used to wear white surgeon's coats all the time and that increased the impression, and he had this queer, ax-like face with this enormous jaw, the biggest jaw I have ever seen on a human being. I once did a talk on Joyce in which I mentioned that he had the biggest chin I had ever seen on a human being, and T. S. Eliot wrote a letter saying that he had often seen chins as big as that on other Irishmen. Well, I didn't know how to reply to that.

So now to get on back to what we were saying about the university novelists versus the natural novelists. The university novelists have been having it their own way for thirty years, and it's about time a natural novelist got back to the job and really told stories about people. Pritchett argued (I wrote this book on the novel—I don't know whether you've seen it—*The Mirror in the Roadway*) that this conception of character has disappeared entirely, the conception of character that I am talking about. You see, I don't believe there's anything else in the world except human beings, they're the best thing you're ever likely to discover, and he says, "Well, this is all finished with." And I know what Pritchett means—the Communists and so on have got rid of it all, there aren't individuals any longer. You get old Cardinal Mindszenty in and you give him the treatment, so he comes out and says what you want him to say. There are no individuals. What I can't understand is why, in America, the last middle-class country, you still cannot beat this loss of faith in the individual.

I've had this argument out. I was reviewing for a London newspaper, and a British intelligence officer who was also a novelist wrote a book in which he defended the use of torture against prisoners. My paper was Conservative, and I asked, "How far can I go?" and they said, "You can go the limit." We asked their lawyers in and they said, "Say what you want to say"—and I did. They were magnificent about it. But that book was reviewed in the Left-Wing journals and they saw nothing wrong with this defense of torture. I know perfectly well you can make a human being say anything or do anything if you torture him enough, and that does not prove that the individual doesn't exist.

INTERVIEWER: Doesn't the unseen and unrevealed, the subconscious, have a bearing on the truth about an individual?

O'CONNOR: We were talking about the twenty-four-hour novel and I say, to me, that's all represented by Joyce, talking about epiphanies, that, in fact, you can never know a character. At some moment he's going to reveal himself unconsciously, and you watch and then you walk out of the room and you write it down, "So-and-so at this point revealed what his real character was." I still maintain that living with somebody, knowing somebody, you know him as well as he can be known—that is to say, you know ninety per cent of him. What happens if you're torturing him or he's dying of cancer is no business of mine and that is not the individual. What a man says when he's dying and in great pain is not evidence. All right, he'll be converted to anything that's handy, but the substance of the character remains with me, that's what matters, the real thing.

INTERVIEWER: As I recall at Harvard, some of the students thought that ignoring the psychological was old-fashioned.

O'CONNOR: And I am old-fashioned! It's the only old-fashionedness you can come back to. You've got to come back eventually to humanism, and that's humanism in the old sense of the word, what the Latins and Greeks thought about human beings, not the American sense of the word, that everybody is conditioned. The Greek and Latin thing says, "No, this is a complete individual." That's the feeling you get from Plutarch, that people are as you see them, and no psychiatrist is going to tell you anything fundamentally different. If he does, he's an ass, that's all. People are as they behave. You're working with a man for years. He's kind in the great majority of the things he does. You say, "He's kind." The psychiatrist says, "No, no, no, he's really cruel," and you're faced with this problem of which you are going to accept—the evidence of your own senses, of your own mind, of your own feeling of history, or this thing which says to you, "You don't understand how a human being works"?

INTERVIEWER: What about the problem of the struggling writer who must make a living?

O'CONNOR: Now, that's something I can't understand about America. It's a big, generous country, but so many students of mine seemed to think they couldn't let anyone else support them. A student of mine had this thing about you mustn't live on your father and I argued with him. I explained that a European writer would live on anybody, would live on a prostitute if he had to, it didn't matter; the great thing was to get the job done. But he didn't believe in this, so he rang up his father and told him he'd had a story refused by *The New Yorker*, and his father said, "I can keep you for the next forty years, don't you think you can get a story in *The New Yorker* in forty years?" Well, this fellow came along and told me this tragic tale. Now, I felt the father was a man I understood and sympathized with, a decent man. But the boy felt he mustn't be supported by his father, so he came down to New York and started selling office furniture.

INTERVIEWER: Why don't you teach?

O'CONNOR: I can't make a living out of it. You can only just get by on the sort of salaries that universities pay. I didn't write a line while I was at Harvard. You've nothing left over to write— I'd just get involved with the students all the way. I was far more pleased with a student's successes than I would have been with my own, and that's wrong. You've got to leave a bit of jealousy in yourself.

INTERVIEWER: Do you think of a novel as a lot of short stories or one big short story?

O'CONNOR: It ought to be one big short story, and not one big short story, but one big novel. That's the real trouble—the novel is not a short story—there's your twenty-four-hour novel, that's what's wrong with it, it's a short story, and that's what's wrong with Hemingway, wrong with most of them; the span is too small. The span of a novel ought to be big. There is this business of the long short story turned out as a novel, and I'm all the time getting them. The span is too brief; there is nothing to test these characters by. Take *Ulysses*, which is twenty-four hours, and I maintain it's a long short story. And it was written as a short story, don't forget that. It was originally entitled "Mr. Hunter's Day." And it's still "Mr. Hunter's Day" and it still is thirty pages. It's all development sideways. That's really what I was talking about: the difference between the novel which is a development, an extension into time, and this novel, which is not a novel, which is an extension sideways. It doesn't lead forward, it doesn't lead your mind forward. *Anglo-Saxon Attitudes* is the same: "So now boys, having finished with this brief moment of our novel, we'll go backward for a while." And all the time they're just going out like that because they're afraid to go forward.

INTERVIEWER: O'Faolain talks about that: Hemingway trying to isolate his hero in time—trying to isolate him to one moment, when he is put to the test.

O'CONNOR: O'Faolain made a good point about Hemingway there. He's saying, "Nothing happened to him before the story begins; nothing happens to him afterward." And I think that's true of most short stories. He's talking about a special aspect of Hemingway—that Hemingway will not allow the character to have had any past. You admit he's had a past, but you say that the whole past is illuminated by the particular event which you are now telling, also the whole future; you can predict a man's development from this. I admit that from the point of view of the short story, you ought to be able to say, "Nothing that happened before this short story is of real importance, nothing that happens after it is likely to be of great importance." But you don't try to cut it off, which is what Hemingway does. You just say, "This is so unimportant that I'm not going to mention it at all."

INTERVIEWER: What do you think about regional influences in American literature?

O'CONNOR: I attribute all good literature in America to New England—including Katherine Anne Porter.

INTERVIEWER: What about Willa Cather?

O'CONNOR: There you get this tremendous nostalgia for plains, the longing for New England, and the longing for a sense of belonging somewhere, so then she runs away to Halifax to try to get it, and when that doesn't do she goes right down to New Mexico in order to get the Catholic tradition. But she's really a New Englander who never settled down. She's a DP writer—and a great writer.

INTERVIEWER: What is the greatest essential of a story?

O'CONNOR: You have to have a theme, a story to tell. Here's a man at the other side of the table and I'm talking to him; I'm going to tell him something that will interest him. As you know perfectly well, our principal difficulty at Harvard was a number of people who'd had affairs with girls or had had another interesting experience, and wanted to come in and tell about it, straight away. That is not a theme. A theme is something that is worth something to everybody. In fact, you wouldn't, if you'd ever been involved in a thing like this, grab a man in a pub and say, "Look,

I had a girl out last night, under the Charles Bridge." That's the last thing you'd do. You grab somebody and say, "Look, an extraordinary thing happened to me yesterday—I met a man—he said this to me—"and that, to me, is a theme. The moment you grab somebody by the lapels and you've got something to tell, that's a real story. It means you want to tell him and think the story is interesting in itself. If you start describing your own personal experiences, something that's only of interest to yourself, then you can't express yourself, you cannot say, ultimately, what you think about human beings. The moment you say this, you're committed.

I'll tell you what I mean. We were down on the south coast of Ireland for a holiday and we got talkin' to this old farmer and he said his son, who was dead now, had gone to America. He'd married an American girl and she had come over for a visit, alone. Apparently her doctor had told her a trip to Ireland would do her good. And she stayed with the parents, had gone around to see his friends and other relations, and it wasn't till after she'd gone that they learned that the boy had died. Why didn't she tell them? There's your story. Dragging the reader in, making the reader a part of the story—the reader is a part of the story. You're saying all the time, "This story is about you—*de te fabula.*"

INTERVIEWER: Do you think the writer should be a reformer or an observer?

O'CONNOR: I think the writer's a reformer; the observer thing is very old, it goes back to Flaubert. I can't write about something I don't admire—it goes back to the old concept of the celebration: you celebrate the hero, an idea.

INTERVIEWER: Why do you use a pseudonym?

O'CONNOR: The real reason was that I was a public official, a librarian in Cork. There was a big row at the time about another writer who had published what was supposed to be a blasphemous story, and I changed my name, my second name being Francis and my mother's name being O'Connor, so that I could officially say that I didn't know who Frank O'Connor was. It satisfied my committee, it satisfied me. The curious thing now is that I'm better known as Frank O'Connor than I'll ever be as Michael O'Donovan. I'd never have interfered with my name except that it was just convenient, and I remember when I did it I intended to change back, but by that time it had become a literary property and I couldn't have changed back without too much trouble.

INTERVIEWER: Have you any particular words of encouragement for young writers?

O'CONNOR: Well, there's this: Don't take rejection slips too seriously. I don't think they ought to send them out at all. I think a very amusing anthology might be gotten up of rejection letters alone. It's largely a question of remembering, when you send something out, that So-and-so is on the other end of this one, and he has certain interests. To give an example of what I mean on this rejection business, I had a story accepted by a magazine. So I wrote it over again as I always do, and sent it back. Well, someone else got it and I got this very nice letter saying that they couldn't use it, but that they'd be very interested in seeing anything else I wrote in the future.

ANTHONY WHITTIER

10. Robert Penn Warren

Robert Penn Warren was born in Guthrie, Kentucky, in 1905. He attended Vanderbilt University, where his early work was published in the literary magazine *Fugitive*. He was associated with the group of Vanderbilt poets and critics known, after the magazine, as the Fugitives, including among others Allen Tate, John Crowe Ransom, Merrill Moore, and Donald Davidson.

After his graduation from Vanderbilt in 1925, Warren won fellowships to the University of California and Yale. In 1930 he was at Oxford on a Rhodes Scholarship. He has taught extensively since then—at Vanderbilt, Southwestern College, Louisiana State, Minnesota, and Yale. In 1934, at Louisiana State, he founded the *Southern Review* with Cleanth Brooks.

Warren's nonfiction works include a biography of John Brown (1929), an article stating his sociological views, which appeared in a collection by twelve Southern writers called *I'll Take My Stand*, and in 1956 a redefinition of his sociological opinions in a little book entitled *Segregation*. His novels are: *Night Rider* (1938), awarded the Houghton Mifflin Literary Fellowship; *At Heaven's Gate* (1943); *All the King's Men* (1946), for which he won a Pulitzer Prize; *World Enough and Time* (1950); *Band of Angels* (1955); and *Blackberry Winter*, a novelette he wrote in 1946. A collection of short stories entitled *Circus in the Attic* was published in 1948, and *Brother to Dragons*, a dramatic poem, in 1953.

Collections of his poetry have appeared under the titles *Thirty-Six Poems* (1935), *Eleven Poems on the Same Theme* (1942), *Selected Poems* (1944), and *Promises: Poems 1954–1956* (1957).

(handwritten margin notes, partially legible: "and they shed much tears I showed a whole as; but" / "Oh I couldn't talk for the showing — oh, I loved Lil!")

(left margin handwritten: "By Court Day" / "you pipe speak & refer to —")

LAETITIA

(To the audience, with the air of ~~someone~~ a person compulsively
going over and over something, almost whispering.)

I made the settlement. They took me down.
I rolled my head on the pillow, and I tried to pray.
Oh, God, even if You're God, and made the world,
And take a mind, with one big huff-and-puff
Could blow the moon and stars off, down the sky,
Like a boy blowing dandelion fuzz -- oh, God,
Even if You're God, even God hasn't got the right
To keep me from knowing the reason things happen to me.
If I don't know that, then I'm nothing, and God, all I want
Is a name to name it, and not be nothing, just nothing, God.

(handwritten: "A please.")

WRITER

So all you demand is definition, too,
Just like poor Lilburn. Well, now would you hate him less
If you thought that he, like you --

(handwritten boxed note: "David's note - develop to place turn japensode")

LAETITIA

Oh, I don't hate him!

(left margin handwritten: "Lil's speech" / "omit line")

Oh, he could be sweet, so sweet. Once we walked in the woods,
'Twas fall, and the sunshine bright, and the trees bright-colored,
And one big sweet-gum golder than the sun.
You know how a sweet-gum is, the leaves like stars.
He cut a branch, and held it in his hand.
Then, "Stop!" he ~~said~~ -- *(handwritten: another - and then --)*

LILBURN

(Suddenly appearing with a sweet-gum bough
of gold, star-shaped leaves)

Stop! ah, Tishie, dear Tishie --
Your hair's all gold, Laetitia, gold, and now --

(He begins putting gold leaves in her hair, like
a coronal.)

The stars are in it gold -- I put them there!

(Standing back to admire his work)

Oh, Tishie, you're an angel from the sky.

(He stares at her a moment, silently, then steps abruptly
to her side, seizes her wrist, leans at her and speaks
in an intense whisper.)

(left margin handwritten, vertical: "D's note: more travel development both - by music")

---

*A work sheet from a verse-play now being written by Robert Penn Warren.
It is based on the narrative poem* Brother to Dragons

Robert Penn Warren

This interview takes place in the apartment of Ralph Ellison at the American Academy in Rome: a comfortable room filled with books and pictures. Mr. Warren, who might be described as a sandy man with a twinkle in his eye, is ensconced in an armchair while the Interviewers, manning tape recorder and notebook, are perched on straight-back chairs. Mrs. Ellison, ice-bowl tinkling, comes into the room occasionally to replenish the glasses: all drink pastis.

INTERVIEWERS: First, if you're agreeable, Mr. Warren, a few biographical details just to get you "placed." I believe you were a Rhodes Scholar—

WARREN: Yes, from Kentucky.

INTERVIEWERS: University of Kentucky?

WARREN: No, I attended Vanderbilt. But I was Rhodes Scholar from Kentucky.

INTERVIEWERS: Were you writing then?

WARREN: As I am now, trying to.

INTERVIEWERS: Did you start writing in college?

WARREN: I had no interest in writing when I went to college. I was interested in reading—oh, poetry and standard novels, you know. My ambitions were purely scientific, but I got cured of that fast by bad instruction in Freshman Chemistry and good instruction in Freshman English.

INTERVIEWERS: What were the works that were especially meaningful for you? What books were—well, doors opening?

WARREN: Well, several things come right away to mind. First of all, when I was six years old, "Horatius at the Bridge" I thought was pretty grand—when they read it to me, to be more exact.

INTERVIEWERS: And others?

WARREN: Yes, "How They Brought the Good News from Ghent to Aix," at about age nine; I thought it was pretty nearly the height of human achievement. I didn't know whether I was impressed by riding a horse that fast or writing the poem. I couldn't distinguish between the two, but I knew there was something pretty fine going on. . . . Then "Lycidas."

INTERVIEWERS: At what age were you then?

WARREN: Oh, thirteen, something like that. By that time I knew it wasn't what was happening in the poem that was important— it was the poem. I had crossed the line.

INTERVIEWERS: What about prose works?

WARREN: Then I discovered Buckle's *History of Civilization*. Did you ever read Buckle?

INTERVIEWERS: Of course, and Motley's *Rise of the Dutch Republic*. Most Southern bookshelves contain that.

WARREN: And Prescott . . . and *The Oregon Trail* is always hovering around there somewhere. Thing that interested me about Buckle was that he had the one big answer to everything: *geography*. History is all explained by geography. I read Buckle and then I could explain everything. It gave me quite a hold over the other kids; they hadn't read Buckle. I had the answer to everything. Buckle was my Marx. That is, he gave you one answer to everything, and the same dead-sure certainty. After I had had my session with Buckle and the one-answer system at the age of thirteen, or whatever it was, I was somewhat inoculated against Marx and his one-answer system when he and the depression hit me and my work when I was about twenty-five. I am not being frivolous about Marx. But when 1 began to hear some of my friends talk about him in 1930, I thought, "Here we go again, boys." I had previously got hold of one key to the universe: Buckle. And somewhere along the way I had lost the notion that there was ever going to be just one key.

But getting back to that shelf of books, the Motley and Prescott and Parkman, et cetera, isn't it funny how unreadable most history written now is when you compare it with those writers?

INTERVIEWERS: Well, there's Samuel Eliot Morison.

WARREN: Yes, a very fine writer. Another is Vann Woodward, he writes very well indeed. And Bruce Catton. But Catton maybe doesn't count, he's not a professional historian. If he wants to write a book on history that happens to be good history and good writing at the same time, there isn't any graduate school to try to stop him.

INTERVIEWERS: It's very interesting that you were influenced by historical writing so early in life. It has always caught one's eye how history is used in your work, for instance *Night Rider*.

WARREN: Well, that isn't a historical novel. The events belonged to my early childhood. I remember the troops coming in when martial law was declared in that part of Kentucky. When I wrote the novel I wasn't thinking of it as history. For one thing, the world it treated still, in a way, survived. You could still talk to the old men who had been involved. In the 1930s I remember going to see a judge down in Kentucky—he was an elderly man then, a man of the highest integrity and reputation—who had lived through that period and who by common repute had been mixed up in it—his father had been a tobacco grower. He got to talking about that period in Kentucky. He said, "Well, I won't say who was and who wasn't mixed up in some of those things, but I will make one observation: I have noticed that the sons of those who were opposed to getting a fair price for tobacco ended up as either bootleggers or brokers." But he was an old-fashioned kind of guy, for whom bootlegging and brokerage looked very much alike. Such a man didn't look "historical" thirty years ago. Now he looks like the thigh bone of a mastodon.

INTERVIEWERS: It seems clear that you don't write "historical" novels; they are always concerned with urgent problems, but the awareness of history seems to be central.

WARREN: That's so. I don't think I do write historical novels. I try to find stories that catch my eye, stories that seem to have issues in purer form than they come to one ordinarily.

INTERVIEWERS: A kind of unblurred topicality?

WARREN: I wrote two unpublished novels in the thirties. *Night Rider* is the world of my childhood. *At Heaven's Gate* was contemporary. My third published, *All the King's Men*, was worlds I had seen. All the stories were contemporary. The novel I'm writing now, and two I plan, are all contemporary.

INTERVIEWERS: *Brother to Dragons* was set in the past.

WARREN: It belonged to a historical setting, but it was not a departure: it was a matter of dealing with issues in a more mythical form. I hate costume novels, but maybe I've written some and don't know it. I have a romantic kind of interest in the objects of American history: saddles, shoes, figures of speech, rifles, et cetera. They're worth a lot. Help you focus. There *is* a kind of extraordinary romance about American history. That's the only word for it—a kind of self-sufficiency. You know, the grandpas and the great-grandpas carried the assumption that somehow their lives and their decisions were important; that as they went up, down, here and there, such a life was important and that it was a man's responsibility to live it.

INTERVIEWERS: In this connection, do you feel that there are certain themes which are basic to the American experience, even though a body of writing in a given period might ignore or evade them?

WARREN: First thing, without being systematic, what comes to mind without running off a week and praying about it, would be that America was based on a big promise—a great big one: the Declaration of Independence. When you have to live with that in the house, that's quite a problem—particularly when you've got to make money and get ahead, open world markets, do all the things you have to, raise your children, and so forth. America is stuck with its self-definition put on paper in 1776, and that was just like putting a burr under the metaphysical saddle of America— you see, that saddle's going to jump now and then and it pricks. There's another thing in the American experience that makes for a curious kind of abstraction. We suddenly had to define ourselves and what we stood for in one night. No other nation ever had to do that. In fact, one man did it—one man in an upstairs room, Thomas Jefferson. Sure, you might say that he was the amanuensis for a million or so people stranded on the edge of the continent and backed by a wilderness, and there's some sense in that notion. But *somebody* had to formulate it—in fact, just overnight, whatever the complicated background of that formulation—and we've been stuck with it ever since. With the very words it used. Do you know the Polish writer Adam Gurowski? [1] He was of a highly placed Polish family; he came and worked as a civil servant in Washington, a clerk, a kind of self-appointed spy on democracy. His book *America*—of 1857, I think—begins by saying that America is unique among nations because other nations are accidents of geography or race, but America is based on an idea. Behind the comedy of proclaiming that idea from Fourth of July platforms there is the solemn notion, *Believe and ye shall be saved.*

---

[1] Adam Gurowski, 1805–1866, author of *America and Europe* (1857) and *My Diary: Notes on the Civil War* (1866) among other works.

That abstraction sometimes does become concrete, is a part of the American experience—and of the American problem—the lag between idea and fact, between word and flesh.

INTERVIEWERS: What about historical time? America has had so much happening in such a short time.

WARREN: Awful lot of foreshortening in it. America lives in two times, chronological time and history. The last widow drawing a pension from the War of 1812 died just a few years ago. My father was old enough to vote when the last full-scale battle against Indians was fought—a couple of regiments, I think, of regulars with artillery.

INTERVIEWERS: From the first your work is explicitly concerned with moral judgments, even during a period of history when much American fiction was concerned with moral questions only in the narrow way of the "proletarian" and "social realism" novels of the 1930s.

WARREN: I think I ought to say that behind *Night Rider* and my next novel, *At Heaven's Gate*, there was a good deal of the shadow not only of the events of that period but of the fiction of that period. I am more aware of that fact now than I was then. Of course only an idiot could have not been aware that he was trying to write a novel about, in one sense, "social justice" in *Night Rider* or, for that matter, *At Heaven's Gate*. But in some kind of a fumbling way I was aware, I guess, of trying to find the dramatic rub of the story at some point a little different from and deeper than the point of dramatic rub in some of the then current novels. But what I want to emphasize is the fact that I was fumbling rather than working according to plan and convictions already arrived at. When you start any book you don't know what, ultimately, your issues are. You try to write to find them. You're fiddling with the stuff, hoping to make sense, whatever kind of sense you can make.

INTERVIEWERS: At least you could say that as a Southerner you were more conscious of what some of the issues were. You couldn't,

I assume, forget the complexity of American social reality, no matter what your aesthetic concerns, or other concerns.

WARREN: It never crossed my mind when I began writing fiction that I could write about anything except life in the South. It never crossed my mind that I knew about anything else; knew, that is, well enough to write about. Nothing else ever nagged you enough to stir the imagination. But I stumbled into fiction rather late. I've got to be autobiographical about this. For years I didn't have much interest in fiction, that is, in college. I was reading my head off in poetry, Elizabethan and the moderns, Yeats, Hardy, Eliot, Hart Crane. I wasn't seeing the world around me—that is, in any way that might be thought of as directly related to fiction. Be it to my everlasting shame that when the Scopes trial was going on a few miles from me I didn't even bother to go. My head was too full of John Ford and John Webster and William Blake and T. S. Eliot. If I had been thinking about writing novels about the South I would have been camping in Dayton, Tennessee—and would have gone about it like journalism. At least the Elizabethans saved me from that. As for starting fiction, I simply stumbled on it. In the spring of 1930 I was at Oxford, doing graduate work. I guess I was homesick and not knowing it. Paul Rosenfeld, who, with Van Wyck Brooks and Lewis Mumford, was then editing the old *American Caravan*, wrote and asked me why I didn't try a long story for them. He had had the patience one evening to listen to me blowing off about night-rider stories from boyhood. So Oxford and homesickness, or at least back-homeward-looking, and Paul Rosenfeld made me write *Prime Leaf*, a novelette which appeared in the *Caravan*, and was later the germ of *Night Rider*. I remember playing hooky from academic work to write the thing, and the discovery that you could really enjoy trying to write fiction. It was a new way of looking at things, and my head was full of recollections of the way objects looked in Kentucky and Tennessee. It was like going back to the age of twelve, going fishing and all that. It was a sense of freedom and excitement.

INTERVIEWERS: When you started writing, what preoccupations, technically and thematically, had you in common with your crowd?

WARREN: I suppose you mean the poets called the Fugitive Group in Nashville—Allen Tate, John Crowe Ransom, Donald Davidson, Merrill Moore, et cetera?

INTERVIEWERS: Yes.

WARREN: Well, in one sense, I don't know what the group had in common. I think there is a great fallacy in assuming that there was a systematic program behind the Fugitive Group. There was no such thing, and among the members there were deep differences in temperament and aesthetic theory. They were held together by geography and poetry. They all lived in Nashville, and they were all interested in poetry. Some were professors, some businessmen, one was a banker, several were students. They met informally to argue philosophy and read each other the poems they wrote. For some of them these interests were incidental to their main concerns. For a couple of others, like Tate, it was poetry or death. Their activity wasn't any "school" or "program." Mutual respect and common interests, that was what held them together—that and the provincial isolation, I guess.

INTERVIEWERS: But did you share with them any technical or thematic preoccupations?

WARREN: The answer can't, you see, apply to the group. But in a very important way, that group was my education. I knew individual writers, poems, and books through them. I was exposed to the liveliness and range of the talk and the wrangle of argument. I heard the talk about techniques, but techniques regarded as means of expression. But most of all I got the feeling that poetry was a vital activity, that it related to ideas and to life. I came into the group rather late. I was timid and reverential, I guess. And I damned well should have been. Anyway, there was little or no talk in those days about fiction. Some of the same people, a little later, however, did give me in a very concrete way a sense of how literature can be related to place and history.

INTERVIEWERS: It's very striking when you consider writing by Southerners before the twenties. Some think that few writers were then in the South as talented or competent, or as confident as today. This strikes me as a very American cultural phenomenon in spite of its specifically regional aspects. Would you say that this was a kind of repetition of what occurred in New England, say, during the 1830s?

WARREN: Yes, I do see some parallel between New England before the Civil War and the South after World War I to the present. The old notion of a shock, a cultural shock, to a more or less closed and static society—you know, what happened on a bigger scale in the Italian Renaissance or Elizabethan England. After 1918 the modern industrial world, with its good and bad, hit the South; all sorts of ferments began. As for individual writers, almost all of them of that period had had some important experience outside the South, then returned there—some strange mixture of continuity and discontinuity in their experience—a jagged quality. But more than mere general cultural or personal shocks, there was a moral shock in the South, a tension that grew out of the race situation. That moral tension had always been there, but it took new and more exacerbated forms after 1920. For one thing, the growing self-consciousness of the Negroes opened up possibilities for expanding economic and cultural horizons. A consequence was that the Southerner's loyalties and pieties—real values, mind you—were sometimes staked against his religious and moral sense, equally real values. There isn't much vital imagination, it seems to me, that doesn't come from this sort of shock, imbalance, need to "relive," redefine life.

INTERVIEWERS: There is, for us, an exciting spiral of redefinition in your own work from *I'll Take My Stand* through the novels to *Segregation*. It would seem that these works mark stages in a combat with the past. In the first, the point of view seems orthodox and unreconstructed. How can one say it? In recent years your work has become more intense and has taken on an element of personal confession which is so definite that one tends to look, for example, on *Segregation* and *Brother to Dragons* as two facets of a single attitude.

WARREN: You've thrown several different things at me here. Let me try to sort them out. First you refer to the Southern Agrarian book *I'll Take My Stand*, of 1930, and then to my recent little book on *Segregation*. My essay in *I'll Take My Stand* was about the Negro in the South, and it was a defense of segregation. I haven't read that piece, as far as I can remember, since 1930, and I'm not sure exactly how things are put there. But I do recall very distinctly the circumstances of writing it. I wrote it at Oxford at about the same time I began writing fiction. The two things were tied together—the look back home from a long distance. I remember the jangle and wrangle of writing the essay and some kind of discomfort in it, some sense of evasion, I guess, in writing it, in contrast with the free feeling of writing the novelette *Prime Leaf*, the sense of seeing something fresh, the holiday sense plus some stirring up of something inside yourself. In the essay, I reckon, I was trying to prove something, and in the novelette trying to find out something, see something, feel something—exist. Don't misunderstand me. On the objective side of things, there wasn't a power under heaven that could have changed segregation in 1929 —the South wasn't ready for it, the North wasn't ready for it, the Negro wasn't. The Court, if I remember correctly, had just reaffirmed segregation too. No, I'm not talking about the objective fact, but about the subjective fact, yours truly, in relation to the objective fact. Well, it wasn't being outside the South that made me change my mind. It was coming back home. In a little while I realized I simply couldn't have written that essay again. I guess trying to write fiction made me realize that. If you are seriously trying to write fiction you can't allow yourself as much evasion as in trying to write essays. But some people can't read fiction. One reviewer—a professional critic—said that *Band of Angels* is an apology for the plantation system. Well, the story of *Band* wasn't an apology *or* an attack. It was simply trying to say something about something. But God Almighty, you have to spell it out for some people, especially a certain breed of professional defender-of-the-good, who makes a career of holding the right thoughts and admiring his own moral navel. Well, that's getting off the point. What else was it you threw at me?

INTERVIEWERS: Would you say that each book marks a redefinition of reality arrived at through a combat with the past? A development from the traditional to the highly personal reality? A confession?

WARREN: I never thought of a combat with the past. I guess I think more of trying to find what there is valuable to us, the line of continuity to us, and *through* us. The specific Southern past, I'm now talking about. As for combat, I guess the real combat is always with yourself, Southerner or anybody else. You fight your battles one by one and do the best you can. Whatever patterns there are develop, aren't planned—the really basic patterns, I mean, the kind you live into. As for confession, that wouldn't have occurred to me, but I do know that in the last ten years or a little more the personal relation to my writing changed. I never bothered to define the change. I quit writing poems for several years; that is, I'd start them, get a lot down, then feel that I wasn't connecting somehow. I didn't finish one for several years, they felt false. Then I got back at it, and that is the bulk of what I've done since *Band of Angels*—a new book of poems which will be out in the summer. When you try to write a book—even objective fiction—you have to write from the inside not the outside—the inside of yourself. You have to find what's there. You can't predict it—just dredge for it and hope you have something worth the dredging. That isn't "confession"—that's just trying to use whatever the Lord lets you lay hand to. And of course you have to have common sense enough and structural sense enough to know what is relevant. You don't choose a story, it chooses you. You get together with that story somehow; you're stuck with it. There certainly is some reason it attracted you, and you're writing it trying to find out that reason; justify, get at that reason. I can always look back and remember the exact moment when I encountered the germ of any story I wrote—a clear flash.

INTERVIEWERS: What is your period of incubation? Months? Years?

WARREN: Something I read or see stays in my head for five or six years. I always remember the date, the place, the room, the road, when I first was struck. For instance, *World Enough and Time*. Katherine Anne Porter and I were both at the Library of Congress as Fellows. We were in the same pew, had offices next to each other. She came in one day with an old pamphlet, the trial of Beauchamp for killing Colonel Sharp. She said, "Well, Red, you better read this." There it was. I read it in five minutes. But I was six years making the book. Any book I write starts with a flash but takes a long time to shape up. All of your first versions are in your head, so by the time you sit down to write you have some line developed in your head.

INTERVIEWERS: What is the relation of sociological research and other types of research to the forms of fiction?

WARREN: I think it's purely accidental. For one writer a big dose of such stuff might be fine, for another it might be poison. I've known a good many people, some of them writers, who think of literature as *material* that you "work up." You don't "work up" literature. They point at Zola. But Zola didn't do that, nor did Dreiser. They may have thought they did, but they didn't. They weren't "working up" something—in one sense, something was working them up. You see the world as best you can—with or without the help of somebody's research, as the case may be. You see as much as you can, and the events and books that are interesting to you should be interesting to you because you're a human being, not because you're trying to be a writer. Then those things may be of some use to you as a writer later on. I don't believe in a schematic approach to material. The business of researching for a book strikes me as a sort of obscenity. What I mean is, researching for a book in the sense of trying to find a book to write. Once you are engaged by a subject, are in your book, have your idea, you may or may not want to do some investigating. But you ought to do it in the same spirit in which you'd take a walk in the evening air to think things over. You can't research to get a book. You stumble on it, or hope to. Maybe you will, if you live right.

INTERVIEWERS: Speaking of craft, how conscious are you of the dramatic structure of your novels when you begin? I ask because in your work there is quite a variety of sub-forms, folklore, set pieces like "The Ballad of Billy Potts" or the Cass Mastern episode in *All the King's Men*. Are these planned as part of the dramatic structure, or do they arise while you are being carried by the flow of invention?

WARREN: I try to think a lot about the craft of other people— that's a result of my long years of teaching. You've been explaining things like how the first scene of *Hamlet* gets off, thinking of how things have been done . . . I suppose some of this sinks down to your gizzard. When it comes to your own work you have made some objective decisions, such as which character is going to tell the story. That's a prime question, a question of control. You have to make a judgment. You find one character is more insistent, he's more sensitive and more pointed than the others. But as for other aspects of structure and craft, I guess, in the actual process of composition or in preliminary thinking, I try to immerse myself in the motive and *feel* toward meanings, rather than plan a structure or plan effects. At some point, you know, you have to try to get one with God and *then* take a hard cold look at what you're doing and work on it once more, trusting in your viscera and nervous system and your previous efforts as far as they've gone. The hard thing, the objective thing, has to be done before the book is written. And if anybody dreams up "Kubla Khan," it's going to be Coleridge. If the work is done the dream will come to the man who's ready for that particular dream; it's not going to come just from dreaming in general. After a thing is done, then I try to get tough and critical with myself.

But damn it, it may sometimes be too late. But that is the fate of man. What I am trying to say is that I try to forget the abstractions when I'm actually composing a thing. I don't understand other approaches that come up when I talk to other writers. For instance, some say their sole interest is experimentation. Well, I think that you learn all you can and try to use it. I don't know what is meant by the word "experiment"; you ought to be playing for keeps.

INTERVIEWERS: Yes, but there is still great admiration of the so-called "experimental writing" of the twenties. What of Joyce and Eliot?

WARREN: What is "experimental writing"? James Joyce didn't do "experimental writing"—he wrote *Ulysses*. Eliot didn't do "experimental writing"—he wrote *The Waste Land*. When you fail at something you call it an "experiment," an élite word for flop. Just because lines are uneven or capitals missing doesn't mean experiment. Literary magazines devoted to experimental writing are usually filled with works by middle-aged or old people.

INTERVIEWERS: Or middle-aged young people.

WARREN: Young fogeys. In one way, of course, all writing that is any good *is* experimental; that is, it's a way of seeing what is possible—what poem, what novel is possible. Experiment—they define it as putting a question to nature, and that is true of writing undertaken with seriousness. You put the question to human nature—and especially your own nature—and see what comes out. It is unpredictable. If it is predictable—not experimental in that sense—then it will be worthless.

INTERVIEWERS: The *Southern Review* contained much fine work, but little that was purely "experimental"—isn't that so?

WARREN: Yes, and there were a lot of good young, or younger, writers in it. Not all Southern either—about half, I should say.

INTERVIEWERS: I remember that some of Algren's first work appeared there.

WARREN: Oh, yes, two early stories, for example; and a longish poem about baseball.

INTERVIEWERS: And the story, "A Bottle of Milk for Mother."

WARREN: And the story "Biceps." And three or four of Eudora's first stories were there—Eudora Welty—and some of Katherine Anne's novelettes—Katherine Anne Porter.

INTERVIEWERS: There were a lot of critics in it—young ones too.

WARREN: Oh yes, younger then, anyway. Kenneth Burke, F. O. Matthiessen, Theodore Spencer, R. P. Blackmur, Delmore Schwartz, L. C. Knights. . . .

INTERVIEWERS: Speaking of critics reminds me that you've written criticism as well as poetry, drama, and fiction. It is sometimes said that the practice of criticism is harmful to the rest; have you found it so?

WARREN: On this matter of criticism, something that appalls me is the idea going around now that the practice of criticism is opposed to the literary impulse—is *necessarily* opposed to it. Sure, it *may* be a trap, it may destroy the creative impulse, but so may drink or money or respectability. But criticism is a perfectly natural human activity, and somehow the dullest, most technical criticism may be associated with full creativity. Elizabethan criticism is all, or nearly all, technical—meter, how to hang a line together—kitchen criticism, how to make the cake. People deeply interested in an art are interested in the "how." Now I don't mean to say that that is the only kind of valuable criticism. Any kind is good that gives a deeper insight into the nature of the thing—a Marxist analysis, a Freudian study, the relation to a literary or social tradition, the history of a theme. But we have to remember that there is no *one, single, correct* kind of criticism, no *complete* criticism. You only have different kinds of perspectives, giving, when successful, different kinds of insights. And at one historical moment one kind of insight may be more needed than another.

INTERVIEWERS: But don't you think that in America now a lot of good critical ideas get lost in terminology, in the gobbledygook style of expression?

WARREN: Every age, every group, has its jargon. When the jargon runs away with the insight, that's no good. Sure, a lot of people think they have the key to truth if they have a lingo. And a lot of modern criticism has run off into lingo, into academicism —the wrong kind of academicism, that pretends to be unacademic. The real academic job is to absorb an idea, to put it into perspective along with other ideas, not to dilute it to lingo. As for lingo, it's true that some very good critics got bit by the bug that you could develop a fixed critical vocabulary. Well, you can't, except within narrow limits. That is a trap of scientism.

INTERVIEWERS: Do you see some new ideas in criticism now emerging?

WARREN: No, I don't see them now. We've had Mr. Freud and Mr. Marx and—

INTERVIEWERS: Mr. Fraser and *The Golden Bough*.

WARREN: Yes, and Mr. Coleridge and Mr. Arnold and Mr. Eliot and Mr. Richards and Mr. Leavis and Mr. Aristotle, et cetera. There have been, or are, many competing kinds of criticism with us—but I don't see a new one, or a new development of one of the old kind. It's an age groping for its issue.

INTERVIEWERS: What about the New Criticism?

WARREN: Let's name some of them—Richards, Eliot, Tate, Blackmur, Winters, Brooks, Leavis (I guess). How in God's name can you get that gang into the same bed? There's no bed big enough and no blanket would stay tucked. When Ransom wrote his book called *The New Criticism*, he was pointing out the vindictive variety among the critics and saying that he didn't agree with any of them. The term is, in one sense, a term without any referent—or with too many referents. It is a term that belongs to the conspiracy theory of history. A lot of people—chiefly aging, conservative professors scared of losing prestige, or young instructors afraid of not getting promoted, middle-brow magazine editors, and the flotsam and jetsam of semi-Marxist social-significance criticism left stranded by history—they all had a communal nightmare called the New Criticism to explain their vague discomfort. I think it was something they ate.

INTERVIEWERS: What do you mean—conspiracy?

WARREN: Those folks all had the paranoidal nightmare that there was a conspiracy called the New Criticism, just to do them personal wrong. No, it's not quite that simple, but there is some truth in this. One thing that a lot of so-called New Critics had in common was a willingness to look long and hard at the literary object. But the ways of looking might be very different. Eliot is a lot closer to Arnold and the Archbishop of Canterbury than he is to Yvor Winters, and Winters is a lot closer to Irving Babbitt than to Richards, and the exegeses of Brooks are a lot closer to Coleridge than to Ransom, and so on. There has been more nonsense talked about this subject than about any I can think of. And a large part of the nonsense, on any side of the question, derives from the assumption that any one kind of criticism is "correct" criticism. There is no correct or complete criticism.

INTERVIEWERS: You had a piece in the *New Republic* once in which you discuss Faulkner's technique. One of the things you emphasize is Faulkner's technique of the "still moment." I've forgotten what you called it exactly—a suspension, in which time seems to hang.

WARREN: That's the frozen moment. Freeze time. Somewhere, almost in a kind of pun, Faulkner himself uses the image of a frieze for such a moment of frozen action. It's an important quality in his work. Some of these moments harden up an event, give it its meaning by holding it fixed. Time fluid versus time fixed. In Faulkner's work that's the drama behind the drama. Take a look at Hemingway; there's no time in Hemingway, there are only moments in themselves, moments of action. There are no parents and no children. If there's a parent he is a grandparent off in America somewhere who signs the check, like the grandfather in *A Farewell to Arms*. You never see a small child in Hemingway. You get death in childbirth but you never see a child. Everything is outside of the time process. But in Faulkner there are always the very old and the very young. Time spreads and is the important thing, the terrible thing. A tremendous flux is there, things flowing away in all directions. Moments not quite ready to be shaped are already there, waiting, and we feel their presence. What you most remember about Jason in *The Sound and the Fury*, say, is the fact that he was the treasurer when the children made and sold kites, and kept the money in his pocket. Or you remember Caddy getting her drawers muddy. Everything is already there, just waiting to happen. You have the sense of the small becoming large in time, the large becoming small, the sweep of time over things—that, and the balance of the frozen, abstracted moment against violent significant action. These frozen moments are Faulkner's game. Hemingway has a different game. In Hemingway there's no time at all. He's out of history entirely. In one sense, he tries to deny history, he says history is the bunk, like Henry Ford.

I am in no sense making an invidious comparison between the two writers—or between their special uses of time. They are both powerfully expressive writers. But it's almost too pat, you know, almost too schematic, the polar differences between those two writers in relation to the question of time. Speaking of pairs of writers, take Proust and Faulkner. There may be a lot written on the subject, but I haven't encountered much of it. They'd make a strange but instructive pair to study—in relation to time.

INTERVIEWERS: Wouldn't you say that there seems to be in the early Hemingway a conscious effort *not* to have a very high center of consciousness within the form of the novel? His characters may have a highly moral significance, but they seldom discuss issues; they prefer to hint.

WARREN: Sure, Hemingway sneaks it in, but he is an intensely conscious and even philosophical writer. When the snuck-in thing or the gesture works, the effect can be mighty powerful. By contrast, French fiction usually has a hero who deals very consciously with the issues. He is his own chorus to the action, as well as the man who utters the equivalent of the Elizabethan soliloquy. Nineteenth-century fiction also dealt with the issues. Those novels could discuss them in terms of a man's relation to a woman, or in terms of whether you're going to help a slave run away, or in terms of what to do about a man obsessed with fighting evil, nature, what have you, in the form of a white whale.

INTERVIEWERS: Your own work seems to have this explicit character. Jack Burden in *All the King's Men* is a conscious center and he is a highly conscious man. He's not there as an omniscient figure, but is urgently trying to discover something. He is involved.

WARREN: Burden got there by accident. He was only a sentence or two in the first version—the verse play from which the novel developed.

INTERVIEWERS: Why did you make the change?

WARREN: I don't know. He was an unnamed newspaper man, a childhood friend of the assassin; an excuse for the young doctor, the assassin of the politician Willie Stark, to say something before he performed the deed. When after two years I picked up the verse version and began to fool with a novel, the unnamed newspaper man became the narrator. It turned out, in a way, that what he thought about the story was more important than the story itself. I suppose he became the narrator because he gave me the kind of interest I needed to write the novel. He made it possible for me to control it. He is an observer, but he is involved.

INTERVIEWERS: For ten years or more it has been said in the United States that problems of race are an obsession of Negro writers, but that they have no place in literature. But how can a Negro writer avoid the problem of race?

WARREN: How can you expect a Southern Negro not to write about race, directly or indirectly, when you can't find a Southern white man who can avoid it?

INTERVIEWERS: I must say that it's usually white Northerners who express a different opinion, though a few Negroes have been seduced by it. And they usually present their argument on aesthetic grounds.

WARREN: I'd like to add here something about the historical element which seems to me important for this general question. The Negro who is now writing protest *qua* protest strikes me as anachronistic. Protest *qua* protest denies the textures of life. The problem is to permit the fullest range of life into racial awareness. I don't mean to imply that there's nothing to protest about, but aside from the appropriate political, sociological, and journalistic concerns, the problem is to see the protest in its relation to other things. Race isn't an isolated thing—I mean as it exists in the U.S.—it becomes a total symbolism for every kind of issue. They all flow into it—and out of it. Well, thank God. It gives a little variety to life. At the same time it proclaims the unity of life. You know the kind of person who puts on a certain expression and then talks about "solving" the race problem. Well, it's the same kind of person and the same kind of expression you meet when you hear the phrase "solve the sex problem." This may be a poor parallel, but it's some kind of parallel. Basically the issue isn't to "solve" the "race problem" or the "sex problem." You don't solve it, you just experience it. Appreciate it.

INTERVIEWERS: Maybe that's another version of William James's "moral equivalent of war." You argue and try to keep the argument clean, all the human complexities in view.

WARREN: What I'm trying to say is this. A few years ago I sat in a room with some right-thinking friends, the kind of people who think you look in the back of the book for every answer—attitude A for situation A, attitude B for situation B, and so on through the damned alphabet. It developed that they wanted a world where everything is exactly alike and everybody is exactly alike. They wanted a production belt of human faces and human attitudes, and the same books on every parlor table.

INTERVIEWERS: Hell, who would want such a world?

WARREN: "Right-thinkers" want it, for one thing. I don't want that kind of world. I want variety and pluralism—and *appreciation*. Appreciation in the context of some sort of justice and decency, and freedom of choice in conduct and personal life. I'd like a country in which there was a maximum of opportunity for any individual to discover his talents and develop his capacities—discover his fullest self and by so doing learn to respect other selves a little. Man is interesting in his differences. It's all a question of what you make of the differences. I'm not for differences *per se,* but you just let the world live the differences, live them out, live them up, and see how things come out. But I feel pretty strongly about attempts to legislate *un*difference. That is just as much tyranny as trying to legislate difference. Apply that to any differences between healthy and unhealthy, criminal and noncriminal. Furthermore, you can't legislate the future of anybody, in any direction. It's not laws that are going to determine what our great-grandchildren feel or do. The tragedy of a big half of American liberalism is to try to legislate virtue. You can't legislate virtue. You should simply try to establish conditions favorable for the growth of virtue. But that will never satisfy the bully-boys of virtue, the plug-uglies of virtue. They are interested in the production-belt stamp of virtue, attitude A in the back of the book, and not in establishing conditions of justice and decency in which human appreciation can find play.

Listen, I'll tell you a story. More than twenty years ago I spent part of a summer in a little town in Louisiana, and like a good number of the population whiled away the afternoons by going to the local murder trials. One case involved an old Negro man who had shot a young Negro woman for talking meanness against his baby-girl daughter. He had shot the victim with both barrels of a twelve-gauge at a range of eight feet, while the victim was in a crap game. There were a dozen witnesses to the execution. Besides that he had sat for half an hour on a stump outside the door of the building where the crap game was going on, before he got down to business. He was waiting, because a friend had lost six dollars to the intended victim and had asked the old man to hold off till he had a chance to win it back. When the friend got the six dollars back, the old man went to work. He never denied what he had done. He explained it all very carefully, and why he had to do it. He loved his baby-girl daughter and there wasn't anything else he could do. Then he would plead not guilty. But if he got tried and convicted—and they couldn't fail to convict—he would get death. If, however, he would plead guilty to manslaughter, he could get off light. But he wouldn't do it. He said he wasn't guilty of anything. The whole town got involved in the thing. Well, they finally cracked him. He pleaded guilty and got off light. Everybody was glad, sure—they weren't stuck with something, they could feel good and pretty virtuous. But they felt bad, too. Something had been lost, something a lot of them could appreciate. I used to think I'd try to make a story of this. But I never did. It was too complete, too self-fulfilling, as fact. But to get back to the old man. It took him three days to crack, and when he cracked he was nothing. Now we don't approve of what he did—a status homicide the sociologists call it, and that is the worst sort of homicide, worse than homicide for gain, because status homicide is irrational, and you can't make sense of it, and it is the mark of a low order of society. But because status homicide is the mark of a low order of society, what are we to think about the old man's three-day struggle to keep his dignity? And are we to deny value to this dignity because of the way "they" live down there?

INTERVIEWERS: You feel, then, that one of the great blocks in achieving serious fiction out of sad experience is the assumption that you're on the right side?

WARREN: Once you start illustrating virtue as such you had better stop writing fiction. Do something else, like Y-work. Or join a committee. Your business as a writer is not to illustrate virtue, but to show how a fellow may move toward it—or away from it.

INTERVIEWERS: Malraux says that "one cannot reveal the mystery of human beings in the form of a plea for the defense."

WARREN: Or in the form of an indictment, either.

INTERVIEWERS: What about the devil's advocate?

WARREN: He can have a role, he can be Jonathan Swift or something.

INTERVIEWERS: I wonder what these right-thinkers feel when they confront a Negro, say, the symbol of the underdog, and he turns out to be a son of a bitch. What do they do—hold a conference to decide how to treat him?

WARREN: They must sure have a problem.

INTERVIEWERS: The same kind of people, they have to consult with themselves to determine if they can laugh at certain situations in which Negroes are involved—like minstrel shows. A whole world of purely American humor got lost in that shuffle, along with some good songs.

WARREN: It's just goddamned hard, you have to admit, though, to sort out things that are symbolically charged. Sometimes the symbolic charge is so heavy you have a hard time getting at the real value really there. You always can, I guess, if the context is right. But hell, a lot of people can't read a context.

INTERVIEWERS: It's like the problem of Shylock in *The Merchant of Venice*.

WARREN: Yes, suppress the play because it might offend a Jew. Or *Oliver Twist*. Well, such symbolic charges just have to be reckoned with and taken on their own terms and in their historical perspective. As a matter of fact, such symbolic charges are present, in one degree or another, in all relationships. They're simply stepped up and specialized in certain historical and social situations. There are mighty few stories you can tell without offending somebody—without some implicit affront. The comic strip of *Li'l Abner*, for instance, must have made certain persons of what is called "Appalachian white" origin feel inferior and humiliated. There are degrees as well as differences in these things. Context is all. And a relatively pure heart. *Relatively* pure—for if you had a pure heart you wouldn't be in the book-writing business in the first place. We're stuck with it in ourselves—what we can write about, if anything; what you can make articulate; what voices you have in your insides and in your ear.

RALPH ELLISON
EUGENE WALTER

Note: There is an integral relationship between this interview and the interview with Ralph Ellison which appeared in issue no. 8 of *The Paris Review*.

11. Alberto Moravia

Alberto Moravia was born Alberto Pincherle in 1907. He had little formal education beyond grammar school and spent much of his youth ill with tuberculosis.

His first novel, *Gli Indifferenti*, was published when he was twenty-two. It attracted wide attention in Europe, but owing to a bad translation (*The Indifferent Ones*, 1932) went almost unnoticed in America. The work was retranslated in 1953 as *The Time of Indifference*, and on its second appearance the *New York Times* said of Moravia that he was "one of the truly important contemporary writers, as unprejudiced, observant, unsentimental and humane as was Stendhal."

Moravia's best-known novels are *The Conformist*, which he considers his most successful to date, and *Woman of Rome*, a book which has been translated into thirteen languages. Because of an underlying theme in his books, the degradation of moral principles during his characters' quest to stay alive, Moravia has often been condemned for sordidness. In 1952 he was placed on the Catholic Index. He has, however, won many honors, among them the Strega Literary Prize and the Legion of Honor, both of which he received in 1952.

Moravia is a prolific and versatile artist. A part-time editor for a Milan publishing house, he is also a constant contributor to *Corriere della sera* and *L'Europeo*.

Atto secondo

Scena prima

Pomeriggio

Camera da letto della duchessa Gorina .

Giustina , Sebastiano .

Una camera grande , con un letto a baldacchino ~~xxxxxxx~~ colonne dorate ,
sormontato da un grande stemma spagnolesco . Mobili barocchi . Molto disordine,
panni in terra , ~~xxxxxxxxxxxxxxxxxxxxxxxxxxxxxxxxxxxxxxxxxxxxxxxxxxx~~ toletta
~~xxxxxxxxxx~~ in tumulto , letto disfatto .

~~xxxxxxxxxxxxxxxxxxxxxxxxxxxxxxxxxxxxxxxxxxxxxxxxxxxxxxxxxxxxxxxxxxxxxxxxxxxxxxxxxxxxxxxxxxxxxxx~~

Nel momento in cui si alza il sipario , la cameriera Giustina sta riordinando
rapidamente la stanza . Pur lavorando , Giustina canta sottovoce una ~~xxxxxxxx~~ *filastrocca*

Giustina : E ti vuol dare un giovan della banda ; e non lo voglio no .

Che tutto il di $\overset{mi}{\text{mi}}$ farà suonar la tromba ; e non lo voglio no .

E ti vuol dare un giovan caffettiere ; e non lo voglio no .

Che tutto il dì $\overset{mi}{\text{mi}}$ farà sciacquar le tazze; e non lo voglio no .

E ti vuol dare un giovan cavaliere ; e lo voglio sì .

Che tutto il di mi porterà a spasso; e lo voglio sì ....

~~Iniquelxxxxxxxxxx~~ *Si* bussa alla porta .

Giustina : Avanti.

Sebastiano:(travestito da ~~xxxxxxxxxx~~, *cameriere*) ~~con i pantaloni neri e giubba bianca~~
Si può ? sono venuto a prendere il vassoio. ~~xxxxxxxxx~~

Giustina :(continuando a cantarellare e guardando con intenzione a Sebastiano)

Un giovan cavaliere ..e lo voglio sì ....Chi sei ? uno dei nuovi ?

Sebastiano : Sì , sono arrivato oggi .

Giustina : (indicando un tavolo sul quale ~~xxxxxxxx~~ posato il vassoio della
colazione mattutina della duchessa) Eccolo, il $\overset{two}{\text{vassoio}}$. Io sono la cameriera
personale della duchessa, mi chiamo Giustina . E tu come ti chiami ?

Sebastiano:(andando a prendere il vassoio) Ricardo .

Giustina : (lanciandogli uno sguardo assassino) Sei un bel ragazzo , sta
attento alla duchessa .

The first page of Act II of Moravia's La Mascherata *(The Fancy Dress Ball)*

Bee W. Dabney

Alberto Moravia

Via dell'Oca lies just off the Piazza del Popolo. A curiously shaped street, it opens out midway to form a largo, tapering at either end, in its brief, cobbled passage from the Lungotevere to a side of Santa Maria dei Miracoli. Its name, Street of the Goose, derives, like those of many streets in Rome, from the signboard of an eating house long forgotten.

On one side, extending unbroken from the Tiberside to Via Ripetta, sprawl the houses of working-class people: a line of narrow doorways with dark, dank little stairs, cramped windows, a string of tiny shops; the smells of candied fruit, repair shops, wines of the Castelli, engine exhaust; the cry of street urchins, the test-roar of a Guzzi, a caterwaul from a court.

On the opposite side the buildings are taller, vaguely out of place, informed with the serene imperiousness of unchipped cornices and balconies overspilling with potted vines, tended creepers: homes of the well-to-do. It is here, on this side, that Alberto Moravia lives, in the only modern structure in the neighborhood, the building jutting like a jade and ivory dike into the surrounding red-gold.

The door is opened by the maid, a dark girl wearing the conventional black dress and white apron. Moravia is behind her in the entry, checking the arrival of a case of wine. He turns. The interviewers may go into the parlor. He'll be in directly.

Moravia's living room, at first sight, is disappointing. It has the elegant, formal anonymity of a Parioli apartment rented by a film actor, but smaller; or that of a reception room at the Swiss Legation, without the travel folders—or reading matter of any sort. There is very little furniture, and this is eighteenth century. Four paintings adorn the walls: two Guttusos, a Martinelli, and, over a wide blue sofa, a Toti Scialoja. At either end of the sofa, an armchair; bracketed between the chairs and sofa, a long low Venetian coffee table inlaid with antique designs of the constellations and signs of the zodiac. The powder blue and old rose of the table are repeated in the colors of the Persian rug beneath. A record cabinet stands against the opposite wall; it contains Bach, Scarlatti, Beethoven's Ninth and some early quartets, Stravinsky, Prokofiev, Monteverdi's Orfeo. The impersonality of the room seems almost calculated. Only the view from the windows recalls the approaching spring; flowers blossom on roof-terraces, the city is warm, red in the westering sun. Suddenly Moravia enters. He is tall, elegant, severe; the geometry of his face, its reflections, are cold, almost metallic; his voice is low, also metallic—one thinks, in each case, of gunmetal. One detects a trace of unease, shyness perhaps, in his manner, but he is at home in his parlor; he settles comfortably on the sofa and crosses his legs.

INTERVIEWERS: May we start at the beginning?

MORAVIA: At the beginning?

INTERVIEWERS: You were born . . .

MORAVIA: Oh. I was born here. I was born in Rome on the twenty-eighth of November, 1907.

INTERVIEWERS: And your education?

MORAVIA: My education, my formal education that is, is practically nil. I have a grammar-school diploma, no more. Just nine years of schooling. I had to drop out because of tuberculosis of the bone I spent, altogether, five years in bed with it, between the ages of nine and seventeen—till 1924.

INTERVIEWERS: Then *"Inverno di malato"* must refer to those years. One understands how—

MORAVIA: You aren't suggesting that I'm Girolamo, are you?

INTERVIEWERS: Well, yes. . . .

MORAVIA: I'm not. Let me say—

INTERVIEWERS *(cautiously)*: It's the same disease.

MORAVIA: Let me say here and now that I do not appear in any of my works.

INTERVIEWERS: Maybe we can return to this a little later.

MORAVIA: Yes. But I want it quite clearly understood: my works are not autobiographical in the usual meaning of the word. Perhaps I can put it this way: whatever is autobiographical is so in only a very indirect manner, in a very general way. I am related to Girolamo, but I am not Girolamo. I do not take, and have never taken, either action or characters directly from life. Events may suggest events to be used in a work later; similarly, persons may suggest future characters; but *suggest* is the word to remember. One writes about what one knows. For instance, I can't say I know America, though I've visited there. I couldn't write about it. Yes, one uses what one knows, but autobiography means something else. I should never be able to write a real autobiography; I always end by falsifying and fictionalizing—I'm a liar, in fact. That means I'm a novelist, after all. I write about what I know.

INTERVIEWERS: Fine. In any case, your first work was *Gli Indifferenti*.

MORAVIA: Yes.

INTERVIEWERS: Will you tell us something about it?

MORAVIA: What do you want to know? I started it in October 1925. I wrote a good deal of it in bed—at Cortina, at Morra's,[1] incidentally. It was published in '29.

INTERVIEWERS: Was there much opposition to it? From the critics, that is? Or, even, from the reading public?

MORAVIA (*taking the defensive*): Opposition? What kind of opposition?

INTERVIEWERS: I mean, coming after D'Annunzio, at the height of Fragmentism and *prosa d'arte* . . .

MORAVIA: Oh. . . . No, there was no opposition to it at all. It was a great success. In fact, it was one of the greatest successes in all modern Italian literature. The greatest, actually; and I can say this with all modesty. There had never been anything like it. Certainly no book in the last fifty years has been greeted with such unanimous enthusiasm and excitement.

INTERVIEWERS: And you were quite young at the time.

MORAVIA: Twenty-one. There were articles in the papers, some of them running to five full columns. It was without precedent, the book's success. (*Pausing*) I may add that nothing approaching it has happened to me since—or, for that matter, to anyone else.

INTERVIEWERS: *Gli Indifferenti* has been interpreted as a rather sharp, even bitter, efficient criticism of the Roman bourgeoisie, and of bourgeois values in general. Was it written in reaction against the society you saw about you?

MORAVIA: No. Not consciously, at least. (*Reconsidering; presently, with finality*) It was not a reaction against anything. It was a novel.

INTERVIEWERS: Those critics who have cast you along with Svevo are wrong, then, you would say?

MORAVIA: Quite. Yes, quite. To tell the truth, Svevo is a writer I don't know at all well. I read him, and then only *Senilità* [*As a*

---

[1] Count Umberto Morra di Lavriano, literary critic, historian, translator, responsible for the introduction of Virginia Woolf's writings to Italy; now director of the Società Italiana per l'Organizzazione Internazionale.

Man Grows Older], and what's the other one?—*La Coscienza di Zeno* [*Confessions of Zeno*]—after I had written *Gli Indifferenti*. There's no question of influence, certainly. Furthermore, Svevo was a conscious critic of the bourgeoisie; my own criticism, whatever there is, is unintentional, occurring entirely by chance. In my view, the function of a writer is not to criticize anyway; only to create living characters. Just that.

INTERVIEWERS: You write, then—?

MORAVIA: I write simply to amuse myself; I write to entertain others and—and, well, to express myself. One has one's own way of expressing oneself, and writing happens to be mine.

INTERVIEWERS: By that, you do not consider yourself a moralist, do you?

MORAVIA: No, I most emphatically do not. Truth and beauty are educatory in themselves. The very fact of representing the left wing, or a "wing" of any sort, implies a partisan position and non-objectivity. For that reason, one is impotent to criticize in a valid sense. Social criticism must necessarily, and always, be an extremely superficial thing. But don't misunderstand me. Writers, like all artists, are concerned to represent reality, to create a more absolute and complete reality than reality itself. They must, if they are to accomplish this, assume a moral position, a clearly conceived political, social, and philosophical attitude; in consequence, their beliefs are, of course, going to find their way into their work. What artists believe, however, is of secondary importance, ancillary to the work itself. A writer survives *in spite of* his beliefs. Lawrence will be read whatever one thinks of his notions on sex. Dante is read in the Soviet Union.

A work of art, on the other hand, has a representative and expressive function. In this representation the author's ideas, his judgments, the author himself, are engaged with reality. Criticism, thus, is no more than a part, an aspect—a minor aspect—of the whole. I suppose, putting it this way, I am, after all, a moralist to some degree. We all are. You know, sometimes you wake up in the morning in revolt against everything. Nothing seems right. And for that day or so, at least until you get over it, you're a moralist. Put it this way: every man is a moralist in his own fashion, but he is many other things besides.

INTERVIEWERS: May we return to *Gli Indifferenti* for just a moment? Did you feel when you were working on it that you faced particular problems of technique?

MORAVIA: There was one big one in my attempt—borrowing a drama technique to begin and end the story within a brief, clearly delimited period, omitting nothing. All the action, in fact, takes place within two days. The characters dine, sleep, entertain themselves, betray one another; and that, succinctly, is all. And everything happens, as it were, "on stage."

INTERVIEWERS: Have you written for the stage?

MORAVIA: A little. There's a stage adaptation of *Gli Indifferenti* which I made with Luigi Squarzina, and I've written one play myself, *La Mascherata* [*The Fancy Dress Party*].

INTERVIEWERS: Based on the book?

MORAVIA: Not exactly. The idea's the same; much of the action has been changed, however. It's being put on in Milan by the Piccolo Teatro.

INTERVIEWERS: Do you intend to continue writing plays?

MORAVIA: Yes. Oh, yes, I hope to go on. My interest in the theater dates back a good many years. Even as a youngster I read, and I continue to read and enjoy, plays—for the most part, the masters: Shakespeare, other of the Elizabethans, Molière, Goldoni, the Spanish theater, Lope de Vega, Calderón. I'm drawn most, in my reading, to tragedy, which, in my opinion, is the greatest of all forms of artistic expression, the theater itself being the most complete of literary forms. Unfortunately, contemporary drama is nonexistent.

INTERVIEWERS: How's that? You mean, perhaps, in Italy.

MORAVIA: No. Simply that there is no modern drama. Not that it's not being staged, but that none has been written.

INTERVIEWERS: But O'Neill, Shaw, Pirandello . . .

MORAVIA: No, none of them. Neither O'Neill, Shaw, Pirandello,

нor anyone else has created drama—tragedy—in the deepest meaning of the word. The basis of drama is language, poetic language.
Even Ibsen, the greatest of modern dramatists, resorted to everyday
language and, in consequence, by my definition failed to create true
drama.

INTERVIEWERS: Christopher Fry writes poetic dramas. You may
have seen *The Lady's Not for Burning* at the Eliseo.

MORAVIA: No.

INTERVIEWERS: You might approve of him.

MORAVIA: I might. I'd have to see first.

INTERVIEWERS: And your film work?

MORAVIA: Script writing, you mean? I haven't actually done
much, and what little I've done I haven't particularly enjoyed.

INTERVIEWERS: Yet it is another art form.

MORAVIA: Of course it is. Certainly. Wherever there is craftsman-
ship there is art. But the question is this: up to what point will the
motion picture permit full expression? The camera is a less complete instrument of expression than the pen, even in the hands of
an Eisenstein. It will never be able to express all, say, that Proust
was capable of. Never. For all that, it is a spectacular medium, over-
flowing with life, so that the work is not entirely a grind. It's the
only really alive art in Italy today, owing to its great financial back-
ing. But to work for motion pictures is exhausting. And a writer is
never able to be more than an idea-man or a scenarist—an under-
ling, in effect. It offers him little satisfaction apart from the pay.
His name doesn't even appear on the posters. For a writer it's a
bitter job. What's more, the films are an impure art, at the mercy
of a welter of mechanisms—*gimmicks,* I think you say in English
—*ficelles.* There is little spontaneity. This is only natural, of course,
when you consider the hundreds of mechanical devices that are
used in making a film, the army of technicians. The whole process
is a cut and dried affair. One's inspiration grows stale working in
motion pictures; and worse, one's mind grows accustomed to forever looking for gimmicks and by so doing is eventually ruined,
shot. I don't like film work in the least. You understand what I

mean: its compensations are not, in a real sense, worth while; hardly worth the money unless you need it.

INTERVIEWERS: Could you tell us a little about *La Romana* [*Woman of Rome*]?

MORAVIA: *La Romana* started out as a short story for the third page.[1] I began it on November 1, 1945. I had intended it to run to no more than three or four typescript pages, treating the relations between a woman and her daughter. But I simply went on writing. Four months later, by March 1, the first draft was finished.

INTERVIEWERS: It was not a case of the tail running away with the dog?

MORAVIA: It was a case, simply, of my thinking initially that I had a short story and finding four months later that it was a novel instead.

INTERVIEWERS: Have there been times when characters have got out of hand?

MORAVIA: Not in anything I've published. Whenever characters get out of control, it's a sign that the work has not arisen from genuine inspiration. One doesn't go on then.

INTERVIEWERS: Did you work from notes on *La Romana?* Rumor has it—

MORAVIA: Never. I never work from notes. I had met a woman of Rome—ten years before. Her life had nothing to do with the novel, but I remembered her, she seemed to set off a spark. No, I have never taken notes or ever even possessed a notebook. My work, in fact, is not prepared beforehand in any way. I might add, too, that when I'm not working I don't think of my work at all. When I sit down to write—that's between nine and twelve every morning, and I have never, incidentally, written a line in the afternoon or at night—when I sit at my table to write, I never know what it's going to be till I'm under way. I trust in inspiration, which sometimes comes and sometimes doesn't. But I don't sit back waiting for it. I work *every* day.

---

[1] In Italian newspapers, the third page is devoted to fiction and articles of general cultural interest, in the leading papers by the country's first writers.

INTERVIEWERS: I suppose you were helped some by your wife. The psychology . . .

MORAVIA: Not at all. For the psychology of my characters, and for every other aspect of my work, I draw solely upon my experience; but understand, never in a documentary, a textbook, sense. No, I met a Roman woman called Adriana. Ten years afterward I wrote the novel for which she provided the first impulse. She has probably never read the book. I only saw her that once; I imagined everything, I invented everything.

INTERVIEWERS: A fantasia on a real theme?

MORAVIA: Don't confuse imagination and fantasy; they are two distinct actions of the mind. Benedetto Croce makes a great distinction between them in some of his best pages. All artists must have imagination, some have fantasy. Science fiction, or—well, Ariosto . . . that's fantasy. For imagination, take *Madame Bovary*. Flaubert has great imagination, but absolutely no fantasy.

INTERVIEWERS: It's interesting that your most sympathetic characters are invariably women: *La Romana, La Provinciale, La Messicana.* . . .

MORAVIA: But that's not a fact. Some of my most sympathetic characters have been men, or boys like Michele in *Gli Indifferenti*, or Agostino in *Agostino*, or Luca in *La Disubbidienza*. I'd say, in fact, that most of my protagonists are sympathetic.

INTERVIEWERS: Marcello Clerici too? [*The Conformist*].

MORAVIA: Yes, Clerici too. Didn't you think him so?

INTERVIEWERS: Anything but—more like Pratolini's *Eroe del nostro tempo*. You don't mean that you actually felt some affection for him?

MORAVIA: Affection, no. More, pity. He was a pitiable character —pitiable because a victim of circumstance, led astray by the times, a *traviato*. But certainly he was not negative. And here we're closer to the point. I have no negative characters. I don't think it's possible to write a good novel around a negative personality.

For some of my characters I have felt affection, though.

INTERVIEWERS: For Adriana.

MORAVIA: For Adriana, yes. Certainly for Adriana.

INTERVIEWERS: Working without notes, without a plan or out line or anything, you must make quite a few revisions.

MORAVIA: Oh, yes, that I *do* do. Each book is worked over several times. I like to compare my method with that of painters centuries ago, proceeding, as it were, from layer to layer. The first draft is quite crude, far from being perfect, by no means finished; although even then, even at that point, it has its final structure, the form is visible. After that I rewrite it as many times—apply as many "layers"—as I feel to be necessary.

INTERVIEWERS: Which is how many as a rule?

MORAVIA: Well, *La Romana* was written twice. Then I went over it a third time, very carefully, minutely, until I had it the way I wanted it, till I was satisfied.

INTERVIEWERS: Two drafts, then, and a final, detailed correction of the second manuscript, is that it?

MORAVIA: Yes.

INTERVIEWERS: And that's usually the case, two drafts?

MORAVIA: Yes. (*Thinking for a moment*) It was three times with *Il Conformista*, too.

INTERVIEWERS: Who do you consider to have influenced you? For example, when you wrote *Gli Indifferenti*?

MORAVIA: It's difficult to say. Perhaps, as regards narrative technique, Dostoevski and Joyce.

INTERVIEWERS: Joyce?

MORAVIA: Well, no—let me explain. Joyce only to the extent that I learned from him the use of the time element bound with action. From Dostoevski I had an understanding of the intricacies of the dramatic novel. *Crime and Punishment* interested me greatly, as technique.

INTERVIEWERS: And other preferences, other influences? Do you feel, for instance, that your realism stems from the French?

MORAVIA: No. No, I wouldn't say so. If there is such a derivation, I'm not at all conscious of it. I consider my literary antecedents to be Manzoni, Dostoevski, Joyce. Of the French, I like, primarily, the eighteenth century, Voltaire, Diderot; then, Stendhal, Balzac, Maupassant.

INTERVIEWERS: Flaubert?

MORAVIA: Not particularly.

INTERVIEWERS: Zola?

MORAVIA: *Not at all!* . . . I've got a splitting headache. I'm sorry. (*Draining his glass*) Here, have some more. Will you take some coffee? Where was I?

INTERVIEWERS: You don't like Zola. Do you read any of the poets?

MORAVIA: I like Rimbaud and Baudelaire very much and some modern poets who are like Baudelaire.

INTERVIEWERS: And in English?

MORAVIA: I like Shakespeare—everybody has to say this, but then it's true, it's necessary. I like Dickens, Poe. Many years ago I tried translating some poems from John Donne. I like the novelists: Butler, there's a beautiful novel. Among the more recent, Thomas Hardy, Joseph Conrad—I think he's a great writer—some of Stevenson, some of Woolf. Dickens is good only in *Pickwick Papers*; the rest is no good. (My next book will be a little like that—no plot.) I have always preferred comic books to tragic books. My great ambition is to write a comic book, but, as you know, it's the most difficult thing of all. How many are there? How many can you name? Not many: *Don Quixote*, Rabelais, *The Pickwick Papers*, *The Golden Ass*, the *Sonnets* of Belli, Gogol's *Dead Souls*, Boccaccio and the *Satyricon*—these are my ideal books. I would give all to have written a book like *Gargantua*. (*He smiles.*) My literary education, as you will have seen by now, has been for the most part classical—classical prose and classical drama. The realists and naturalists, to be perfectly frank, don't interest me very much.

INTERVIEWERS: They do interest, apparently, and have had a considerable influence upon the young writers who have appeared since the war. Especially the Americans seem to have been an influence: Hemingway, Steinbeck, Dos Passos. . . .

MORAVIA: Yes, that's quite so from what I know of postwar Italian writing. But the influence has been indirect: distilled through Vittorini. Vittorini has been the greatest of all influences upon the younger generation of Italian writers. The influence is American just the same, as you suggest; but Vittorini-ized American. I was once judge in a competition held by *L'Unita* to award prizes for fiction. Out of fifty manuscripts submitted, a good half of them were by young writers influenced by Vittorini—Vittorini and the sort of "poetic" prose you can find in Hemingway in places, and in Faulkner.

INTERVIEWERS: Still, editing *Nuovi argomenti* you must see a great deal of new writing.

MORAVIA: How I wish I did! Italian writers are lazy. All in all, I receive very little. Take our symposium on Communist art. We were promised twenty-five major contributions. And how many did we get? Just imagine—three. It's really a task running a review in Italy. What we need, and don't get, are literary and political essays of length, twenty to thirty pages. We get lots of little four- and five-page squibs; only that's not what we're looking for.

INTERVIEWERS: But I meant fiction. Editing *Nuovi argomenti*, you must know more about modern Italian fiction than you admit.

MORAVIA: No; quite truthfully, I know only those writers everybody knows. Besides, you don't have to read everything to know what you like. I'd rather not name any names; there would be terrible gaps and *gaffes*.

INTERVIEWERS: How do you account for the big empty spaces in the novel tradition of Italy? Could you tell us a little about the novel in Italy?

MORAVIA: That's a pretty large question, isn't it? (*He frowns, then smiles.*) But I'll try to answer. I think one could say that Italy has *had* the novel, way back. When the bourgeois was really bourgeois, in the thirteenth and fourteenth centuries, narrative was fully developed (remember that all that painting was narrative too) but since the Counter Reformation, Italian society doesn't like to look at itself in a mirror. The main bulk of narrative literature is, after all, criticism in one form or another. In Italy when they say something is beautiful that's the last word: Italians prefer beauty to truth. The art of the novel, too, is connected with the growth and development of the European bourgeoisie. Italy hasn't yet achieved a modern bourgeoisie. Italy is really a very old country; in some ways it looks new because it's so old. Culturally, now, it follows the rest of Europe: does what the others do, but later. (*He pauses, thoughtfully.*) Another thing—in our literary history, there are great writers—titans—but no middle-sized ones. Petrarch wrote in the thirteenth century, then for four centuries everybody imitated him. Boccaccio completely exhausted the possibilities of the Italian short story in the fourteenth century. Our golden centuries were then, our literary language existed then, had crystallized. England and France had their golden centuries much later. Take, for example, Dante. Dante wrote a pure Italian, is still perfectly understandable. But his contemporary Chaucer wrote in a developing tongue: today he must be practically translated for the modern reader. That's why most modern Italian writers are not very Italian, and must look abroad for their masters: because their tradition is so far back there, is really medieval. In the last ten years, they've looked to America for their masters.

INTERVIEWERS: Will you tell us something now about your *Racconti romani?*

MORAVIA: There's not much I can say about them. They describe the Roman lower classes and petite bourgeoisie in a particular period after the war.

INTERVIEWERS: Is that all? I mean, there's nothing you can add to that?

MORAVIA: What *can* I add? Well, no, really—really there's quite a bit I can say. There's always a lot I can say about my last publication. Ask me questions and I'll try to answer whatever you ask.

INTERVIEWERS: To be truthful, I've read only one of them. I don't usually see the *Corriere della sera*, and the book itself is rather expensive. . . .

MORAVIA (*smiling*): Twenty-four hundred lire.

INTERVIEWERS: In any case, you have not heretofore, or at least

not often, dealt with the lower classes and petite bourgeoisie.
These stories are a clear departure from your previous work. Perhaps you might say something about any problems in particular
that you faced in writing them.

MORAVIA: Each of my books is the result, if not of pre-design,
of highly involved thought. In writing the *Racconti romani* there
were specific problems I had to cope with—problems of language.
Let me begin this way: up to the *Racconti romani* all of my works
had been written in the third person, even when, as in *La Romana*
and since—in the novel I have just finished—told in the first person. By third person I mean simply expressing oneself in a sus-
tained literary style, the style of the author. I've explained this, by
the way, in a note to the Penguin edition of *Woman of Rome*. In
the *Racconti romani*, on the other hand, I adopted for the first
time the language of the character, the language of the first person; but then again, not the language precisely, rather the *tone* of
the language. There were advantages and disadvantages in taking
this tack. Advantages for the reader in that he was afforded greater
intimacy; he entered directly into the heart of things; he was not
standing outside peeping in. The method was essentially photo-
graphic. The great disadvantage of the first person consists of the
tremendous limitations imposed upon what the author can say. I
could deal only with what the subject himself might deal with,
speak only of what the subject might speak of. I was even further
restricted by the fact that, say, a taxi driver could not speak with
any real knowledge even of a washerwoman's work, whereas in the
third person I might permit myself to speak of whatever I wished.
Adriana, the Woman of Rome, speaking in my third-first person,
could speak of anything in Rome that I myself, also a Roman,
could speak of.

The use of the first-person mode in treating the Roman lower
classes implies, of course, the use of dialect. And the use of dialect
imposes stringent limitations upon one's material. You cannot say
in dialect all that you may say in the language itself. Even Belli,

the master of *romanesco*, could speak of certain things, but was prevented from speaking of others. The working classes are narrowly restricted in their choice of expression, and personally I am not particularly predisposed to dialect literature. Dialect is an inferior form of expression because it is a less cultivated form. It does have its fascinating aspects, but it remains cruder, more imperfect, than the language itself. In dialect one expresses chiefly, and quite well, primal urges and exigent necessities—eating, sleeping, drinking, making love, and so forth.

In the *Racconti romani*—there are sixty-one in the volume, though I've written more than a hundred of them now; they are my chief source of income—the spoken language is Italian, but the construction of the language is irregular, and there is here and there an occasional word in dialect to capture a particular vernacular nuance, the flavor and raciness of *romanesco*. It is the only book in which I've tried to create comic characters or stories—for a time everybody thought I had no sense of humor.

I've tried in these stories, as I have said, to depict the life of the sub-proletariat and the *très petite bourgeoisie* in a period just after the last war, with the black market and all the rest. The genre is picaresque. The *picaro* is a character who lives exclusively as an economic being, the Marxist archetype, in that his first concern is his belly: eating. There is no love, genuine romantic love; rather, and above all, the one compelling fact that he must eat or perish. For this reason, the *picaro* is also an arid being. His life is one of trickery, deception, dishonesty if you will. The life of feelings, and with it the language of sensibility, begin on a rather more elevated level.

INTERVIEWERS: Themes have a way of recurring throughout your work.

MORAVIA: Of course. Naturally. In the works of every writer with any body of work to show for his effort, you will find recurrent themes. I view the novel, a single novel as well as a writer's entire corpus, as a musical composition in which the characters

are themes, from variation to variation completing an entire
parabola; similarly for the themes themselves. This simile of a
musical composition comes to mind, I think, because of my approach to my material; it is never calculated and pre-designed, but
rather instinctive: worked out by ear, as it were.

INTERVIEWERS: One last book now. We can't discuss them all.
But will you tell us something about *La Mascherata?* That, and
how it ever got by the censors.

MORAVIA: Ah, now that you mention it, that was one time when
I *was* concerned to write social criticism. The only time, however.
In 1936, I went to Mexico, and the Hispano-American scene suggested to me the idea for a satire. I returned and for several years
toyed with the idea. Then, in 1940, I went to Capri and wrote it.
What happened afterward—you asked about the censors—is an
amusing story. At least it seems amusing now. It was 1940. We
were in the full flood of war, Fascism, censorship, et cetera, et
cetera. The manuscript, once ready, like all manuscripts, had to
be submitted to the Ministry of Popular Culture for approval.
This Ministry, let me explain, was overrun by grammar-school
teachers who received three hundred lire, about six or seven thousand now, for each book they read. And, of course, to preserve
their sinecures, whenever possible they turned in negative judgments. Well, I submitted the manuscript. But whoever read it,
not wishing to take any position on the book, passed it to the
Under Secretary; the Under Secretary, with similar qualms, passed
it to the Secretary; the Secretary to the Minister; and the Minister,
finally—to Mussolini.

INTERVIEWERS: I suppose, then, you were called on the carpet?
MORAVIA: Not at all. Mussolini ordered the book to be published.
INTERVIEWERS: Oh!
MORAVIA: And it was. A month later, however, I received an un-
signed communication notifying me that the book was being
withdrawn. And that was that. The book didn't appear again till
after the Liberation.

INTERVIEWERS: Was that your only tilt with the censors?

MORAVIA: Oh, no; not by any means! I've been a lifelong anti-Fascist. There was a running battle between me and the Fascist authorities beginning in '29 and ending with the German occupation in 1943, when I had to go into hiding in the mountains, near the southern front, where I waited nine months until the Allies arrived. Time and again my books were not allowed to be mentioned in the press. Many times by order of the Ministry of Culture I lost jobs I held on newspapers, and for some years I was forced to write under the pen name of Pseudo.

Censorship is an awful thing! (*Leaning forward to push back his cognac glass and vigorously stroking the glass top of the coffee table with his forefinger*) And a damned hardy plant once it takes root! The Ministry of Culture was the last to close up shop. I sent *Agostino* to them two months before the fall of Fascism, two months before the end. While all about them everything was toppling, falling to ruin, the Ministry of Popular Culture was doing business as usual. Approval looked not to be forthcoming; so one day I went up there, to Via Veneto—you know the place; they're still there, incidentally; I know them all—to see what the trouble was. They told me that they were afraid that they wouldn't be able to give approval to the book. My dossier was lying open on the desk, and when the secretary left the room for a moment I glanced at it. There was a letter from the Brazilian cultural attaché in it, some poet, informing the Minister that in Brazil I was considered a subversive. In Brazil of all places! But that letter, that alone, was enough to prevent the book's publication. Another time—it was for *Le Ambizioni sbagliate* [*The Wheel of Fortune*] —when I went up, I found the manuscript scattered all over the place, in several different offices, with a number of different people reading *parts* of it! Censorship is monstrous, a monstrous thing! I can tell you all you want to know about it.

They started out, however, rather liberal. With time they grew worse. Besides filling up the Ministry with timid grammar-school teachers, the censors were also either bureaucrats or failed writers; and heaven help you if your book fell into the hands of one of those "writers"!

INTERVIEWERS: And how is it for the writer today? You said the censors were "still there."

MORAVIA: The writer has nothing to fear. He can publish whatever he wishes. It's those in the cinema, and in the theater, who have it bad.

INTERVIEWERS: What about the Index?

MORAVIA: The Index isn't really censorship, at least not in Italy. The Vatican is one thing and Italy is another, two separate and distinct states. If it were to come to power in Italy, or if it were to gain the power that it has in Ireland or Spain, *then* it would be very serious.

INTERVIEWERS: One would have thought, however, by your protest when you were placed on the Index, that you regarded it as an abridgment of your freedom as a writer.

MORAVIA: No, it wasn't that. I was certainly upset, but mostly because I disliked the scandal.

INTERVIEWERS: Anyway, it must have increased your sales. I remember it was about then that Bompiani started bringing out your collected works in de-luxe editions.

MORAVIA: No, in Italy the Index doesn't affect one's sales one way or the other. I've always sold well, and there was no appreciable rise in sales after the Index affair.

INTERVIEWERS: You do not see the possibility of Italy's falling to a new totalitarian regime?

MORAVIA: There's the possibility, but a quite remote one. If we were to come under a new totalitarianism, writers, I now believe, would have no decent recourse but to give up writing altogether.

INTERVIEWERS: Incidentally, what do you think of the future of the novel?

MORAVIA: Well, the novel as we knew it in the nineteenth century was killed off by Proust and Joyce. They were the last of the nineteenth-century writers—great writers. It looks now as if we were going toward the *roman à idée* or toward the documentary novel—either the novel of ideas, or else the novel of life as it goes on, with no built-up characters, no psychology. It's also apparent that a good novel can be of any kind, but the two forms that are prevalent now are the essay-novel and the documentary novel or personal experience, *quelque chose qui arrive.* Life has taken two ways in our time: the crowd and the intellectuals. The day of the crowd is all accident; the day of the intellectual is all philosophy. There is no bourgeoisie now, only the crowd and the intellectuals.

INTERVIEWERS: What about "literature as scandal" that so concerns the French?

MORAVIA (*smiling*): Oh, it's going on thirty years now that they've been scandalizing one another.

INTERVIEWERS: And in your own work, do you see a new direction?

MORAVIA: I'll go on writing novels and short stories.

INTERVIEWERS: You do not foresee a time, then, when you will occupy your mornings otherwise.

MORAVIA: I do not foresee a time when I shall feel that I have nothing to say.

ANNA MARIA DE DOMINICIS
BEN JOHNSON

12. Nelson Algren

The Man with the Golden Arm received the National Book Award as the most distinguished American novel published in 1949. Nelson Algren's other books include three novels, *Somebody in Boots* (1935), *Never Come Morning* (1942), and *A Walk on the Wild Side* (1956); a volume of short stories called *The Neon Wilderness* (1948); and his impressions of a city, *Chicago: City on the Make* (1951). For most of his life he has lived in or near Chicago, which has provided the setting for much of his work.

Algren was born in 1909 in Detroit. After being graduated from the University of Illinois, he spent the depression years wandering through the American Southwest as a migratory worker. His first short story was based on letters written a friend from an abandoned Sinclair filling station just outside Rio Hondo. Entitled "So Help Me," it was sold to *Story Magazine* for twenty-five dollars.

Before the war Algren worked on a WPA Writer's Project, and also served as a worker on venereal-disease control for the Chicago Board of Health. After his discharge from the Army—where he served as a medical corpsman in Europe—he returned to Chicago's West Side and started work on *The Man with the Golden Arm*.

Algren lives at present in Gary, Indiana, outside Chicago, working in a bungalow—writing, as Budd Schulberg has described him, "like no one else in America today . . . from a brilliant, sordid, uncompromising, and twisted imagination."

The pimps alone didn't seem to ccatch on that the country was progressing downward to new rates of normality. They had been progressing
downward for some time without even knowing that ~~that they were~~
they were in style. Now of a sudden they discovered themselves with
more girls than beds to put them on. ~~~~
~~with scarcely Twenties a week or a month behind in their own~~ Scarcely-
Twenties looking for a Daddy, any old Daddy who'd tell them where to lie
down. ~~The~~ landlords and landladies passed them on to the cabbies and the
cabbies passed them on to the pimps. *It was then)* Between prostitution and Prohibition, *that*
finally
the ancient color line was breached.

Negro bellboys had gained a virtual monopoly on the delivery of illicit
either
alcohol and had found that white male guests ~~usually~~ wanted a woman with
the bottle or a bottle with the woman. The errand-boys' work evolved
into soliciting ~~for the white women, and as a solicitor the bellboy~~
~~claimed his natural privileges.~~ Immediately, he looked with scorn upon
ponce
his own women. Like the Negro ~~pimp~~ was harder on
people than was the
his own ~~~~ ~~the white~~ ~~~~-pander.
He saw now *He was*
~~but he the young Negro saw~~, at first hand, that what his ~~father~~
had told him, ~~in order to make a believer of him,~~ was not true after all;
never acted
that "good" white folks ~~didn't ever act like~~ bad black ones. For he *say's me*
with *do-right* *howling like*
and wanted the best ~~~~ names in town, the ~~big family~~ names, ~~the supporters~~
wolves in the Saturday stews *who panties on take*
~~of church and Prohibition itself~~ ~~~~ *in the Saturday night stews with*
bedpost, ~~out the~~ ~~panties on the floor,~~ *yet knew*
~~the pants on the bedpost and the bottles on the floor,~~ *back with his family,*
come Sunday ~~~~Do-Right Daddy would be ~~in his pew with his wife and~~
town. *mornings in the pew with best names in*
~~family in time for the Sunday morning service.~~
The Negro ~~began doing because~~ *He saw*
~~~~ the white woman ~~was~~ there and then. He
gave her the choice of moving over or being turned in to the law. The
solicitor
errand boy became an informer as well as ~~~~ times weren't
he felt,
as bad as the papers made out.

Bee W. Dabney

Nelson Algren

*The interview took place in a dark and untidy Greenwich Village
walk-up flat in the fall of 1955. A number of visitors dropped in
to listen to Algren. Word had spread that he was giving an interview, and in that quarter of the city Algren is highly respected.*

*He makes his living writing, has no set routine for working at it,
nor seriously feels the need of one; he finds that he works best, or
most frequently, at night, and he composes on the typewriter. He
strikes one as a man who feels and means just what he says, and
often says it in the same way he dresses—with a good-humored
nonchalance that is at once uniquely American and, in the latter-
day sense, quite un-American: his tie, if he ever wore one, would very
likely be as askew as his syntax often is. He is a man who betrays
no inclination whatsoever towards politeness, but he has a natural
generosity and compassion. To talk with Algren is to have a conversation brought very quickly to that rarefied level where values
are actually declared.*

INTERVIEWERS: Did you have any trouble getting *The Man with the Golden Arm* published?

ALGREN: No, no. Nothing was easier, because I got paid before I wrote it. It got a very lucky deal because they had an awful lot of money, the publishers did, during the war. Doubleday had a big backlog. I was working for Harper's—that is, I'd *done* one novel. Under the way they operate—well, it's a very literary house; I mean, they'd give you, oh, maybe a five-hundred-dollar advance and then you're on your own. And then if the book goes on two years—well, but I mean, *you* take the risk. They pay in literary prestige, they have an editor who once edited something by Thomas Wolfe or something; they figure that way. And I didn't see it, just didn't know what the score was, you see. So a guy from Doubleday came along, and I said what I wanted was enough to live on by the week for a year. And he said, "what do you call enough to live on?" and I said, "Fifty dollars," which seemed like a lot to me then—and he said, "Well, how about sixty dollars for *two* years?" He raised it himself, see; I mean, they were author-stealing, of course, and ah—well, I had a very bad contract at Harper's anyhow. So they gave me that sixty-a-week deal for two years, which was very generous then, and—I told them I was going to write a *war* novel. But it turned out to be this *Golden Arm* thing. I mean, the war kind of slipped away, and these people with the hypos came along—and that was it. But they had so much money it was fantastic. It's very hard to get out of the habit of thinking you're going to kill them if you ask for fifty a week.

INTERVIEWERS: Which of your books sold the most?

ALGREN: That was the only book that sold. The others never sold much except in paperbacks.

INTERVIEWERS: Do you think of *The Man with the Golden Arm* as being very autobiographical?

ALGREN: Oh, to some extent I drew on some people I knew in a half way. I made some people up and ah . . . the "Dealer" was . . . sort of a mixture; I got two, I dunno, two, three guys in mind. I know a couple guys around there. I knew *one* guy especially had a lot of those characteristics, but it's never clearly one person.

INTERVIEWERS: Well, anyway, you do think of some *one* person who could have started you thinking about Frankie Machine, since, apparently, you had at first planned an entirely different book.

ALGREN: The only connection I can make is . . . well, I was thinking about a war novel, and I had a buddy—little Italian bookie—pretty good dice-shooter, and he always used that phrase. We'd go partners—he's a *fairly* good crap-shooter—I mean, he's always good for about three passes. And then I'd say, "Pick it up, Joe, pick it up," and he'd say, "*Don't* worry, gotta golden arm." Then he'd come out with a crap. He never picked it up at all— but that's where I got that title. That was a guy I knew in the Army. It has no connection, it just happened to fit in later.

INTERVIEWERS: How do you think you arrived at it thematically —rather than a war novel?

ALGREN: Well, if you're going to write a war novel, you have to do it while you're *in* the war. If you don't do the thing while you're there—at least the way I operate—you can't do it. It slips away. Two months after the war it was gone; but I was living in a *living* situation, and . . . I find it pretty hard to write on any-thing in the past . . . and this thing just got more real; I mean, the neighborhood I was living in, and these people, were a lot more *real* than the Army was.

INTERVIEWERS: What was the neighborhood you were living in?

ALGREN: Near Division Street.

INTERVIEWERS: Was this one of those books that "wrote itself"?

ALGREN: No. No, it didn't write itself. But I didn't have to con-trive it. I mean, the situation hits you and you react to it, that's all.

INTERVIEWERS: Did it occur to you that this might be an un-usual treatment of tragedy, using a protagonist like Frankie Machine?

ALGREN: No, I didn't think of it that way at all. I didn't think of it essentially as a tragedy. I was just going along with that situation, and—well, I'd already *written* the book; I mean, I'd spent almost two years on the book before I ever ran into a drug addict. I wasn't acquainted with that situation at all. I had the book written about a *card-dealer*, but there wasn't any dope angle at all. It crossed my mind once or twice that that would be dramatic as hell, but I didn't know anything about it. I thought it would be better to lay off if you don't *know*, and I didn't see how you'd go about finding out about something like that deliberately, so I dropped it. Somehow I didn't fit it in. You see, I'd sent the book to the agent, and the agent said she liked it and all that, but it needed a *peg*, it didn't seem to be hung on anything. But it's real curious when I think of it now how obvious a thing is you don't see it. I mean, I was thinking about what to hang this book on, and I was hanging with these guys by that time. Well, one of these guys is a guy I know a long time—a guy done a lot of time, just a Polish guy used to drink a lot, that's all—and he said, "Let's go out for a beer," so we go down on Madison Street. And it was late, I remember it was about two in the morning and I wanted to get in—it was raining—and he said, "Well, I just live across the street," so we ducked, you know, through doors, up, around, up— and first thing I see this guy standing behind the curtain, I see his arm swinging, but I was so full of beer I didn't make anything too *clear* about it. It didn't dawn on me then, but it bothered me that somebody should be there swinging his arm up and down, you know, and somebody said, "Jack is having trouble," or something like that.

I was sort of bothered—I didn't quite know—and then a bunch of them come over, and I had a hell of a time putting that situation together. I didn't get it; they would come in and out with little cigar boxes under their arms, and a guy would say to me, "We're just having breakfast, would you like some breakfast?" and I'd say, "No, I guess I had breakfast." So he said, "You want to see how it's done?" I said, "Hell no, I don't want to see how it's done." I felt—well, I have an aversion to needles, anyway; I had it in the Army—but I felt, you know, if you want to do it, that's *your* business. I mean, if a guy goes into the can with a cigar box under his arm, I don't want no part of *that*, I don't *want* to see it.

Well, then I see that Jack is on junk, but he says with him it don't make any difference, he can knock it off any time, you know? Just happens to be one of these guys it don't get the better of. So I said, "Well, he's lucky, I guess he knows what he's doing." Well, I'd go over there. I'd stop and buy, you know, a few bottles of beer or something like that—I mean there was never anything to eat or drink in the joint. That bothered me—maybe one can of beans on the shelf—people that don't eat and don't drink. So I'd bring up half a dozen bottles of beer or something, and nobody'd want a beer. I didn't get it. There'd never be anything to eat, so I'd say, "Let's go down and get something to *eat*." So a girl comes down with me, and I was going to the butcher shop—get some meat and potatoes—she went to the bakery and got chocolate rolls, sweet rolls, rolls with sugar on them. I say, "Jesus, that's *desert*." I said, "What the hell, don't you people *eat*?" And she just says, "Got a sweet tooth."

Well, it got plain enough. Sometimes it made me mad—I always thought I was getting fooled, see. I mean, these guys would come on with, "Lemme have a—" you know, hit you for a few bucks, try you out, and I'd come up; I was a *fairly* good mark, not *too* good a mark. So this one guy says, "*You* know what I do. Sure I hit it a little for kicks, but when it starts getting the better of me, that's all." You know the kind of guy, just naturally strong. I mean, I believed him. Then his wife calls up: "Jack is sick." So I said, "Why don't you get a doctor?" And she said, "Well, he can't exactly get a doctor," and, "Why don't they come by and get you in a cab because he wants his own doctor"—or something. So two of these goofs come by in a cab and we go up north, in a hotel, out, got nine bucks, up and down, around a corner, ducking up and down, then back to Jack, and poor son of a bitch, he come out and he was bawling. This was the strong guy—he was crying and just pouring sweat. I guess he lost about fifteen pounds that day. He came out with a real sheepish look, like "Well, you know, it happens to everybody." So I felt a little contemptuous of him. Then these other people had come in, and I had different reactions with one or two of them, like this one guy I used in—well, he wasn't Frankie Machine, but when I think of him I think of this guy. He had a pushed-in kind of mug. I felt much more sympathetic toward him because—see, Jack was on it, but he was *for* it, too; I mean, he really wanted it to be that way—but this guy was on it, but he didn't want to be. He was against it. There was a girl there, too, who was like that, never should've been on it. So the swindle got faster and faster. I had an ideal place for them to come up and fix, so I didn't think anything of it. They'd just come up and fix, and that was it. I got along with them pretty good—but it took me a remarkably long time to make any connection between that and the book. I didn't want to go over to their place because it took time from the book; I felt I shouldn't have been goofing off like that. But I enjoyed going over there. We'd sit around and they'd always have music; they didn't always go right for the needle, you know, a lot of times they didn't have it. Then I began to feel very dimly that maybe there was something there usable. I thought about it very—timidly, and finally I said to the agent, "You think that, uh—do you think it's too sensational?" She said, "No, use it." She insisted that I use it, so I hung it on there; I hung it on there without really knowing a great deal about it. It was an afterthought. I got the mood of the thing, but I didn't have much time to, you know, do it thoroughly. I know a little bit more about it now, but what I learned, I learned after the book came out.

INTERVIEWERS: Did you ever feel that you should try heroin, in connection with writing a book about users?

ALGREN: No. No, I think you can do a thing like that best from a detached position.

INTERVIEWERS: Were you ever put down by any of these people as an eavesdropper?

ALGREN: No, they were mostly amused by it. Oh, they thought

it was a pretty funny way to make a living, but—well, one time, after the book came out, I was sitting in this place, and there were a couple of junkies sitting there, and this one guy was real *proud* of the book; he was trying to get this other guy to read it, and finally the other guy said he had *read* it, but he said, "You know it ain't so, it ain't like that." There's a part in the book where this guy takes a shot, and then he's talking for about four pages. This guy says, "You know it ain't like that, a guy takes a fix and he goes on the nod, I mean, you know that." And the other guy says, "Well, on the other hand, if he *really* knew what he was talking about, he couldn't write the book, he'd be out in the can." So the other guy says, "Well, if you mean, is it all right for squares, sure, it's all right for squares." So, I mean, you have to compromise. But the book was somehow incidental to my relationship with them, inasmuch as they always had some hassle going on, and—well, this needle thing wasn't always up front, you know. I mean, these were people you just went to hear a band with. It was only now and then it'd come to you—like it might suddenly occur to you that one of your friends is crippled or something—it would come to you that the guy's on stuff. But it didn't stay with you very much.

INTERVIEWERS: Were you conscious of having a model for Zosh?

ALGREN: No, no, I think that was kind of an invented thing. One of those things you pick up in the papers—sometimes there's a story about a woman chasing the old man around with a mattress-board all night—that sort of thing. I get a lot of things from the papers.

INTERVIEWERS: Do you ever plot a thing out mechanically?

ALGREN: I did it with this last book, *A Walk on the Wild Side*, but that was the first time I tried it. Up to now, I'd just go along with the story and then sort of prop it up—plots that don't really stand up, but now in this last one . . . Whether the book itself stands up as a literary thing I don't know—but I *was* surprised when I went through it that I'd contrived better because the plot dovetailed and that was the first time I was able to do that. This

Golden Arm thing is really very creaky as far as plot goes, it's more
of a cowboy-and-Indian thing, a cops-and-robbers thing.

INTERVIEWERS: Do you write in drafts?

ALGREN: Yes, but each draft gets a little longer. I don't try to
write the whole thing in one draft.

INTERVIEWERS: How much do you usually write before you begin
to rewrite?

ALGREN: Very little, I dunno, maybe five pages. I've always
figured the only way I could finish a book and get a plot was just
to keep making it longer and longer until something happens—you
know, until it finds its own plot—because you can't outline and
then fit the thing into it. I suppose it's a slow way of working.

INTERVIEWERS: Do you think of any particular writers as having
influenced your style, or approach?

ALGREN: Well, I used to like Stephen Crane a lot and, it goes
without saying, Dostoevski—that's the only Russian I've ever reread. No, that ain't all, there's Kuprin.

INTERVIEWERS: How about American writers?

ALGREN: Well, Hemingway is pretty hard not to write like.

INTERVIEWERS: Do you think you write like that?

ALGREN: No, but you get the feeling from it—the feeling of
economy.

INTERVIEWERS: How about Farrell?

ALGREN: Well, I don't feel he's a good writer. Since *Studs Loni-
gan*, I don't know of anything of his that's new or fresh or well
written. Frankly, I just don't see him. I *missed* Farrell, let's put
it that way.

INTERVIEWERS: Some of the reviews have linked you and Farrell.

ALGREN: I don't think he's a writer, really. He's too journalistic
for my taste. I don't get anything besides a social study, and not
always well told, either. He has the same lack that much lesser-
known writers have. He hits me the same way as, say . . . a guy
like Hal Ellson. Do you know him? Well, he's a New York writer
who does this gang stuff. He's written some very good books, but
they're just straight case studies, you know what I mean?

INTERVIEWERS: How about Horace McCoy?

ALGREN: No, no. I didn't mean to put Farrell down there. No, Farrell, I think, is a real earnest guy—but I mention this Ellson because Ellson does the same thing. But, I mean, there's something awfully big left out. It isn't enough to do just a case study, something stenographic. Farrell is stenographic, and he isn't even a real good stenographer. He's too sloppy. In his essays he compares himself with Dreiser, but I don't think he's in Dreiser's league. He's as *bad* a writer as Dreiser—but he doesn't have the compassion that makes Dreiser's bad writing important.

INTERVIEWERS: Do you have a feeling of camaraderie, or solidarity, with any contemporary writers?

ALGREN: No, I couldn't say so. I don't know many writers.

INTERVIEWERS: How do you avoid it?

ALGREN: Well, I dunno, but I do have the feeling that other writers can't help you with writing. I've gone to writers' conferences and writers' sessions and writers' clinics, and the more I see of them, the more I'm sure it's the wrong direction. It isn't the place where you learn to write. I've always felt strongly that a writer shouldn't be engaged with other writers, or with people who make books, or even with people who read them. I think the farther away you get from the literary traffic, the closer you are to sources. I mean, a writer doesn't really *live*, he observes.

INTERVIEWERS: Didn't Simone de Beauvoir dedicate a book to you?

ALGREN: Yeah, I showed her around Chicago. I showed her the electric chair and everything.

INTERVIEWERS: Do you vote? Locally, there around Gary?

ALGREN: No. No, I don't.

INTERVIEWERS: Still you do frequently get involved in these issues, like the Rosenbergs, and so on.

ALGREN: Yes, that's true.

INTERVIEWERS: What do your publishers think of that?

ALGREN: Well, they don't exactly give me any medals for caution.

INTERVIEWERS: Do you think there's been any sort of tradition of isolation of the writer in America, as compared to Europe?

ALGREN: We don't have any tradition at *all* that I know of. I don't think the isolation of the American writer is a tradition; it's more that geographically he just *is* isolated, unless he happens to live in New York City. But I don't suppose there's a small town around the country that doesn't have a writer. The thing is that here you get to be a writer differently. I mean, a writer like Sartre *decides*, like any professional man, when he's fifteen, sixteen years old, that instead of being a doctor he's going to be a writer. And he absorbs the French tradition and proceeds from there. Well, here you get to be a writer when there's absolutely nothing else you can do. I mean, I don't know of any writers here who just started out to be writers, and then became writers. They just happen to fall into it.

INTERVIEWERS: How did you fall into it?

ALGREN: Well, I fell into it when I got out of a school of journalism in '31 in the middle of the depression. I had a little card that entitled me to a job because I'd gone to this school of journalism, you see. I was just supposed to present this card to the editor. I didn't know whether I wanted to be a sports columnist, a foreign correspondent, or what; I was willing to take what was open. Only, of course, it wasn't. Things were pretty tight. Small towns would send you to big cities, and big cities would send you to small towns; it was a big hitchhiking time, so I wound up in New Orleans selling coffee—one of these door-to-door deals —and one of the guys on this crew said we ought to get out of there because he had a packing shed in the Rio Grande Valley. So we bummed down to the Rio Grande. Well, he didn't have a packing shed, he *knew* somebody who had one—one of those things, you know—but what he did do, he promoted a Sinclair gasoline station down there. It was a farce, of course, it was an abandoned station in the middle of nowhere; I mean, there was no chance of selling gas or anything like that, but I suppose it looked good for the Sinclair agent to write up to Dallas and say he had a couple guys rehabilitating the place. There was nothing to the station, it didn't even have any windows. But we had to dig pits for the gas, and then one day the Sinclair guy comes up with a hundred gallons of gas and wanted somebody to take legal responsibility for it. So my partner hands me the pencil and says, "Well, you can write better than I can, you been to school," and I was sort of proud of that, so I signed for it.

Then my partner had the idea that I should stay there and take care of the station, just keep up a front, you know, in case the Sinclair guy came around, and he'd go out—he had an old Studebaker—and buy up produce from the Mexican farmers very cheap, and bring it back and we'd sell it at the station—turn the station into a produce stand. I mean, we were so far out on this highway that the agent couldn't really check on us—we were way out; there were deer and wild hogs and everything out there—and in three weeks we'd be rich. That was *his* idea. But the only thing he brought back was black-eyed peas. He paid about two dollars for a load of black-eyed peas—well, that was like buying a load of cactus—but he wouldn't admit he'd make a mistake. So, he went around to the big Piggly-Wiggly store and they said they'd take *some* of the peas if they were shelled. So he set me to shelling the peas. I shelled those damn peas till I was nearly blind. In the meantime, he'd left town, out to promote something else.

Then one day he showed up with another guy, in a much better-looking car—he'd left the old Studebaker there at the station—and I saw them out there by the pit fooling around with some sort of contraption, but it didn't dawn on me, and then it turned out they were siphoning the gas into this guy's car. Well, they left town before I knew what was happening. When I caught on I was being swindled, of course, I was very indignant about it, and I wrote letters that took in the whole South. I gave the whole Confederacy hell. Oh, it was nowhere, just nowhere, nowhere. So I wrote a couple letters like that—and I was very serious at the time, and some of that got into the letters. Ultimately, I got out of there. I poured a lot of water into the empty tank, but I felt like a fugitive because I didn't account to the Sinclair guy. It was a terrible farce, but later when I got home—I don't know how much later—I read the letters again, and there was a story in them, all right. So I rewrote it and *Story Magazine* published it, and I was off. But that's what I mean by "falling into it." Because I was really trying to become a big oil man.

INTERVIEWERS: Have you consciously tried to develop a style?

ALGREN: Well, I haven't consciously tried to develop it. The only thing I've consciously tried to do was put myself in a position to hear the people I wanted to hear talk talk. I used the police line-up for I don't know how many years. But that was accidental too, like that junky deal—you don't exactly seek it out, you're there and it dawns on you. I got a newspaper man to loan me his card, but that was only good for one night. But then I finally got rolled. I didn't get myself deliberately rolled; I was just over on the South Side and got rolled. But they gave me a card, you know, to look for the guys in the line-up, and I used that card for something like seven years. They finally stopped me—the card got ragged as hell, pasted here and there, you couldn't read it— the detective at the door stopped me and said, "What happened, you mean you're still looking for the guy?" This was like seven years later, and I said, "Hell yes, I lost fourteen dollars," so he let me go ahead.

INTERVIEWERS: Do you think, then, that you're more interested in idiom, than in idea? And isn't that generally characteristic of American writers?

ALGREN: That's cutting it pretty close, all right. I think of a tragic example: Dick Wright. I think he made . . . a very bad mistake. I mean, he writes out of passion, out of his belly; but he won't admit this, you see. He's trying to write as an intellectual, which he isn't basically; but he's trying his best to write like a Frenchman. Of course, it isn't strictly an American-European distinction, the belly and the head; you find the same distinction here. A book like Ralph Ellison's, for example, or Peter Matthiessen's, stays better with me than the opposite thing, a book like Saul Bellow's. Bellow's is a book done with great skill and great control, but there isn't much fire. I depend more on the stomach. I always think of writing as a *physical* thing. I'm not trying to generalize, it just happens to be that way with me.

INTERVIEWERS: Can you relate *The Man with the Golden Arm* to an idea?

ALGREN: No, unless a feeling can be an idea. I just had an over-all *feeling*, I didn't have any particular theory about what I ought to do. Living in a very dense area, you're conscious of how the people underneath live, and you have a certain feeling toward them—so much so that you'd rather live among them than with the business classes. In a historical sense, it might be related to an idea, but you write out of—well, I wouldn't call it indignation, but a kind of *irritability* that these people on top should be so contented, so absolutely unaware of these other people, and so sure that their values are the right ones. I mean, there's a certain satisfaction in recording the people underneath, whose values are as sound as theirs, and a lot funnier, and a lot truer in a way. There's a certain over-all satisfaction in kind of scooping up a shovelful of these people and dumping them in somebody's parlor.

INTERVIEWERS: Were you trying to dramatize a social problem?

ALGREN: Well, there's always something wrong in any society. I think it would be a mistake to aim at any solution, you know; I mean, the most you can do is—well, if any writer can catch the *routine lives* of people just *living* in that kind of ring of fire to show how you can't go out of a certain neighborhood if you're addicted, or for other reasons, that you can't be legitimate, but that within the limitation you can succeed in making a life that is routine—with human values that seem to be a little more real, a little more intense, and human, than with people who are freer to come and go—if somebody could write a book about the routine of these circumscribed people, just their everyday life, without any big scenes, without any violence, or cops breaking in, and so on, just day-to-day life—like maybe the woman is hustling and makes a few bucks, and they get a little H just to keep from getting sick, and go to bed, and get up—just an absolutely prosaic life without any particular drama to it in their eyes—if you could just do that straight, without anybody getting arrested—there's always a little danger of that, of course—but to have it just the way these thousands of people live, very quiet, commonplace routine . . . well, you'd have an awfully good book.

INTERVIEWERS: On the point of style again, you seem to favor phrases, almost more than sentences.

ALGREN: I always thought my sentences were pretty good. But I do depend on phrases quite a bit.

INTERVIEWERS: Do you try to write a poetic prose?

ALGREN: No. No, I'm not writing it, but so many people say things poetically, they say it for you in a way you never could. Some guy just coming out of jail might say, "I did it from bell to bell," or like the seventeen-year-old junkie, when the judge asked him what he did all day, he said, "Well, I find myself a doorway to lean against, and I take a fix, and then I lean, I just lean and dream." They always say things like that.

INTERVIEWERS: What do you think of Faulkner?

ALGREN: Well, I can get lost in him awful easy. But he's powerful.

INTERVIEWERS: It's interesting that Hemingway once said that Faulkner and you were the two best writers in America.

ALGREN: Yeah, I remember when he said that. He said, "After Faulkner . . ." I was very hurt.

INTERVIEWERS: You said that the plot of *The Man with the Golden Arm* was "creaky." How much emphasis are you going to put on plot in your future writing?

ALGREN: Well, you have to prop the book up somehow. You've got to frame it, or otherwise it becomes just a series of episodes.

INTERVIEWERS: You gave more attention to plot in this book you've just finished.

ALGREN: This one I plotted a great deal more than any other. In the first place because it's more of a contrived book. I'm trying to write a reader's book, more than my own book. When you're writing your own book, you don't have to plot; it's just when you write for the reader. And since I'm dealing with the past, the thirties, I have to contrive, whereas, with a living situation, I wouldn't have to.

INTERVIEWERS: Do you think that this one came off as well as *The Man with the Golden Arm?*

ALGREN: Mechanically and, I think, technically, it's done more carefully, and probably reads better than previous books.

INTERVIEWERS: You make this distinction between a "reader's book" and a book for yourself. What do you think the difference is?

ALGREN: It's the difference between writing by yourself and writing on a stage. I mean, if the book were your own, you'd be satisfied just to have the guy walk down the sidewalk and fall on his head. In a reader's book, you'd have him turn a double somersault. You're more inclined to clown, I think, in a reader's book. You've got one ear to the audience for yaks. It's just an obligation you have to fulfill.

INTERVIEWERS: Obligation to whom?

ALGREN: Well, you're talking economics now. I mean, the way I've operated with publishers is that I live on the future. I take as much money as I can get for as long as I can get it, you know, a year or two years, and by the end of that time your credit begins to have holes in it, and—well, you have to come up. After all, they're businessmen. Of course, you can get diverted from a book you *want* to write. I've got a book about Chicago on the West Side—I did a hundred pages in a year, and I still figure I need three years on it—but I was under contract for this other one, so it took precedence. I didn't want to contract for the first one, because I just wanted to go along as far as I could on it without having any pressure on me. The one I contracted for is the one I finished, and now I'm going back to the one I want to do.

INTERVIEWERS: Did you enjoy writing *The Man with the Golden Arm* more than you did this last one?

ALGREN: Well, it seemed more important. I wouldn't say I en-

joyed it more, because in a way this was a much easier book to do.
The lumber is all cut for you. The timber and the dimensions are
all there, you know you're going to write a four-hundred-page
book; and in that way your problems are solved, you're limited.
Whereas, with a book like that *Man with the Golden Arm*, you
cut your own timber, and you don't know where you're building,
you don't have any plan or anything.

INTERVIEWERS: Do you find that you take more care with a
thing like that?

ALGREN: No, I always take great care. I think I'm very careful,
maybe too careful. You can get too fussy. I do find myself getting
bogged down wondering whether I should use a colon or a semi-
colon, and so on, and I keep trying each one out. I guess you can
overdo that.

INTERVIEWERS: Do you think that writing a book out of economic obligation could affect your other work?

ALGREN: No, it won't have anything to do with that at all. One
is a matter of *living* and reacting from day to day, whereas the
book I just finished could be written anywhere there's a typewriter.

INTERVIEWERS: Do you think your writing improves?

ALGREN: I think technically it does. I reread my first book, and
found it—oh, you know, "poetic," in the worst sense.

INTERVIEWERS: Do you feel that any critics have influenced
your work?

ALGREN: None could have, because I don't read them. I doubt
anyone does, except other critics. It seems like a sealed-off field
with its own lieutenants, pretty much preoccupied with its own
intrigues. I got a glimpse into the uses of a certain kind of
criticism this past summer at a writers' conference—into how the
avocation of assessing the failures of better men can be turned
into a comfortable livelihood, providing you back it up with a
Ph.D. I saw how it was possible to gain a chair of literature on no
qualification other than persistence in nipping the heels of Hemingway, Faulkner, and Steinbeck. I know, of course, that there

are true critics, one or two. For the rest all I can say is, "Deal around me."

INTERVIEWERS: How about this movie, *The Man with the Golden Arm?*

ALGREN: Yeah.

INTERVIEWERS: Did you have anything to do with the script?

ALGREN: No. No, I didn't last long. I went out there for a thousand a week, and I worked Monday, and I got fired Wednesday. The guy that hired me was out of town Tuesday.

ALSTON ANDERSON
TERRY SOUTHERN

13. Angus Wilson

Angus Wilson was born at Bexhill, in Sussex, on August 11, 1913. After attending Westminster School, he studied medieval history at Merton College, Oxford. His academic career was followed by a succession of employments which included tutoring, secretarial work, catering, social organizing, and running a restaurant. In 1937 he took a post with the British Museum, and after spending the war years employed at the Foreign Office, he returned to the position of deputy superintendent of the Reading Room. Late in the war he had suffered a nervous breakdown and, as a therapeutic measure, had begun to write short stories. It was a practice he continued after the war on week ends from his Museum work. In 1949 the stories were published in a volume called *The Wrong Set*. The collection attracted immediate attention for its savage characterizations of the contemporary world—marked by Wilson's mockery of hypocrisy and sham. A second collection, *Such Darling Dodos*, followed in 1950. In 1952, with the appearance of his first novel, *Hemlock and After*, Wilson's reputation was established as one of the most promising of postwar British novelists.

Wilson's second novel, *Anglo-Saxon Attitudes*, was published in 1956. Cyril Connolly reported in London's *Sunday Times* that it was a novel "such as we have not seen since Huxley's *Point Counter Point*." It was as well received in the United States. Charles Rolo of the *Atlantic Monthly* was moved to describe the author as a ". . . writer with unusual resources of wit and intelligence—a writer, moreover, who is virtually incapable of producing a dull page."

Wilson's works also include an examination of Zola's novels (*Emile Zola*, 1952), a satiric insight into the twenties entitled *For Whom the Cloche Tolls* (1954), and a third volume of short stories—*A Bit off the Map* (1957).

Wilson resigned from his Museum post in 1955. He divides his time between London and a Suffolk cottage, where his hobby is gardening.

Something about Kennie's symbiotic obsession must
fit the pattern of Colonel L's delusion. Huggett simply
points the way by his dismissal of human activity.
Tristram gives the outside view. Clara is an
educated counterpose to Kennie.

Kennie has combined delusions of grandeur, knowingness,
utter self contempt & almost feeblemindedness.

Huggett has delusions of grandeur coupled with a very
salty cynicism.

Colonel L. has delusions of grandeur & behind all is a
complete blank. Otherwise he has only the surface of
his old manners.

Reg talks like this to K.
"My Myshkin, my divine idiot — only you mustn't
come the creeping Jesus, you know. You must have the
perverseness of Stavrogin and the cunning of Lebedeyev".
Huggett is a clerk in a travel bureau. But Huggett shuts
him up.

Huggett — "Reg is under the
impression that he has a mission to reincarnate the
all too mouldering flesh of D. H. Lawrence. What
Lawrence said was largely dotto, in Reg's mouth
it becomes so many scrabbobbles, so go and blow your bubbles
elsewhere, little boy".

---

*A page from Angus Wilson's working notebook. The notes refer to characters
in his story "A Bit Off the Map"*

Rosalie Seidler

Angus Wilson

A London apartment in Dolphin Square, just downriver from Chelsea. Dolphin Square—and this came as something of a surprise—is a huge block of service apartments, with restaurant (where we ate lunch), indoor swimming pool, shops, bars, etc.— the layout and décor of this part strongly reminiscent of an ocean liner. The apartment itself, on the ground floor and looking out on the central court, was small, comfortable, tidy, uneccentric; there were books but not great heaps of them; the pictures included a pair of patriotic prints from the First World War ("The period fascinates me"). For Wilson it is just a place to stay when he has to be in London: his real home is a cottage in Suffolk, five miles from the nearest village ("I find I hate cities more and more. I used to need people, but now I can be much more alone"). The electric fire was on, although the late September day was fine and quite mild. Wilson explained that he had just got back from

*Asia—Japan (where he had been a guest of honor at the P.E.N.
Conference), the Philippines, Cambodia, Thailand—and found
England cold.*

*Although one does not think of Wilson as a small man, he is
rather below the average height. His face is mobile but somewhat
plumper than in most of the published photographs, the hair
white at the front shading to gray at the back, the forehead lined,
the eyebrows rather prominent, the eyes pale gray and serious—
but not solemn: Wilson's manner has a liveliness and warmth
that is immediately engaging. He talks quickly, confidently yet
unaffectedly, eagerly—obviously enjoying it. The conversation before and during lunch was mainly about Japan—it had been his
first visit to Asia and he had clearly been impressed—and about
other writers. Now, after lunch, Wilson agrees to talk about himself.*

INTERVIEWER: When did you start writing?

WILSON: I never wrote anything—except for the school magazine—until November 1946. Then I wrote a short story one week
end—"Raspberry Jam"—and followed that up by writing a short
story every week end for twelve weeks. I was then thirty-three. My
writing started as a hobby: that seems a funny word to use—but,
yes, hobby. During the war, when I was working at the Foreign
Office, I had a bad nervous breakdown, and after the war I decided
that simply to return to my job at the British Museum would be
too depressing. Writing seemed a good way of diversifying my
time. I was living in the country and commuting to London then
and I could only do it at week ends. That's why I started with
short stories: this was something I could finish, realize completely,
in a week end.

INTERVIEWER: Had you never thought of becoming a writer before that time?

WILSON: No, I never had any intention of becoming a writer.
I'd always thought that far too many things were written, and
working in the Museum convinced me of it. But I showed some

of my stories to Robin Ironside, the painter, and he asked if he could show them to Cyril Connolly, who took two for *Horizon*. Then a friend of mine at Secker and Warburg said, "Let us have a look at them," and they said that if I gave them twelve stories they would publish them. This was *The Wrong Set*. They told me there wasn't much sale for short stories and so on, but the book was surprisingly successful both here and in America. After that I went on writing—reviews, broadcasts, more short stories. The thing grew and grew, and when I came to write *Hemlock and After* I had to do it in one of my leaves. I did it in four weeks. But when I wanted to write a play—that was a different matter. I knew it would take longer to write and that I'd have to revise it, attend rehearsals, and so on. And I was still a full-time civil servant at the British Museum. To resolve the conflict I resigned. It was rather ironic really. When I left school I wanted a permanent job, and I got it at the Museum. Now at the age of forty-two I no longer wanted a permanent job. It meant giving up my pension, and that isn't easy at that age. But so far I haven't regretted it.

INTERVIEWER: Do you find writing comes easily to you?

WILSON: Yes. I write very easily. I told you *Hemlock* took four weeks. *Anglo-Saxon Attitudes* took four months, and an awful lot of that time was taken up just with thinking. The play—*The Mulberry Bush*, the only thing I've rewritten several times—was different again. My latest book of short stories, *A Bit off the Map*, took longer too, and my new novel is proving a bit difficult. But I'm not unduly worrried. When one starts writing it's natural for the stuff to come rolling off the stocks—is that the right image?— rather easily. And, of course, the fact that it comes harder doesn't necessarily mean that it's worse. When Dickens published his novels in serial form he always added in his letter to the reader: "I send you this labor of love." After *Bleak House* he couldn't; it hadn't been a labor of love. But the later Dickens novels are certainly none the worse for that.

INTERVIEWER: Do you work every day?

WILSON: Goodness, no. I did that when I was a civil servant and I don't propose to do so now. But when I'm writing a book I do work every day.

INTERVIEWER: To a schedule?

WILSON: Not really. No. I usually work from eight to two, but if it's going well I may go on to four. Only if I do I'm extremely exhausted. In fact, when the book is going well the only thing that stops me is sheer exhaustion. I wouldn't like to do what Elizabeth Bowen once told me she did—write *something* every day, whether I was working on a book or not.

INTERVIEWER: Do you usually work on one book at a time?

WILSON: Oh, yes. I've never worked on more than one book at a time, and I don't think it would be good.

INTERVIEWER: About how many words a day do you write?

WILSON: Oh—between one and two thousand. Sometimes more. But the average would be one or two thousand.

INTERVIEWER: Longhand, typewriter, or dictation?

WILSON: Longhand. I can't type. And I'm sure it wouldn't work for me to dictate, though I did think of it when I was doing the play; it might help with the dialogue. But the trouble is I'm too histrionic a person anyway, and even when I'm writing a novel I act out the scenes.

INTERVIEWER: Aloud?

WILSON: Very often. Especially dialogue.

INTERVIEWER: Do you make notes?

WILSON: Books of them. The gestatory period before I start to write is very important to me. That's when I'm persuading myself of the truth of what I want to say, and I don't think I could persuade my readers unless I'd persuaded myself first.

INTERVIEWER: What sort of notes?

WILSON: Oh, notes about the ages of the characters, where they live, little maps, facts about their lives before the book starts. Names are very important to me, too. Look at these notes for *The Mulberry Bush*, for example. There are statements of themes, like this: "James and Rose are the core of the tradition." And questions—I'm always asking myself questions—like "What are Kurt's motives here?" I set myself problems and try to find ways out of them. Then the thing begins to take shape—this note, for example: "The first act ends in row between Ann and Simon." Then comes the first version of the first act. It's the same with the novels: I write notes like "But this isn't what the book is really about. What it *is* about is . . . ," and so on.

INTERVIEWER: Why do you feel the need for so many notes?

WILSON: Two reasons. To convince myself, as I said before. And to keep a kind of check on myself. Once one starts writing, the histrionic gifts—the divine passion or whatnot—are liable to take control and sweep you away. It's a matter of setting things on their right course. Then it's much easier to write as the spirit moves.

INTERVIEWER: Do you do careful or rapid first drafts?

WILSON: Oh, I only do one draft. I never do any other. I correct as I go along. And there is very little correction; the changes in the draft are mainly deletions. Occasionally a new paragraph goes in. Take the end of *Hemlock*, for example. It's rather a Dickens ending, accounting for all the characters. At the end I found Ron's mother, Mrs. Wrigley, wasn't accounted for, so I put in the paragraph about her. It's rather like Dickens at the end of *Dombey and Son*. After he'd sent the manuscript to his publishers he sent them a note: "Please put in a paragraph about Diogenes the dog: something on these lines. . . ." I like to have everyone accounted for, too.

INTERVIEWER: What is the difference for you between a short story and a novel?

WILSON: Short stories and plays go together in my mind. You take a point in time and develop it from there; there is no room for development backwards. In a novel I also take a point in time, but feel every room for development backwards. All fiction for me is a kind of magic and trickery—a confidence trick, trying to make people believe something is true that isn't. And the novelist, in particular, is trying to convince the reader that he is seeing society as a whole.

This is why I use such a lot of minor characters and subplots, of course. It isn't willful love of subplots for their own sake, willful Victorianism, but because they enable me to suggest the existence of a wider society, the ripples of a society outside. And more important is this thing about fiction as trickery. The natural habit of any good and critical reader is to disbelieve what you are telling him and try to escape out of the world you are picturing. Some novelists try to make the magic work by taking you deep down inside one person. I try to multiply the worlds I put into the books—so that, like the ripples of the stone thrown into the brook, you feel the repercussions going farther and farther out, and at the same time bringing more in. The reader is more inclined to believe in Gerald and Ingeborg because someone so different as Mrs. Salad is affected by them. I've always thought this had something to do with the endings of Shakespeare's tragedies. An entirely new lot of people come in—Fortinbras in *Hamlet*, for example, and it's the same with *Macbeth* and *Lear*. You believe in the tragedies more because these others from outside confirm them. The worst kind of nightmare is the one where you dream you've woken up and it's still going on. The third reason for all the characters is the Proustian one, which seems to me very good, that the strangest and most unlikely lives are in fact interdependent. This is especially true in times like our own when the old boundaries and demarcations are becoming blurred.

INTERVIEWER: What about short stories?

WILSON: You can't do this sort of thing with short stories. They have a kind of immediate ethical text. Many of mine have punning titles. I take a platitude—"the wrong set," for example: the point is that no one knows what the wrong set is, and one person's wrong set is another's right set. And you get the pay-off, which is something I like. A play is rather like this, but has more depth. And plays and short stories are similar in that both start when all but the action has finished.

INTERVIEWER: I think you've seen what Frank O'Connor said about *Anglo-Saxon Attitudes* when he was interviewed for this series. He criticizes your "exploitation of every known form of technique in the modern novel"—techniques taken, he says, from the cinema and from *Point Counter Point*—and the whole modern tendency to concentrate the action of a novel around the actual moment of crisis instead of covering a longer period and "demonstrating the hero in all his phases." *Anglo-Saxon Attitudes*, he says, "would have been a good novel if it had begun twenty years earlier." I'm sure you will have something to say to this.

WILSON: Yes, indeed. I thought his remarks very curious. He implies that I'm in the twentieth-century experimental tradition. It's very flattering, of course—"every known form of technique in the modern novel"—but I wasn't aware of using any techniques, except that the book was concerned with echoes of memory. I think the reader should be unaware of techniques, though it's the critic's job to see them, of course. O'Connor seems not to have noticed that the techniques used in *Anglo-Saxon Attitudes* are not just flashbacks as in the cinema, nor just episodic as in *Point Counter Point*—I've recently reread that and can see no shape in it at all. If you examine the flashbacks in *Anglo-Saxon Attitudes*— and they took me a lot of trouble, I may say—you'll see that it is an ironic picking up of phrases. Marie Hélène says, "Life consists, I believe, in accepting one's duty, and that means often to accept the second best." This leads Gerald to remember his courtship of Ingeborg: he accepted the second best then, and it has ruined both his life and hers. This is an ironic comment on the cynical realism of Marie Hélène. It's not just cinema, you see, it's very carefully planned, though I say it myself.

INTERVIEWER: What about O'Connor's remark that it should have started twenty years earlier?

WILSON: If it had started twenty years earlier it would have been a simply enormous book—a kind of chronicle novel, I suppose: *The Story of a Disappointed Man*. Where O'Connor goes wrong is in thinking that I'm concerned at all with the hero as such. I'm only concerned with the hero as an illustration of the inevitability of decline if life is denied. After all, there's a definite statement in the book: Gerald's life goes wrong in two ways—with the historical fraud, and with his wife and children. And when he tries to "face the truth"—in the conventional phrase—he can do this in relation to the fraud all right, but he can't remake his life with his wife and children. This shows up the platitude of "facing the truth." Gerald is only freed in that he faces the *result* of his *not* having faced the truth—he accepts his loneliness. A matter of theoretical morality can be put right, but this can't be done where human beings are involved.

INTERVIEWER: Other people besides O'Connor have commented on certain technical similarities between your work and Huxley's. I gather you don't feel you owe him any particular debt?

WILSON: Consciously, of course, I'm in great reaction against Huxley—and against Virginia Woolf. But I read them a great deal when young, and what you read in adolescence can go very deep. I've been much more influenced by Dickens, Proust, Zola. And the ceremony in *Hemlock* is obviously influenced by that scene in *The Possessed* where the poet, who is Turgenev, comes in and makes a fool of himself. Zola has certainly influenced me a great deal in the form and shape of my novels. From Proust I get the feeling about paradox and the truth of improbability—especially the latter.

INTERVIEWER: Are your characters based on observation?

WILSON: Oh, yes. I don't see how else you can do it. But not taken from life. Every character is a mixture of people you've known. Characters come to me—and I think this is behind the Madeleine business in Proust—when people are talking to me. I feel I have heard this, this tone of voice, in other circumstances. And, at the risk of seeming rude, I have to hold on to this and chase it back until it clicks with someone I've met before. The second secretary at the embassy in Bangkok may remind me of the chemistry assistant at Oxford. And I ask myself, what have they in common? Out of such mixtures I can create characters. All my life I've always known a lot of people. Some say my novels are narrow, but I really can't see what they mean. I thought they were pretty wide myself.

INTERVIEWER: Some people think you have an unnecessarily large number of vicious characters.

WILSON: I really don't know why people find my characters unpleasant. I believe—perhaps it would be different if I were religious—that life is very difficult for most people and that most people make a fair job of it. The opportunities for heroism are limited in this kind of world: the most people can do is sometimes not to be as weak as they've been at other times. When Evelyn Waugh reviewed *Hemlock and After* he was very percipient about techniques, but described the characters as "young cad," "mother's darling," and so on—terms it would never occur to me to use. I told him I thought the people he described in those terms had behaved rather well. Terence—the "young cad"—is on the make, certainly, but he behaves rather well in spite of that. And Eric does half break away from his mother—which is quite an achievement in the circumstances.

Of course, all my characters are very self-conscious, aware of what they are doing and what they are like. There's heroism in going on at all while knowing how we are made. Simple, naïve people I'm impatient of, because they haven't faced up to the main responsibility of civilized man—that of facing up to what he is and to the Freudian motivations of his actions. Most of my characters have a Calvinist conscience, and this is something which in itself makes action difficult. The heroism of my people, again, is in their success in making a relationship with other human beings, in a humanistic way, and their willingness to accept some sort of pleasure principle in life as against the gnawings of a Calvinist conscience and the awareness of Freudian motivations. These people are fully self-conscious, and the only ones who are at all evil—apart from Mrs. Curry, who is something quite different, a kind of embodiment of evil—are those like Marie Hélène and Ingeborg who substitute for self-awareness and self-criticism a simple way of living, Marie Hélène's hard and practical, Ingeborg's soft and cosy. They accept a *pattern* of behavior and morality instead of self-awareness. Characters can be heroic even though they can squeeze only a minimum of action out of the situation. That is how I see it, anyway, though I realize some people might find my characters rather inactive.

INTERVIEWER: I noticed earlier that you sometimes seem to speak of your characters as existing outside the novel—the kind of thing the Leavises so object to. And Elizabeth Sands makes a brief appearance in *Anglo-Saxon Attitudes*.

WILSON: Yes, my friends have criticized my putting Elizabeth Sands in there—"Hugh Walpole," they say. I told E. M. Forster this and he said, "Ah yes—but Balzac too, you know." I'm on Leavis's side really, but he always writes as a critic, never as a creator. And the writer can't visualize his characters within a framework, although the creation of a work of art demands putting them within a framework. The use of a character for artistic creation is one thing; the author's knowledge of that character is another. Otherwise you'd remove the element of choice, which is the essence of the creative act. What if George Eliot had seen *Middlemarch* whole, in a lump? There'd be no choice. At some point she must have imagined what Mr. Casaubon's housekeeper was like and decided to leave her out. It's not instantaneous vision, and I don't think Leavis himself would expect it to be. Of course it was self-indulgence to bring Elizabeth Sands into *Anglo-Saxon Attitudes*: I felt that many people would like *Anglo-Saxon Attitudes* better than *Hemlock and After*—and for the wrong reasons —and I wanted to show them that the worlds of the two books were the same.

INTERVIEWER: You think *Hemlock and After* has been underrated?

WILSON: Yes. I think that in the long run *Hemlock and After* is a better book than *Anglo-Saxon Attitudes*, if not so competently carried out. *Hemlock* is both a more violent and a more compassionate book. I know this is a sentimental cliché, but I do feel toward my books very much as a parent must toward his children. As soon as someone says, "I *did* like your short stories, but I don't like your novels," or, "Of course you only really came into your own with *Anglo-Saxon Attitudes*"—then immediately I want to defend all my other books. I feel this especially about *Hemlock and After* and *Anglo-Saxon Attitudes*—one child a bit odd but exciting, the other competent but not really so interesting. If people say they like one book and not the other, then I feel they can't have understood the one they don't like.

INTERVIEWER: The publisher's blurb for your new volume of short stories, *A Bit off the Map*, begins: "In an England where the lines of class and caste are becoming blurred and the traditional values have lost much of their force, the characters in Angus Wilson's new stories seek—sometimes cheerfully, sometimes with desperation—to get their true bearings on the map of society." Wouldn't this comment apply pretty much to all your books?

WILSON: Yes, I suppose it would. But you'll realize when they appear that each of these stories is designed to show a specific example of such blurrings of the class lines and of the false answers people provide today to get back some sense of position in society. These new stories are all satirical of the old philosophies which have now become fashionable again—neo-Toryism, Colin Wilson's Nietzscheanism, and so on—of people seeking after values which now no longer apply.

INTERVIEWER: Do you think of yourself primarily as a satirist?

WILSON: No, I don't. Satire for me is something more abstract —*Animal Farm, Erewhon,* that sort of thing. I'm much more traditional than that—which is why I was so surprised at Frank O'Connor's putting me with the experimental writers. I've deliberately tried to get back to the Dickens tradition. I use irony as one main approach, perhaps overdoing it. It's been said that too much irony is one of the great dangers of the English tradition, and perhaps I've fallen into that trap. I don't think of *Point Counter Point* as satire: it's comedy of manners—and you could call my work that. But satire implies an abstract philosophy that I don't have; there's nothing I want to say in the way that Butler wanted to say something about machines, for example.

INTERVIEWER: In writing about Anglo-Saxon attitudes, then, you aren't seeking to change them?

WILSON: Oh, no. I don't think it's the novelist's job to give answers. He's only concerned with exposing the human situation, and if his books do good incidentally that's all well and good. It's rather like sermons.

INTERVIEWER: Isn't a sermon intended to do good?

WILSON: Only to the individual, not to society. It's designed to touch the heart—and I hope my books touch the heart now and again.

INTERVIEWER: But you definitely don't think a novelist should have a social purpose?

WILSON: I don't think a writer *should* have anything. I have certain social and political views, and I suppose these may appear in my work. But as a novelist I'm concerned solely with what I've discovered about human emotions. I attack not specific things, but only people who are set in one way of thinking. The people in my books who come out well may be more foolish, but they have retained an immediacy toward life, not a set of rules applied to life in advance.

INTERVIEWER: What do you think, then, of the "angry young men"?

WILSON: Of course they don't really belong together—though it's largely their own fault that they have been lumped together. They thought popular journalism was a good way to propagate their ideas, and the popular journalists themselves have naturally written of them as a group. The only thing I have against them —while knowing and liking them personally—is the element of strong self-pity, which I do think is a very ruinous element in art. Whatever they write about—when Osborne writes about his feeling for the underprivileged, for example—you get the feeling that they are really complaining about the way *they* have been treated.

And, apart from Colin Wilson, they are so concerned to say that they won't be taken in—we'll be honest and not lay claim to any higher feelings than those we're quite sure we have—that one sometimes wishes they'd be a bit more hypocritical. After all, if you think of yourself in that way you come to think of everyone else in that way and reduce everything to the level of a commercial traveler talking in a bar, knowing life only too well—and in fact people are often better than they make themselves out to be. Their point of view is Iago's, and Iago disguised a very black heart—I don't accuse the angry young men of being black-hearted, of course—beneath his guise of a cynical plain man's point of view. It isn't quite good enough for serious artists.

INTERVIEWER: What do you feel about writing for the stage? Do you feel the novelist has anything to learn from it?

WILSON: Yes. One learns a great deal about what can be omitted, even from a novel, because the play is such a compact form. The best modern plays—by Tennessee Williams, John Osborne, and so on—have tremendous and wonderful power. But the play of ideas—Ibsen and so on—is a little too much at a discount these days.

INTERVIEWER: Do you intend to write for the stage again?

WILSON: Certainly. I want to try to produce more purely theatrical emotion. And I hope to do that and still try for the ideas and the wit of dialogue that I think I got in *The Mulberry Bush*, which seemed a little untheatrical to some people. I want to get more theatrical power, not to write like Williams, but to bring back something of the Ibsen and Shaw tradition.

INTERVIEWER: What about the cinema?

WILSON: I should be only too pleased if my books were turned into films, but I can't imagine myself writing original film scripts —I don't know the necessary techniques, and I rarely even go to the cinema these days. When writing a play you have to realize that the final production won't be only your own work. You have to cooperate with the producer, the actors, and so on. And I'm prepared for that. But in the cinema the writer is quite anonymous, and I feel—for good reasons or bad—that I must be responsible for what I've written and collect the praise or blame for it. Once a book is done I don't care what other people do with it. *The Mulberry Bush* is being televised soon, and the producer rang me up to say it would have to be cut to ninety minutes. I told him to go ahead and do what he wanted: he knows television and I don't. But I couldn't have made a sketch of *The Mulberry Bush* and let it be played about with, if you see the difference.

INTERVIEWER: What plans do you have for the future?

WILSON: I'm in the course of writing another novel. And, as I've just said, I want to do another play. Then I want to do a book of literary essays on nineteenth-century writers, about whom I have a lot to say that I think hasn't been said. And I want to do a book—not fiction—about the home front during the 1914 war. Of all the terrible things that have happened in my lifetime I still think of the trench warfare of the 1914 war as the worst. And the home front was in the strange position of being concerned and yet unconcerned at the same time. The predicament of these people seems likely to connect closely with the predicament of many of the characters in my novels: Bernard Sands and Gerald Middleton, for example, are both concerned with tragedy yet become observers of it by their withdrawal.

INTERVIEWER: Would you say something more about your new novel?

WILSON: I'm sorry, but I don't like to talk about my books in advance. It isn't just that any short account of a novel seems ridiculous by the side of the real thing. But, as I've said before, fiction writing is a kind of magic, and I don't care to talk about a novel I'm doing because if I communicate the magic spell, even in an abbreviated form, it loses its force for me. And so many people have talked out to me books they would otherwise have written. Once you have talked, the act of communication has been made.

MICHAEL MILLGATE

14. William Styron

William Styron was born in 1925 in Newport News, Virginia, a section which provided the locale for his first novel, *Lie Down in Darkness*. He studied in William Blackburn's writing class at Duke University, and later in Hiram Haydn's course at New York's New School. Under Haydn's guidance, Styron finished *Lie Down in Darkness*, a first novel which appeared in 1951 and won him immediate standing among the best of contemporary writers. The critic John W. Aldridge wrote: "It would be a disservice to Styron, and worse than meaningless in these times, to say that he has produced a work of genius . . . yet one can say that he has produced a first novel containing some of the elements of greatness, one with which the work of no other young writer of twenty-five can be compared."

In 1950, Styron was recalled to the Marines, and the experience gave him the background for a brilliant novella-length story called "The Long March." Originally published in the first issue of the literary magazine *discovery*, the story was in 1956 published as a book by Random House.

For *Lie Down in Darkness* Styron won the 1952 Prix de Rome for Literature. He was married in Rome, and has since returned with his wife to Roxbury, Connecticut, where he is at work on a novel about Americans in Europe.

Abruptly he was conscious of a dry, parched thirst, and, ~~turning~~ to his feet. ~~He~~ put on a robe, and hobbled out into the hallway toward the water-cooler. There he saw Mannix, naked except for a towel around his waist, making his slow and agonized way down the hall. He was hairy and enormous, and as he inched his way toward the shower-room, clawing at the wall for support, his face with its clenched eyes and taut, drawn-down mouth was one of tortured and gigantic suffering. The swelling at his ankle was the size of a grapefruit, an ugly blue, and his leg he dragged behind him, a dead-weight no longer capable of motion.

Culver started to limp toward him, said, "Al—"; in an effort to help him along, but just then a Negro maid, bespectacled, bandannaed, came shuffling along with a mop, stopped, seeing him, too, and said, "Oh my, you poor man. What you been doin'?" Do it hurt?" Culver halted.

"Do it hurt?" she repeated, "Oh I bet it does. Deed it does." Mannix looked up at her from the short yards that separated them, silent, blinking. Culver would remember this: the two of them communicating across that chasm one unspoken moment of sympathy and understanding before the woman, ~~full-throated~~, said again, "Deed it does," and before, almost precisely the same instant, the towel slipped away slowly from Mannix's waist and fell with a soft plop to the floor; Mannix then, standing there, heaving dizzily and clutching for support at the wall, a mass of scars and naked as the day he emerged from his mother's womb, save for the soap which he clutched feebly in one hand. He seemed to have neither the strength nor the ability to lean down and retrieve the towel, and so he merely stood there huge and naked in the slanting dusty light and blinked ~~and~~ finally, a sour apologetic smile. "Deed it does." he said.

THE END

oh deal
it does Negro
"Deed it does," crowed.

The last manuscript page of William Styron's "The Long March"

William Pène du Bois

William Styron

William Styron was interviewed in Paris, in early autumn, at Patricks, a café on the Boulevard Montparnasse which has little to distinguish it from its neighbors—the Dome, the Rotonde, Le Chapelain—except a faintly better brand of coffee. Across the Boulevard from the café and its sidewalk tables, a red poster portrays a skeletal family. They are behind bars, and the caption reads: TAKE YOUR VACATION IN HAPPY RUSSIA. *The lower part of the poster has been ripped and scarred and plastered with stickers shouting:* LES AMÉRICANS EN AMÉRIQUE! U.S. GO HOME! *An adjoining poster advertises carbonated water.* PERRIER! *it sings.* L'EAU QUI FAIT PSCHITT! *The sun reflects strongly off their vivid colors, and Styron, shading his eyes, peers down into his coffee. He is a young man of good appearance, though not this afternoon; he is a little paler than is healthy in this quiet hour when the denizens of the quarter lie hiding, their weak night eyes insulted by the light.*

INTERVIEWERS: You were about to tell us when you started to write.

STYRON: What? Oh, yes. Write. I figure I must have been about thirteen. I wrote an imitation Conrad thing, "Typhoon and the Tor Bay" it was called, you know, a ship's hold swarming with crazy Chinks. I think I had some sharks in there too. I gave it the full treatment.

INTERVIEWERS: And how did you happen to start? That is, why did you want to write?

STYRON: I wish I knew. I wanted to express myself, I guess. But after "Typhoon and the Tor Bay" I didn't give writing another thought until I went to Duke University and landed in a creative writing course under William Blackburn. He was the one who got me started.

INTERVIEWERS: What value has the creative writing course for young writers?

STYRON: It gives them a start, I suppose. But it can be an awful waste of time. Look at those people who go back year after year to summer writers' conferences, you get so you can pick them out a mile away. A writing course can only give you a start, and help a little. It can't teach writing. The professor should weed out the good from the bad, cull them like a farmer, and not encourage the ones who haven't got something. At one school I know in New York which has a lot of writing courses there are a couple of teachers who moon in the most disgusting way over the poorest, most talentless writers, giving false hope where there shouldn't be any hope at all. Regularly they put out dreary little anthologies, the quality of which would chill your blood. It's a ruinous business, a waste of paper and time, and such teachers should be abolished.

INTERVIEWERS: The average teacher can't teach anything about technique or style?

STYRON: Well, he can teach you something in matters of technique. You know—don't tell a story from two points of view and that sort of thing. But I don't think even the most conscientious and astute teachers can teach anything about style. Style comes only after long, hard practice and writing.

INTERVIEWERS: Do you enjoy writing?

STYRON: I certainly don't. I get a fine warm feeling when I'm doing well, but that pleasure is pretty much negated by the pain of getting started each day. Let's face it, writing is hell.

INTERVIEWERS: How many pages do you turn out each day?

STYRON: When I'm writing steadily—that is, when I'm involved in a project which I'm really interested in, one of those rare pieces which has a foreseeable end—I average two-and-a-half or three pages a day, longhand on yellow sheets. I spend about five hours at it, of which very little is spent actually writing. I try to get a feeling of what's going on in the story before I put it down on paper, but actually most of this breaking-in period is one long, fantastic daydream, in which I think about anything but the work at hand. I can't turn out slews of stuff each day. I wish I could. I seem to have some neurotic need to perfect each paragraph— each sentence, even—as I go along.

INTERVIEWERS: And what time of the day do you find best for working?

STYRON: The afternoon. I like to stay up late at night and get drunk and sleep late. I wish I could break the habit but I can't. The afternoon is the only time I have left and I try to use it to the best advantage, with a hangover.

INTERVIEWERS: Do you use a notebook?

STYRON: No, I don't feel the need for it. I've tried, but it does no good, since I've never used what I've written down. I think the use of a notebook depends upon the individual.

INTERVIEWERS: Do you find you need seclusion?

STYRON: I find it's difficult to write in complete isolation. I think it would be hard for me on a South Sea island or in the Maine woods. I like company and entertainment, people around. The actual process of writing, though, demands complete, noiseless privacy, without even music; a baby howling two blocks away will drive me nuts.

INTERVIEWERS: Does your emotional state have any bearing on your work?

STYRON: I guess like everybody I'm emotionally fouled up most of the time, but I find I do better when I'm relatively placid. It's hard to say, though. If writers had to wait until their precious psyches were completely serene there wouldn't be much writing done. Actually—though I don't take advantage of the fact as much as I should—I find that I'm simply the happiest, the placidest, *when* I'm writing, and so I suppose that that, for me, is the final answer. When I'm writing I find it's the only time that I feel completely self-possessed, even when the writing itself is not going too well. It's fine therapy for people who are perpetually scared of nameless threats as I am most of the time—for jittery people. Besides, I've discovered that when I'm not writing I'm prone to developing certain nervous tics, and hypochondria. Writing alleviates those quite a bit. I think I resist change more than most people. I dislike traveling, like to stay settled. When I first came to Paris all I could think about was going home, home to the old James River. One of these days I expect to inherit a peanut farm. Go back home and farm them old peanuts and be real old Southern whisky gentry.

INTERVIEWERS: Your novel was linked to the Southern school of fiction. Do you think the critics were justified in doing this?

STYRON: No, frankly, I don't consider myself in the Southern school, whatever that is. *Lie Down in Darkness*, or most of it, was set in the South, but I don't care if I never write about the South again, really. Only certain things in the book are particularly Southern. I used leitmotivs—the Negroes, for example—that run throughout the book, but I would like to believe that my people would have behaved the way they did anywhere. The girl, Peyton, for instance, didn't have to come from Virginia. She would have wound up jumping from a window no matter where she came from. Critics are always linking writers to "schools." If they couldn't link people to schools, they'd die. When what they condescendingly call "a genuinely fresh talent" arrives on the scene, the critics rarely try to point out what makes him fresh or genuine but concentrate instead on how he behaves in accordance with their preconceived notion of what school he belongs to.

INTERVIEWERS: You don't find that it's true of most of the so-called Southern novels that the reactions of their characters are universal?

STYRON: Look, I don't mean to repudiate my Southern background completely, but I don't believe that the South alone produces "universal" literature. That universal quality comes far more from a single writer's mind and his individual spirit than from his background. Faulkner's a writer of extraordinary stature more because of the great breadth of his vision than because he happened to be born in Mississippi. All you have to do is read one issue of the *Times Book Review* to see how much junk comes out regularly from south of the Mason-Dixon line, along with the good stuff. I have to admit, though, that the South has a definite literary tradition, which is the reason it probably produces a better quality of writing, proportionately. Perhaps it's just true that Faulkner, if he had been born in, say, Pasadena, might very well still have had that universal quality of mind, but instead of writing *Light in August* he would have gone into television or written universal ads for Jantzen bathing suits.

INTERVIEWERS: Well, why do you think this Southern tradition exists at all?

STYRON· Well, first, there's that old heritage of Biblical rhetoric and story-telling. Then the South simply provides such wonderful material. Take, for instance, the conflict between the ordered Protestant tradition, the fundamentalism based on the Old Testament, and the twentieth century—movies, cars, television. The poetic juxtapositions you find in this conflict—a crazy colored preacher howling those tremendously moving verses from Isaiah 40, while riding around in a maroon Packard. It's wonderful stuff and comparatively new, too, which is perhaps why the renaissance of Southern writing coincided with these last few decades of the machine age. If Faulkner had written in the 1880s he would have been writing, no doubt, safely within the tradition, but his novels would have been genteel novels, like those of George Washington Cable or Thomas Nelson Page. In fact, the modern South is such powerful material that the author runs the danger of capturing the local color and feeling that's enough. He gets so bemused by decaying mansions that he forgets to populate them with people. I'm beginning to feel that it's a good idea for writers who come from the South, at least some of them, to break away a little from all them magnolias.

INTERVIEWERS: You refer a number of times to Faulkner. Even though you don't think of yourself as a "Southern" writer, would you say that he influenced you?

STYRON: I would certainly say so. I'd say I had been influenced as much, though, by Joyce and Flaubert. Old Joyce and Flaubert have influenced me stylistically, given me arrows, but then a lot of the contemporary works I've read have influenced me as a craftsman. Dos Passos, Scott Fitzgerald, both have been valuable in teaching me how to write the novel, but not many of these modern people have contributed much to my *emotional* climate. Joyce comes closest, but the strong influences are out of the past —the Bible, Marlowe, Blake, Shakespeare. As for Flaubert, *Madame Bovary* is one of the few novels that moves me in every way, not only in its style, but in its total communicability, like the effect of good poetry. What I really mean is that a great book should leave you with many experiences, and slightly exhausted at the end. You live several lives while reading it. Its writer should, too. Without condescending, he should be conscious of himself as a reader, and while he's writing it he should be able to step outside of it from time to time and say to himself, "Now if I were just *reading* this book, would I like this part here?" I have the feeling that that's what Flaubert did—maybe too much, though, finally, in books like *Sentimental Education*.

INTERVIEWERS: While we're skirting this question, do you think Faulkner's experiments with time in *The Sound and the Fury* are justified?

STYRON: Justified? Yes, I do.

INTERVIEWERS: Successful, then?

STYRON: No, I don't think so. Faulkner doesn't give enough help to the reader. I'm all for the complexity of Faulkner, but not for the confusion. That goes for Joyce, too. All that fabulously beautiful poetry in the last part of *Finnegans Wake* is pretty much lost to the world simply because not many people are ever going to put up with the chaos that precedes it. As for *The Sound and the Fury*, I think it succeeds in spite of itself. Faulkner often simply stays too damn intense for too long a time. It ends up being great stuff, somehow, though, and the marvel is how it could be so wonderful being pitched for so long in that one high, prolonged, delirious key.

INTERVIEWERS: Was the problem of time development acute in the writing of *Lie Down in Darkness*?

STYRON: Well, the book started with the man, Loftis, standing at the station with the hearse, waiting for the body of his daughter to arrive from up North. I wanted to give him density, but all the tragedy in his life had happened in the past. So the problem was to get into the past, and this man's tragedy, without breaking the story. It stumped me for a whole year. Then it finally occurred to me to use separate moments in time, four or five long dramatic scenes revolving around the daughter, Peyton, at different stages in her life. The business of the progression of time seems to me one of the most difficult problems a novelist has to cope with.

INTERVIEWERS: Did you prefigure the novel? How much was planned when you started?

STYRON: Very little. I knew about Loftis and all his domestic troubles. I had the funeral. I had the girl in mind, and her suicide in Harlem. I thought I knew why, too. But that's all I had.

INTERVIEWERS: Did you start with emphasis on character or story?

STYRON: Character, definitely. And by character I mean a person drawn full-round, not a caricature. E. M. Forster refers to "flat" and "round" characters. I try to make all of mine round. It takes an extrovert like Dickens to make flat characters come alive. But story as such has been neglected by today's introverted writers. Story and character should grow together; I think I'm lucky so far in that in practically everything I've tried to write these two elements have grown together. They must, to give an impression of life being lived, just because each man's life is a story, if you'll pardon the cliché. I used to spend a lot of time worrying over word order, trying to create beautiful passages. I still believe in the value of a handsome style. I appreciate the sensibility which can produce a nice turn of phrase, like Scott Fitzgerald. But I'm not interested any more in turning out something shimmering and impressionistic—Southern, if you will—full of word-pictures, damn Dixie baby-talk, and that sort of thing. I guess I just get more and more interested in people. And story.

INTERVIEWERS: Are your characters real-life or imaginary?

STYRON: I don't know if that's answerable. I really think frankly, though, that most of my characters come closer to being entirely imaginary than the other way round. Maybe that's because they all seem to end up, finally, closer to being like myself than like people I've actually observed. I sometimes feel that the characters I've created are not much more than sort of projected facets of myself, and I believe that a lot of fictional characters have been created that way.

INTERVIEWERS: How far removed must you be from your subject matter?

STYRON: Pretty far. I don't think people can write immediately, and well, about an experience emotionally close to them. I have a feeling, for example, that I won't be able to write about all the time I've spent in Europe until I get back to America.

INTERVIEWERS: Do you feel yourself to be in competition with other writers?

STYRON: No, I don't. "Some of my best friends are writers." In America there seems to be an idea that writing is one big cat-and-dog fight between the various practitioners of the craft. Got to hole up in the woods. Me, I'm a farmer, I don't know no writers. Hate writers. That sort of thing. I think that just as in everything else writers can be too cozy and cliquish and end up nervous and incestuous and scratching each other's backs. In London once I was at a party where everything was so literary and famous and intimate that if the place had suddenly been blown up by dynamite it would have demolished the flower of British letters. But I think that writers in the U.S. could stand a bit more of the attitude that prevailed in France in the last century. Flaubert and Maupassant, Victor Hugo and Musset, they didn't suffer from knowing each other. Turgenev knew Gogol. Chekhov knew Tolstoi and Andreiev, and Gorki knew all three. I think it was Henry James who said of Hawthorne that he might have been even better than he was if he had occasionally communicated a little bit more with others working at the same sort of thing. A lot of this philosophy of isolation in America is a dreary pose. I'm not advocating a Writers' Supper Club on Waverly Place, just for chums in the business, or a union, or anything like that, but I do think that writers in America might somehow benefit by the attitude that, what the hell, we're all in this together, instead of all my pals are bartenders on Third Avenue. As a matter of fact, I do have a pal who's a bartender on Third Avenue, but he's a part-time writer on the side.

INTERVIEWERS: In general, what do you think of critics, since they are a subject which must be close to a writer's heart?

STYRON: From the writer's point of view, critics should be ignored, although it's hard not to do what they suggest. I think it's unfortunate to have critics for friends. Suppose you write something that stinks, what are they going to say in a review? Say it stinks? So if they're honest they do, and if you were friends you're still friends, but the knowledge of your lousy writing and their articulate admission of it will be always something between the two of you, like the knowledge between a man and his wife of some shady adultery. I know very few critics, but I usually read their reviews. Bad notices always give me a sense of humility, or perhaps humiliation, even when there's a tone of envy or sour grapes or even ignorance in them, but they don't help me much. When *Lie Down in Darkness* came out, my home-town paper scraped up the local literary figure to review the book, a guy who'd written something on hydraulics, I think, and he came to the conclusion that I was a decadent writer. Styron is a decadent writer, he said, because he writes a line like "the sea sucking at the shore," when for that depraved bit he should have substituted "the waves lapping at the shore." Probably his hydraulic background. No, I'm afraid I don't think much of critics for the most part, although I have to admit that some of them have so far treated me quite kindly. Look, there's only one person a writer should listen to, pay any attention to. It's not any damn critic. It's the reader. And that doesn't mean any compromise or sell-out. The writer must criticize his own work as a reader. Every day I pick up the story or whatever it is I've been working on and read it through. If I enjoy it as a reader then I know I'm getting along all right.

INTERVIEWERS: In your preface to the first issue of this magazine you speak of there being signs in the air that this generation can and will produce literature to rank with that of any other generation. What are these signs? And do you consider yourself, perhaps, a spokesman for this new generation?

STYRON: What the hell is a spokesman, anyway? I hate the idea of spokesmen. Everybody, especially the young ones, in the writing game jockeying into position to give a name for a generation. I must confess that I was guilty of that in the preface, too. But don't you think it's tiresome, really, all these so-called spokesmen trumpeting around, elbowing one another out of the way to see who'll be the first to give a new and original name to twenty-five million people: the Beat Generation, or the Silent Generation, and God knows what-all? I think the damn generation should be let alone. And that goes for the eternal idea of competition— whether the team of new writers can beat the team of Dos Passos, Faulkner, Fitzgerald, and Hemingway. As I read in a review not long ago, by some fellow reviewing an anthology of new writing which had just that sort of proprietary essay in it and which compared the new writers with the ones of the twenties, the reviewer said, in effect, what the hell, there's plenty of *Lebensraum* and *Liebestraum* for everybody.

INTERVIEWERS: But you *did* say, in the preface, just what we were speaking of—that this generation can and will—

STYRON (*interrupting*): Yes, can and will produce literature equal to that of any other generation, especially that of the twenties. It was probably rash to say, but I don't see any reason to recant. For instance, I think those "signs in the air" are apparent from just three first novels, those being *From Here to Eternity, The Naked and the Dead,* and *Other Voices, Other Rooms.* It's true that a first novel is far from a fair standard with which to judge a writer's potential future output, but aren't those three novels far superior to the first novels of Dos Passos, Faulkner, and Fitzgerald? In fact I think one of those novels—*The Naked and the Dead*—is so good by itself that it can stand up respectably well with the *mature* work of any of those writers of the twenties. But there I go again, talking in competition with the older boys. Anyway, I think that a lot of the younger writers around today are stuffed with talent. A lot of them, it's true, are shameless and terrible self-promoters—mainly the members of what a friend of mine calls "the fairy axis"—but they'll drop by the wayside and don't count for much anyway. The others, including the ones I've mentioned, plus people like Salinger and Carson McCullers and Hortense Calisher—all those have done, and will go on doing, fine work, unless somebody drops an atom bomb on them, or they get locked up in jail by Velde and that highly cultured crowd.

INTERVIEWERS: Speaking of atom bombs and Representative Velde, among other such contemporary items, do you think—as some people have been saying—that the young writer today works at a greater disadvantage than those of preceding—uh—generations?

STYRON: Hell no, I don't. Writers ever since writing began have had problems, and the main problem narrows down to just one word—life. Certainly this might be an age of so-called faithlessness and despair we live in, but the new writers haven't cornered any market on faithlessness and despair, any more than Dostoevski or Marlowe or Sophocles did. Every age has its terrible aches and pains, its peculiar new horrors, and every writer since the beginning of time, just like other people, has been afflicted by what that same friend of mine calls "the fleas of life"—you know, colds, hangovers, bills, sprained ankles, and little nuisances of one sort or another. *They* are the constants of life, at the core of life, along with nice little delights that come along every now and then. Dostoevski had them and Marlowe had them and we all have them, and they're a hell of a lot more invariable than nuclear fission or the Revocation of the Edict of Nantes. So is Love invariable, and Unrequited Love, and Death and Insult and Hilarity. Mark Twain was as baffled and appalled by Darwin's theories as anyone else, and those theories seemed as monstrous to the Victorians as atomic energy, but he still wrote about riverboats and old Hannibal, Missouri. No, I don't think the writer today is any worse off than at any other time. It's true that in Russia he might as well be dead and that in Youngstown, Ohio, that famous police chief, whatever his name is, has taken to inspecting and banning books. But in America he can still write practically anything he pleases, so long as it isn't libelous or pornographic. Also in America he certainly doesn't have to starve, and there are few writers so economically strapped that they can't turn out work regularly. In fact, a couple of young writers—and good writers—are damn near millionaires.

INTERVIEWERS: Then you believe in success for a writer? Financial, that is, as well as critical?

STYRON: I sure do. I certainly have sympathy for a writer who hasn't made enough to live comfortably—comfortably, I mean, not necessarily lavishly—because I've been colossally impoverished at times, but impoverished writers remind me of Somerset Maugham's remark about multilingual people. He admired them, he said, but did not find that their condition made them necessarily wise.

INTERVIEWERS: But getting back to the original point--in *Lie Down in Darkness* didn't your heroine commit suicide on the day the atom bomb was dropped on Hiroshima? This seems to us to be a little bit more than fortuitous symbolism, and perhaps to indicate a sense of that inescapable and overpowering despair of our age which you just denied was our peculiar lot.

STYRON: That was just gilding the lily. If I were writing the same thing now I'd leave that out and have her jump on the Fourth of July. Really, I'm not trying to be rosy about things like the atom bomb and war and the failure of the Presbyterian Church. Those things are awful. All I'm trying to say is that those things don't alter one bit a writer's fundamental problems, which are Love, Requited and Unrequited, Insult, et cetera.

INTERVIEWERS: Then you believe that young writers today have no cause to be morbid and depressing, which is a charge so often leveled at them by the critics?

STYRON: Certainly they do. They have a perfect right to be anything they honestly are, but I'd like to risk saying that a great deal of this morbidity and depression doesn't arise so much from political conditions, or the threat of war, or the atom bomb, as from the terrific increase of the scientific knowledge which has come to us about the human self—Freud, that is, abnormal psychology, and all the new psychiatric wisdom. My God, think of how morbid and depressing Dostoevski would have been if he could have gotten hold of some of the juicy work of Dr. Wilhelm Stekel, say *Sadism and Masochism*. What people like John Webster and, say, Hieronymus Bosch felt intuitively about some of the keen horrors which lurk in the human mind, we now have neatly catalogued and clinically described by Krafft-Ebing and the Menningers and Karen Horney, and they're available to any fifteen-year-old with a pass-card to the New York Public Library. I don't say that this new knowledge is *the* cause of the so-called morbidity and gloom, but I do think it has contributed to a new trend toward the introspective in fiction. And when you get an eminent journal like *Time* magazine complaining, as it often has, that to the young writers of today life seems short on rewards and that what they write is a product of their own neuroses, in its silly way the magazine is merely stating the status quo and obvious truth. The good writing of any age has always been the product of *someone's* neurosis, and we'd have a mighty dull literature if all the writers that came along were a bunch of happy chuckleheads.

INTERVIEWERS: To sort of round this out, we'd like to ask finally what might sound like a rather obvious question. That is, what should be the purpose of a young writer? Should he, for instance, be *engagé*, not concerned as much with the story aspects of the novel as with the problems of the contemporary world?

STYRON: It seems to me that only a great satirist can tackle the world problems and articulate them. Most writers write simply out of some strong interior need, and that I think is the answer. A great writer, writing out of this need, will give substance to and perhaps even explain all the problems of the world without even knowing it, until a scholar comes along a hundred years after he's dead and digs up some symbols. The purpose of a young writer is to write, and he shouldn't drink too much. He shouldn't think that after he's written one book he's God Almighty and air all his immature opinions in pompous interviews. Let's have another cognac and go up to Le Chapelain.

PETER MATTHIESSEN
GEORGE PLIMPTON

15. Truman Capote

Truman Capote (born Truman Streckfus Persons in 1925) was brought up in the South, sent to school in Greenwich, Connecticut, and until his stories began to be accepted held diverse jobs as a movie-script reader, dancer on a river-boat, and an office boy for *The New Yorker.*

At nineteen, he won an O. Henry prize for his short story "Miriam," and in 1948 won another O. Henry award for "Shut a Final Door." Random House published a collection of his short stories (*A Tree of Night*) in 1949.

In 1948 Capote won national attention with his first novel, *Other Voices, Other Rooms,* a book elaborately furnished with the grotesques of the Gothic tradition set against the background of the Deep South. Carlos Baker wrote of the author's method: "He knows that in one condition of the human spirit the sound of a voice may be epochal and the sense of something or someone breathing behind the wall of another room can bring the listener near the edge of cataclysm."

A second novel, *The Grass Harp,* appeared in 1951. An adaptation presented on Broadway in 1952 had an unsuccessful run, though praised by Brooks Atkinson as "the most creative contribution of the season." In 1954 Capote wrote the book for another Broadway show, a lavish but not very successful musical based on his short story, "The House of Flowers."

Although Capote lives on Brooklyn Heights, he spends much of the year traveling. He has written a travel book called *Local Color,* describing his trips through the South, Portugal, and France; in 1956 he recounted his experiences with the *Porgy and Bess* troupe in Russia in the highly praised *The Muses Are Heard.*

She spent entire days slopping about in her tiny, sweatbox kitchen (José says I'm a fabulous cook. Better than the Colony. Who would have thought I had such a great natural talent. A month ago I couldn't scramble eggs.") And she still couldn't, for that matter. The simpler dishes, steak, a proper salad, were beyond her; instead, she fed José outré soups (brandied black terrapin poured into avocado shells), dubious innovations (chicken and rice served with a chocolate sauce: An East Indian ~~spic~~ speciality, darling."), Nero-ish novelties

---

A manuscript page from Truman Capote's short novel Breakfast at Tiffany's

Rosalie Seidler

Truman Capote

Truman Capote lives in a big yellow house in Brooklyn Heights, which he has recently restored with the taste and elegance that is generally characteristic of his undertakings. As I entered he was head and shoulders inside a newly arrived crate containing a wooden lion.

"There!" he cried as he tugged it out to a fine birth amid a welter of sawdust and shavings. "Did you ever see anything so splendid? Well, that's that. I saw him and I bought him. Now he's all mine."

"He's large," I said. "Where are you going to put him?"

"Why, in the fireplace, of course," said Capote. "Now come along into the parlor while I get someone to clear away this mess."

The parlor is Victorian in character and contains Capote's most intimate collection of art objects and personal treasures, which,

*for all their orderly arrangement on polished tables and bamboo
bookcases, somehow remind you of the contents of a very astute
little boy's pockets. There is, for instance, a golden Easter egg
brought back from Russia, an iron dog, somewhat the worse for
wear, a Fabergé pillbox, some marbles, blue ceramic fruit, paper-
weights, Battersea boxes, picture postcards, and old photographs.
In short everything that might seem useful or handy in a day's
adventuring around the world.*

*Capote himself fits in very well with this impression at first
glance. He is small and blond, with a forelock that persists in falling down into his eyes, and his smile is sudden and sunny. His
approach to anyone new is one of open curiosity and friendliness.
He might be taken in by anything and, in fact, seems only too
ready to be. There is something about him, though, that makes
you feel that for all his willingness it would be hard to pull any
wool over his eyes and maybe it is better not to try.*

*There was a sound of scuffling in the hall and Capote came in,
preceded by a large bulldog with a white face.*

"This is Bunky," he said.

Bunky sniffed me over and we sat down.

INTERVIEWER: When did you first start writing?

CAPOTE: When I was a child of about ten or eleven and lived
near Mobile.

I had to go into town on Saturdays to the dentist and I joined
the Sunshine Club that was organized by the Mobile Press Regis-
ter. There was a children's page with contests for writing and for
coloring pictures, and then every Saturday afternoon they had a
party with free Nehi and Coca-Cola. The prize for the short-story
writing contest was either a pony or a dog, I've forgotten which,
but I wanted it badly. I had been noticing the activities of some
neighbors who were up to no good, so I wrote a kind of *roman à
clef* called "Old Mr. Busybody" and entered it in the contest. The
first installment appeared one Sunday, under my real name of
Truman Streckfus Persons. Only somebody suddenly realized that

I was serving up a local scandal as fiction, and the second install-ment never appeared. Naturally, I didn't win a thing.

INTERVIEWER: Were you sure then that you wanted to be a writer?

CAPOTE: I realized that I *wanted* to be a writer. But I wasn't sure I *would* be until I was fifteen or so. At that time I had im-modestly started sending stories to magazines and literary quarter-lies. Of course no writer ever forgets his first acceptance; but one fine day when I was seventeen, I had my first, second, and third, all in the same morning's mail. Oh, I'm here to tell you, dizzy with excitement is no mere phrase!

INTERVIEWER: What did you first write?

CAPOTE: Short stories. And my more unswerving ambitions still revolve around this form. When seriously explored, the short story seems to me the most difficult and disciplining form of prose writ-ing extant. Whatever control and technique I may have I owe en-tirely to my training in this medium.

INTERVIEWER: What do you mean exactly by "control"?

CAPOTE: I mean maintaining a stylistic and emotional upper hand over your material. Call it precious and go to hell, but I believe a story can be wrecked by a faulty rhythm in a sentence—especially if it occurs toward the end—or a mistake in paragraph-ing, even punctuation. Henry James is the maestro of the semi-colon. Hemingway is a first-rate paragrapher. From the point of view of ear, Virginia Woolf never wrote a bad sentence. I don't mean to imply that I successfully practice what I preach. I try, that's all.

INTERVIEWER: How does one arrive at short-story technique?

CAPOTE: Since each story presents its own technical problems, obviously one can't generalize about them on a two-times-two-equals-four basis. Finding the right form for your story is simply to realize the most *natural* way of telling the story. The test of whether or not a writer has divined the natural shape of his story is just this: after reading it, can you imagine it differently, or does it silence your imagination and seem to you absolute and final?

As an orange is final. As an orange is something nature has made just right.

INTERVIEWER: Are there devices one can use in improving one's technique?

CAPOTE: Work is the only device I know of. Writing has laws of perspective, of light and shade, just as painting does, or music. If you are born knowing them, fine. If not, learn them. Then rearrange the rules to suit yourself. Even Joyce, our most extreme disregarder, was a superb craftsman; he could write *Ulysses because* he could write *Dubliners*. Too many writers seem to consider the writing of short stories as a kind of finger exercise. Well, in such cases, it is certainly only their fingers they are exercising.

INTERVIEWER: Did you have much encouragement in those early days, and if so, by whom?

CAPOTE: Good Lord! I'm afraid you've let yourself in for quite a saga. The answer is a snake's nest of no's and a few yes's. You see, not altogether but by and large, my childhood was spent in parts of the country and among people unprovided with any semblance of a cultural attitude. Which was probably not a bad thing, in the long view. It toughened me rather too soon to swim against the current—indeed, in some areas I developed the muscles of a veritable barracuda, especially in the art of dealing with one's enemies, an art no less necessary than knowing how to appreciate one's friends.

But to go back. Naturally, in the milieu aforesaid, I was thought somewhat *eccentric*, which was fair enough, and *stupid*, which I suitably resented. Still, I despised school—or schools, for I was always changing from one to another—and year after year failed the simplest subjects out of loathing and boredom. I played hooky at least twice a week and was always running away from home. Once I ran away with a friend who lived across the street—a girl much older than myself who in later life achieved a certain fame. Because she murdered a half-dozen people and was electrocuted at Sing Sing. Someone wrote a book about her. They called her the Lonely Hearts Killer. But there, I'm wandering again. Well, finally, I guess I was around twelve, the principal at the school I was attending paid a call on my family, and told them that in his opinion, and in the opinion of the faculty, I was "subnormal." He thought it would be sensible, the humane action, to send me to some special school equipped to handle backward brats. Whatever they may have privately felt, my family as a whole took official umbrage, and in an effort to prove I wasn't subnormal, pronto packed me off to a psychiatric study clinic at a university in the East where I had my I.Q. inspected. I enjoyed it thoroughly and —guess what?—came home a genius, so proclaimed by science. I don't know who was the more appalled: my former teachers, who refused to believe it, or my family, who didn't want to believe it— they'd just hoped to be told I was a nice normal boy. Ha ha! But as for me, I was exceedingly pleased—went around staring at myself in mirrors and sucking in my cheeks and thinking over in my mind, my lad, you and Flaubert—or Maupassant or Mansfield or Proust or Chekhov or Wolfe, whoever was the idol of the moment.

I began writing in fearful earnest—my mind zoomed all night every night, and I don't think I really slept for several years. Not until I discovered that whisky could relax me. I was too young, fifteen, to buy it myself, but I had a few older friends who were most obliging in this respect and I soon accumulated a suitcase full of bottles, everything from blackberry brandy to bourbon. I kept the suitcase hidden in a closet. Most of my drinking was done in the late afternoon; then I'd chew a handful of Sen Sen and go down to dinner, where my behavior, my glazed silences, gradually grew into a source of general consternation. One of my relatives used to say, "Really, if I didn't know better, I'd swear he was dead drunk." Well, of course, this little comedy, if such it was, ended in discovery and some disaster, and it was many a moon before I touched another drop. But I seem to be off the track again. You asked about encouragement. The first person who ever really helped me was, strangely, a teacher. An English teacher I had in high school, Catherine Wood, who backed my ambitions in every way, and to whom I shall always be grateful. Later on, from the time I first began to publish, I had all the encouragement anyone could ever want, notably from Margarita Smith, fiction editor of *Mademoiselle*, Mary Louise Aswell of *Harper's Bazaar*, and Robert Linscott of Random House. You would have to be a glutton indeed to ask for more good luck and fortune than I had at the beginning of my career.

INTERVIEWER: Did the three editors you mention encourage you simply by buying your work, or did they offer criticism, too?

CAPOTE: Well, I can't imagine anything *more* encouraging than having someone buy your work. I never write—indeed, am physically incapable of writing—anything that I don't think will be paid for. But, as a matter of fact, the persons mentioned, and some others as well, were all very generous with advice.

INTERVIEWER: Do you like anything you wrote long ago as well as what you write now?

CAPOTE: Yes. For instance, last summer I read my novel *Other Voices, Other Rooms* for the first time since it was published eight years ago, and it was quite as though I were reading something by a stranger. The truth is, I am a stranger to that book; the person who wrote it seems to have so little in common with my present self. Our mentalities, our interior temperatures are entirely different. Despite awkwardness, it has an amazing intensity, a real voltage. I am very pleased I was able to write the book when I did, otherwise it would never have been written. I like *The Grass Harp* too, and several of my short stories, though not "Miriam," which is a good stunt but nothing more. No, I prefer "Children on Their Birthdays" and "Shut a Final Door," and oh, some others, especially a story not too many people seemed to care for, "Master Misery," which was in my collection *A Tree of Night*.

INTERVIEWER: You recently published a book about the *Porgy and Bess* trip to Russia. One of the most interesting things about the style was its unusual detachment, even by comparison to the reporting of journalists who have spent many years recording events in an impartial way. One had the impression that this version must have been as close to the truth as it is possible to get through another person's eyes, which is surprising when you consider that most of your work has been characterized by its very personal quality.

CAPOTE: Actually, I don't consider the style of this book, *The Muses Are Heard*, as markedly different from my fictional style. Perhaps the content, the fact that it is about real events, makes it seem so. After all, *Muses* is straight reporting, and in reporting one is occupied with literalness and surfaces, with implication without comment—one can't achieve immediate depths the way one may in fiction. However, one of the reasons I've wanted to do reportage was to prove that I could apply my style to the realities of journalism. But I believe my fictional method is equally detached—emotionality makes me lose writing control: I have to exhaust the emotion before I feel clinical enough to analyze and project it, and as far as I'm concerned that's one of the laws of achieving true technique. If my fiction seems more personal it is because it depends on the artist's most personal and revealing area: his imagination.

INTERVIEWER: How do you exhaust the emotion? Is it only a matter of thinking about the story over a certain length of time, or are there other considerations?

CAPOTE: No, I don't think it is merely a matter of time. Suppose you ate nothing but apples for a week. Unquestionably you would exhaust your appetite for apples and most certainly know what they taste like. By the time I write a story I may no longer have any hunger for it, but I feel that I thoroughly know its flavor. The *Porgy and Bess* articles are not relevant to this issue. That was reporting, and "emotions" were not much involved—at least not the difficult and personal territories of feeling that I mean. I seem to remember reading that Dickens, as he wrote, choked with laughter over his own humor and dripped tears all over the page when one of his characters died. My own theory is that the writer should have considered his wit and dried his tears long, long before setting out to evoke similar reactions in a reader. In other words, I believe the greatest intensity in art in all its shapes is achieved with a deliberate, hard, and cool head. For example, Flaubert's *A Simple Heart*. A warm story, warmly written; but it could only be the work of an artist muchly aware of true techniques, i.e., necessities. I'm sure, at some point, Flaubert must-have felt the story very deeply—but *not* when he wrote it. Or, for a more contemporary example, take that marvelous short novel of Katherine Anne Porter's, *Noon Wine*. It has such intensity, such a sense of happening-now, yet the writing is so controlled, the inner rhythms of the story so immaculate, that I feel fairly certain Miss Porter was at some distance *from* her material.

INTERVIEWER: Have your best stories or books been written at a comparatively tranquil moment in your life or do you work better because, or in spite, of emotional stress?

CAPOTE: I feel slightly as though I've never lived a tranquil moment, unless you count what an occasional Nembutal induces. Though, come to think of it, I spent two years in a very romantic house on top of a mountain in Sicily, and I guess this period could be called tranquil. God knows, it was quiet. That's where I wrote *The Grass Harp*. But I must say an iota of stress, striving toward deadlines, does me good.

INTERVIEWER: You have lived abroad for the last eight years. Why did you decide to return to America?

CAPOTE: Because I'm an American, and never could be, and have no desire to be, anything else. Besides, I like cities, and New York is the only real city-city. Except for a two-year stretch, I came back to America every one of those eight years, and I never entertained expatriate notions. For me, Europe was a method of acquiring perspective and an education, a stepping stone toward maturity. But there *is* the law of diminishing returns, and about two years ago it began to set in: Europe had given me an enormous lot, but suddenly I felt as though the process were reversing itself—there seemed to be a taking away. So I came home, feeling quite grown up and able to settle down where I belong—which doesn't mean I've bought a rocking chair and turned to stone.

No indeed. I intend to have footloose escapades as long as fron-
tiers stay open.

INTERVIEWER: Do you read a great deal?

CAPOTE: Too much. And anything, including labels and recipes
and advertisements. I have a passion for newspapers—read all the
New York dailies every day, and the Sunday editions, and several
foreign magazines too. The ones I don't buy I read standing at
news stands. I average about five books a week—the normal-length
novel takes me about two hours. I enjoy thrillers and would like
someday to write one. Though I prefer first-rate fiction, for the last
few years my reading seems to have been concentrated on letters
and journals and biographies. It doesn't bother me to read while
I am writing—I mean, I don't suddenly find another writer's style
seeping out of my pen. Though once, during a lengthy spell of
James, my own sentences *did* get awfully long.

INTERVIEWER: What writers have influenced you the most?

CAPOTE: So far as I consciously know, I've never been aware of
direct literary influence, though several critics have informed me
that my early works owe a debt to Faulkner and Welty and
McCullers. Possibly. I'm a great admirer of all three; and Katherine Anne Porter, too. Though I don't think, when really ex-
amined, that they have much in common with each other, or me,
except that we were all born in the South. Between thirteen and
sixteen are the ideal if not the only ages for succumbing to
Thomas Wolfe—he seemed to me a great genius then, and still
does, though I can't read a line of it now. Just as other youthful
flames have guttered: Poe, Dickens, Stevenson. I love them in
memory, but find them unreadable. These are the enthusiasms
that remain constant: Flaubert, Turgenev, Chekhov, Jane Austen,
James, E. M. Forster, Maupassant, Rilke, Proust, Shaw, Willa
Cather—oh the list is too long, so I'll end with James Agee, a
beautiful writer whose death over two years ago was a real loss.
Agee's work, by the way, was much influenced by the films. I
think most of the younger writers have learned and borrowed from
the visual, structural side of movie technique. I have.

INTERVIEWER: You've written for the films, haven't you? What was that like?

CAPOTE: A lark. At least the one picture I wrote, *Beat the Devil*, was tremendous fun. I worked on it with John Huston while the picture was actually being made on location in Italy. Sometimes scenes that were just about to be shot were written right on the set. The cast were completely bewildered—sometimes even Huston didn't seem to know what was going on. Naturally the scenes had to be written out of a sequence, and there were peculiar moments when I was carrying around in my head the only real outline of the so-called plot. You never saw it? Oh, you should. It's a marvelous joke. Though I'm afraid the producer didn't laugh. The hell with them. Whenever there's a revival I go to see it and have a fine time.

Seriously, though, I don't think a writer stands much chance of imposing himself on a film unless he works in the warmest rapport with the director or is himself the director. It's so much a director's medium that the movies have developed only one writer who, working exclusively as a scenarist, could be called a film genius. I mean that shy, delightful little peasant, Zavattini. What a visual sense! Eighty per cent of the good Italian movies were made from Zavattini scripts—all of the De Sica pictures, for instance. De Sica is a charming man, a gifted and deeply sophisticated person; nevertheless he's mostly a megaphone for Zavattini, his pictures are absolutely Zavattini's creations: every nuance, mood, every bit of business is clearly indicated in Zavattini's scripts.

INTERVIEWER: What are some of your writing habits? Do you use a desk? Do you write on a machine?

CAPOTE: I am a completely horizontal author. I can't think unless I'm lying down, either in bed or stretched on a couch and with a cigarette and coffee handy. I've got to be puffing and sipping. As the afternoon wears on, I shift from coffee to mint tea to sherry to martinis. No, I don't use a typewriter. Not in the beginning. I write my first version in longhand (pencil). Then I do a complete revision, also in longhand. Essentially I think of myself as a stylist, and stylists can become notoriously obsessed with the placing of a comma, the weight of a semicolon. Obsessions of this sort, and the time I take over them, irritate me beyond endurance.

INTERVIEWER: You seem to make a distinction between writers who are stylists and writers who aren't. Which writers would you call stylists and which not?

CAPOTE: What is style? And "what" as the Zen Koan asks, "is the sound of one hand?" No one really *knows*; yet either you *know* or you don't. For myself, if you will excuse a rather cheap little image, I suppose style is the mirror of an artist's sensibility —more so than the *content* of his work. To some degree all writers have style—Ronald Firbank, bless his heart, had little else, and thank God he realized it. But the possession of style, *a* style, is often a hindrance, a negative force, not as it should be, and as it is —with, say, E. M. Forster and Colette and Flaubert and Mark Twain and Hemingway and Isak Dinesen—a reinforcement. Dreiser, for instance, has *a* style—but oh, *Dio buono!* And Eugene O'Neill. And Faulkner, brilliant as he is. They all seem to me triumphs over strong but negative styles, styles that do not really add to the communication between writer and reader. Then there is the styleless stylist—which is very difficult, very admirable, and *always* very popular: Graham Greene, Maugham, Thornton Wilder, John Hersey, Willa Cather, Thurber, Sartre (remember, we're *not* discussing content), J. P. Marquand, and so on. But yes, there *is* such an animal as a nonstylist. Only they're not writers; they're typists. Sweaty typists blacking up pounds of bond paper with formless, eyeless, earless messages. Well, who are some of the younger writers who seem to know that style exists? P. H. Newby, Françoise Sagan, somewhat. Bill Styron, Flannery O'Connor—she has some fine moments, that girl. James Merrill. William Goyen—if he'd stop being hysterical. J. D. Salinger—especially in the colloquial tradition. Colin Wilson? Another typist.

INTERVIEWER: You say that Ronald Firbank had little else but style. Do you think that style alone can make a writer a great one?

CAPOTE: No, I don't think so—though, it could be argued, what happens to Proust if you separate him from his style? Style has never been a strong point with American writers. This though some of the best have been Americans. Hawthorne got us off to a fine start. For the past thirty years Hemingway, stylistically speaking, has influenced more writers on a world scale than anyone else. At the moment, I think our own Miss Porter knows as well as anyone what it's all about.

INTERVIEWER: Can a writer learn style?

CAPOTE: No, I don't think that style is consciously arrived at, any more than one arrives at the color of one's eyes. After all, your style *is* you. At the end the personality of a writer has so much to do with the work. The personality has to be humanly there. Personality is a debased word, I know, but it's what I mean. The writer's individual humanity, his word or gesture toward the world, has to appear almost like a character that makes contact with the reader. If the personality is vague or confused or merely literary, *ça ne va pas*. Faulkner, McCullers—they project their personality at once.

INTERVIEWER: It is interesting that your work has been so widely appreciated in France. Do you think style can be translated?

CAPOTE: Why not? Provided the author and the translator are artistic twins.

INTERVIEWER: Well, I'm afraid I interrupted you with your short story still in penciled manuscript. What happens next?

CAPOTE: Let's see, that was second draft. Then I type a third draft on yellow paper, a very special certain kind of yellow paper. No, I don't get out of bed to do this. I balance the machine on my knees. Sure, it works fine; I can manage a hundred words a minute. Well, when the yellow draft is finished, I put the manuscript away for a while, a week, a month, sometimes longer. When I take it out again, I read it as coldly as possible, then read it aloud to a friend or two, and decide what changes I want to make and whether or not I want to publish it. I've thrown away rather a few short stories, an entire novel, and half of another. But if all goes well, I type the final version on white paper and that's that.

INTERVIEWER: Is the book organized completely in your head before you begin it or does it unfold, surprising you as you go along?

CAPOTE: Both. I invariably have the illusion that the whole play of a story, its start and middle and finish, occur in my mind simultaneously—that I'm seeing it in one flash. But in the working-out, the writing-out, infinite surprises happen. Thank God, because the surprise, the twist, the phrase that comes at the right moment out of nowhere, is the unexpected dividend, that joyful little push that keeps a writer going.

At one time I used to keep notebooks with outlines for stories. But I found doing this somehow deadened the idea in my imagination. If the notion is good enough, if it truly belongs to *you*, then you can't forget it—it will haunt you till it's written.

INTERVIEWER: How much of your work is autobiographical?

CAPOTE: Very little, really. A little is *suggested* by real incidents or personages, although everything a writer writes is in some way autobiographical. *The Grass Harp* is the only true thing I ever wrote, and naturally everybody thought it all invented, and imagined *Other Voices, Other Rooms* to be autobiographical.

INTERVIEWER: Do you have any definite ideas or projects for the future?

CAPOTE (*meditatively*): Well, yes, I believe so. I have always written what was easiest for me until now: I want to try something else, a kind of controlled extravagance. I want to use my mind more, use many more colors. Hemingway once said anybody can write a novel in the first person. I know now exactly what he means.

INTERVIEWER: Were you ever tempted by any of the other arts?

CAPOTE: I don't know if it's art, but I was stage-struck for years and more than anything I wanted to be a tap-dancer. I used to practice my buck-and-wing until everybody in the house was ready to kill me. Later on, I longed to play the guitar and sing in night clubs. So I saved up for a guitar and took lessons for one whole winter, but in the end the only tune I could really play was a beginner's thing called "I Wish I Were Single Again." I got so tired of it that one day I just gave the guitar to a stranger in a bus station. I was also interested in painting, and studied for three years, but I'm afraid the fervor, *la vrai chose*, wasn't there.

INTERVIEWER: Do you think criticism helps any?

CAPOTE: Before publication, and if provided by persons whose judgment you trust, yes, of course criticism helps. But after something is published, all I want to read or hear is praise. Anything less is a bore, and I'll give you fifty dollars if you produced a writer who can honestly say he was ever helped by the prissy carpings and condescensions of reviewers. I don't mean to say that none of the professional critics are worth paying attention to—but few of the good ones review on a regular basis. Most of all, I believe in hardening yourself against opinion. I've had, and continue to receive, my full share of abuse, some of it extremely personal, but it doesn't faze me any more. I can read the most outrageous libel about myself and never skip a pulsebeat. And in this connection there is one piece of advice I strongly urge: never demean yourself by talking back to a critic, never. Write those letters to the editor in your head, but don't put them on paper.

INTERVIEWER: What are some of your personal quirks?

CAPOTE: I suppose my superstitiousness could be termed a quirk. I have to add up all numbers: there are some people I never telephone because their number adds up to an unlucky figure. Or I won't accept a hotel room for the same reason. I will not tolerate the presence of yellow roses—which is sad because they're my favorite flower. I can't allow three cigarette butts in the same ashtray. Won't travel on a plane with two nuns. Won't begin or end anything on a Friday. It's endless, the things I can't and won't. But I derive some curious comfort from obeying these primitive concepts.

INTERVIEWER: You have been quoted as saying your preferred pastimes are "conversation, reading, travel, and writing, in that order." Do you mean that literally?

CAPOTE: I think so. At least I'm pretty sure conversation will always come first with me. I like to listen, and I like to talk. Heavens, girl, can't you *see* I like to talk?

PATI HILL

16. Françoise Sagan

Françoise Sagan is the *nom de plume* of Françoise Quoirez. She derived her name from Proust's favorite author, the Princesse de Sagan. The daughter of a prosperous engineer of Spanish extraction, Mademoiselle Sagan was born in 1935 in the little town of Cajac in the Department of Lot and was brought up with her brother and sister in the upper-middle-class quarter of Paris which borders on the Parc Monceau. After being graduated from a Paris school, she entered the Sorbonne in 1952. In July, at the end of the school year, she failed her examinations and started work on *Bonjour tristesse*. The book was finished by the end of August, was published by Editions Juillard in 1954, and was awarded the Prix des Critiques for that year. Immediately a success, *Bonjour tristesse* sold over 700,000 copies in France and was translated into fourteen languages. It was followed in 1956 by *Un Certain sourire* (A Certain Smile). *Dans un mois, dans un an* (*Those without Shadows*) was published in 1957. In America her first two books have sold more than two million copies. In addition to her novels, Mademoiselle Sagan has written lyrics for the singer Juliette Greco, movie scripts, and a commentary for a collection of photographs of New York City. She lives in a Paris apartment and often works alone in the country outside the city.

In the spring of 1957 she was nearly killed in a sports-car crash. Sports cars are her hobby; a bare foot on the accelerator, she drives at speeds so reckless that European press reports on her driving have been about as voluminous as the critiques of her writing.

One of the final manuscript pages from Françoise Sagan's Un Certain sourire
(A Certain Smile)

Bee W. Dabney

Françoise Sagan

Françoise Sagan now lives in a small and modern ground-floor apartment of her own on the Rue de Grenelle, where she is busily writing a film script and some song lyrics as well as a new novel. But when she was interviewed early last spring just before the publication of Un Certain sourire, *she lived across the city in her parents' apartment on the Boulevard Malesherbes in a neighborhood which is a stronghold of the well-to-do French bourgeoisie. She met the interviewers in the comfortably furnished living room, seated them in large chairs drawn up to a marble fireplace, and offered them scotch from a pint bottle which was unquestionably, somehow, her own contribution to the larder. Her manner is shy, but casual and friendly, and her gamine face crinkles easily into an attractive, rather secret smile. She wore a simple black sweater and gray skirt; if she is a vain girl the only indication of it was her high-heeled shoes, which were of elegantly worked light gray*

*leather. She speaks in a high-pitched but quiet voice and she clearly
does not enjoy being interviewed or asked to articulate in a formal
way what are, to her, natural assumptions about her writing. She
is sincere and helpful, but questions which are pompous or elaborate, or about personal life, or which might be interpreted as chal-
lenging her work, are liable to elicit only a simple "oui" or "non,"
or "je ne sais pas—je ne sais pas du tout"—and then an amused,
disconcerting smile.*

INTERVIEWERS: How did you come to start *Bonjour tristesse*
when you were eighteen? Did you expect it would be published?

SAGAN: I simply started it. I had a strong desire to write and
some free time. I said to myself, "This is the sort of enterprise
very, very little girls of my age devote themselves to; I'll never be
able to finish it." I wasn't thinking about "literature" and literary
problems, but about myself and whether I had the necessary will
power.

INTERVIEWERS: Did you let it drop and then take it up again?

SAGAN: No, I wanted passionately to finish it—I've never
wanted anything so much. While I was writing I thought there
might be a chance of its being published. Finally, when it was
done, I thought it was hopeless. I was surprised by the book and
by myself.

INTERVIEWERS: Had you wanted to write for a long time before?

SAGAN: Yes. I had read a lot of stories. It seemed to me impossible not to want to write one. Instead of leaving for Chile with
a band of gangsters, one stays in Paris and writes a novel. That
seems to me the great adventure.

INTERVIEWERS: How quickly did it go? Had you thought out the
story in advance?

SAGAN: For *Bonjour tristesse* all I started with was the idea of a
character, the girl, but nothing really came of it until my pen was
in hand. I have to start to write to have ideas. I wrote *Bonjour
tristesse* in two or three months, working two or three hours a day.

Un Certain sourire was different. I made a number of little notes
and then thought about the book for two years. When I started in
writing, again two hours a day, it went very fast. When you make
a decision to write according to a set schedule and really stick to
it, you find yourself writing very fast. At least I do.

INTERVIEWERS: Do you spend much time revising the style?

SAGAN: Very little.

INTERVIEWERS: Then the work on the two novels didn't take
more than five or six months in all?

SAGAN: Yes (*smiling*), it's a good way to make a living.

INTERVIEWERS: You say the important thing at the start is a
character?

SAGAN: A character, or a few characters, and perhaps an idea for
a few of the scenes up to the middle of the book, but it all changes
in the writing. For me writing is a question of finding a certain
rhythm. I compare it to the rhythms of jazz. Much of the time
life is a sort of rhythmic progression of three characters. If one
tells oneself that life is like that, one feels it less arbitrary.

INTERVIEWERS: Do you draw on the people you know for your
characters?

SAGAN: I've tried very hard and I've never found any resemblance between the people I know and the people in my novels. I
don't search for exactitude in portraying people. I try to give to
imaginary people a kind of veracity. It would bore me to death to
put into my novels the people I know. It seems to me that there
are two kinds of trickery: the "fronts" people assume before one
another's eyes, and the "front" a writer puts on the face of reality.

INTERVIEWERS: Then you think it is a form of cheating to take
directly from reality?

SAGAN: Certainly. Art must take reality by surprise. It takes
those moments which are for us merely a moment, plus a moment,
plus another moment, and arbitrarily transforms them into a special series of moments held together by a major emotion. Art
should not, it seems to me, pose the "real" as a preoccupation.

Nothing is more unreal than certain so-called "realist" novels—
they're nightmares. It is possible to achieve in a novel a certain
sensory truth—the true feeling of a character—that is all.

Of course the illusion of art is to make one believe that great
literature is very close to life, but exactly the opposite is true. Life
is amorphous, literature is formal.

INTERVIEWERS: There are certain activities in life with highly
developed forms, for instance horse racing. Are the jockeys less
real because of that?

SAGAN: People possessed by strong passions for their activities,
as jockeys may seem to be, don't give me the impression of being
very real. They often seem like characters in novels, but *without*
novels, like *The Flying Dutchman*.

INTERVIEWERS: Do your characters stay in your mind after the
book is finished? What kind of judgments do you make about
them?

SAGAN: When the book is finished I immediately lose interest
in the characters. And I *never* make moral judgments. All I would
say is that a person was droll, or gay, or, above all, a bore. Making
judgments for or against my characters bores me enormously, it
doesn't interest me at all. The only morality for a novelist is the
morality of his *esthétique*. I write the books, they come to an end,
and that's all that concerns me.

INTERVIEWERS: When you finished *Bonjour tristesse* did it
undergo much revising by an editor?

SAGAN: A number of general suggestions were made about the
first book. For example, there were several versions of the ending
and in one of them Anne didn't die. Finally it was decided that
the book would be stronger in the version in which she did.

INTERVIEWERS: Did you learn anything from the published
criticism of the book?

SAGAN: When the articles were agreeable I read them through.
I never learned anything at all from them but I was astonished
by their imagination and fecundity. They saw intentions I never
had.

INTERVIEWERS: How do you feel now about *Bonjour tristesse?*

SAGAN: I like *Un Certain sourire* better, because it was more difficult. But I find *Bonjour tristesse* amusing because it recalls a certain stage of my life. And I wouldn't change a word. What's done is done.

INTERVIEWERS: Why do you say *Un Certain sourire* is a more difficult book?

SAGAN: I didn't hold the same trump cards in writing the second book: no seaside summer-vacation atmosphere, no intrigue naïvely mounting to a climax, none of the gay cynicism of Cécile. And then it was difficult simply because it was the second book.

INTERVIEWERS: Did you find it difficult to switch from the first person of *Bonjour tristesse* to the third-person narrative of *Un Certain sourire?*

SAGAN: Yes, it is harder, more limiting and disciplining. But I wouldn't make as much of that difficulty as some writers apparently do.

INTERVIEWERS: What French writers do you admire and feel important to you?

SAGAN: Oh, I don't know. Certainly Stendhal and Proust. I love their mastery of the narrative, and in some ways I find myself in definite need of them. For example, after Proust there are certain things that simply cannot be done again. He marks off for you the boundaries of your talent. He shows you the possibilities that lie in the treatment of character.

INTERVIEWERS: What strikes you particularly about Proust's characters?

SAGAN: Perhaps the things that one does not know about them as much as the things one knows. For me, that is literature in the very best sense: after all the long and slow analyses one is far from knowing all the thoughts and facts and sides of Swann, for example—and that is as it should be. One has no desire at all to ask "Who was Swann?" To know who was Proust is quite enough. I don't know if that's clear: I mean to say that Swann belongs completely to Proust and it is impossible to imagine a Balzacian Swann, while one might well imagine a Proustian Marsay.

INTERVIEWERS: Is it possible that novels get written because the novelist imagines himself in the role of a novelist writing a novel?

SAGAN: No, one assumes the role of hero and then seeks out "the novelist" who can write his story.

INTERVIEWERS: And one always finds the same novelist?

SAGAN: Essentially, yes. Very broadly, I think one writes and rewrites the same book. I lead a character from book to book, I continue along with the same ideas. Only the angle of vision, the method, the lighting, change. Speaking very, very roughly, it seems to me there are two kinds of novels—there is that much choice. There are those which simply tell a story and sacrifice a great deal to the telling—like the books of Benjamin Constant which *Bonjour tristesse* and *Un Certain sourire* resemble in construction. And then there are those books which attempt to discuss and probe the characters and events in the book—*un roman où l'on discute*. The pitfalls of both are obvious: in the simple narrative it often seems that the important questions are passed over. In the longer classical novel the digressions can impair the effectiveness.

INTERVIEWERS: Would you like to write "*un roman où l'on discute*"?

SAGAN: Yes, I would like to write—in fact I'm now planning—a novel with a larger cast of characters—there will be three heroines —and with characters more diffuse and elastic than Dominique and Cécile and the others in the first two books. The novel I would like to write is one in which the hero would be freed from the demands of the plot, freed from the novel itself and from the author.

INTERVIEWERS: To what extent do you recognize your limits and maintain a check on your ambitions?

SAGAN: Well, that is a pretty disagreeable question, isn't it? I recognize limitations in the sense that I've read Tolstoi and Dostoevski and Shakespeare. That's the best answer, I think. Aside from that I don't think of limiting myself.

INTERVIEWERS: You've very quickly made a lot of money. Has it changed your life? Do you make a distinction between writing novels for money and writing seriously, as some American and French writers do?

SAGAN: Of course the success of the books has changed my life somewhat because I have a lot of money to spend if I wish, but as far as my position in life is concerned, it hasn't changed much. Now I have a car but I've always eaten steaks. You know, to have a lot of money in one's pocket is nice, but that's all. The prospect of making more or less money would never affect the way I write —I write the books, and if money appears afterward, *tant mieux.*

Mlle. Sagan interrupted the interviewers to say that she had to leave to work on a radio program. She apologized and got up to go. It was difficult to believe, once she had stopped talking, that the slight, engaging girl had, with a single book, reached more readers than most novelists do in a lifetime. Rather, one would have thought her a schoolgirl rushing off to the Sorbonne as she called down the apartment hall to her mother, "Au revoir, maman. Je sors travailler mais je rentre de bonne heure."

BLAIR FULLER
ROBERT B. SILVERS

For a complete list of books available from Penguin in the United States, write to Dept. DG, Penguin Books, 299 Murray Hill Parkway, East Rutherford, New Jersey 07073.

For a complete list of books available from Penguin in Canada, write to Penguin Books Canada Limited, 2801 John Street, Markham, Ontario L3R 1B4.

If you live in the British Isles, write to Dept. EP, Penguin Books Ltd, Harmondsworth, Middlesex.